D0385383

COMPARATIVE RELIGION

Dr Bouquet, who was born in 1884, was Lecturer on the History and Comparative Study of Religions in the University of Cambridge from 1932 to 1955. A scholar of Trinity College, and Lady Kay Scholar of Jesus College, he graduated in 1905 and took a First in Theology. After spending some years in pastoral work and serving as an Army Chaplain 1915–19, he returned to Cambridge in 1922, taking his D.D. in the same year. Since then, among other activities, he has successively held the Hulsean and Stanton Lectureships in the University. He has been a delegate to several Anglo-Scandinavian Theological Conferences. For the years 1939–41 he was President of the Cambridge University Theological Society. In 1957 (Michaelmas term) he was Upton Lecturer at Oxford on the History of Religion. In 1955 he was invited to lecture in the University of Delhi, and again in 1961, and in 1957–8 he was engaged in research at Andhra University in India. He has been a visiting lecturer at Harvard, Princeton, UCLA, and Middlebury College, Vermont. He has been a delegate to the International Conferences on the History of Religion at Amsterdam (1950), Rome (1955), Marburg (1960), and Claremont, California (1963). He was the President of the Cambridge University Judo Club for over 30 years and is now Honorary Vice-President. From 1922 to 1945 he was Vicar of All Saints Church, Cambridge.

COMPARATIVE
RELIGION

A SHORT OUTLINE

BY

A. C. BOUQUET

PENGUIN BOOKS

Penguin Books Ltd, Harmondsworth, Middlesex, England
Penguin Books Inc., 7110 Ambassador Road, Baltimore, Maryland 21207, U.S.A.
Penguin Books Australia Ltd, Ringwood, Victoria, Australia

—

First published 1941
Second edition 1945
Third edition 1950, reprinted 1951
Fourth edition 1953, reprinted 1954
Fifth edition 1956, reprinted 1958
Sixth edition 1962
Reprinted 1964
Seventh edition 1967
Reprinted with revisions 1969
Reprinted 1971

—

Copyright © A. C. Bouquet, 1941, 1962

—

Made and printed in Great Britain
by Cox & Wyman Ltd,
London, Reading and Fakenham
Set in Monotype Bembo

PREFACE TO THE SEVENTH EDITION

IT is over twenty years since this book was first written, and I well remember correcting the proofs during the course of the battle of Britain, and putting the galleys under the dining-room table every time we heard German planes overhead. Since then one has tried with each succeeding edition (six of them) to bring the text and bibliography more and more up to date and to free them from errors. But even now, as the 1960 Marburg conference has shown, progress in the study of the subject is still being made and new vistas are being opened up.

1. The publication by the Ministry of Works of the handbook on Stonehenge and Avebury, with its account of the re-dating of the former as the result of the discovery of engravings of axes upon some of the great stones, and its repudiation of any connexion of this open-air sanctuary with the Druids, marks a decisive stage in our study of ancient megalithic temples; though I fear we are no nearer to finding out how they were used, unless the ceremonies at the open-air temple of Heaven at Peking (finally discontinued after about 1915) throw any light on the matter. The importance of radio-carbon analysis in dating ancient remains cannot be too strongly emphasized.

2. The correlation of the practices of the palaeolithic hunters of central Europe with those still surviving in various parts of the world by Professor Johannes Maringer and others has raised again in a more serious form the question whether early man had arrived already at the conception of a single Supreme Being, although his high-god may have been merely a quasi-personal dispenser of hunting luck.

3. The appearance in 1958 of an important set of lectures on Zoroastrianism by Professor J. Duchesne-Guillemin of Liège, and another (1961) by Professor R. C. Zaehner of Oxford raises again the question as to what primitive Zoroastrianism really was. Was Zarathustra a true and uncompromising monotheist, or did he stand on the border between monotheism, pluralism, and dualism? And was there any monotheism in Iran *before* Zarathustra?

4. The rather exciting documentary finds at Qumran and Nag Hammadi are throwing fresh light upon the background against which the Christian movement emerged. Readers will find sane comments upon the Qumran scrolls in the recently published paper by Professor F. F. Bruce of Manchester, in the proceedings of the 1960 Conference of the M.C.U., held at Cambridge; and the Nag Hammadi collection of Gnostic documents is also referred to by Professor S. G. F. Brandon of Manchester in the same proceedings, while Professor van Unnik has broadcast about them, and his more detailed study is now being made accessible in English. Other works are referred to in the bibliography.

5. Professor Arnold Toynbee's final volume is a fresh though severely criticized attempt at reconstructing a general theory of religion.

6. Renewed conversations between Hindus and Christians, between Buddhists and Christians and between Christians and Muslims give promise of bearing fruit. Their interruption by the post-war emergence of Barthian and Kraemerite modes of thought ('there is *no* point of contact') seems likely to give way to a fresh emphasis upon and a further development of the doctrine of the Logos as it occurs in the early Greek Fathers. Even Kraemer himself came to admit 'a dialogue' *must* take place between East and West.

7. My remarks about Islam in the republic of Turkey now need a slight modification. In recent years there has been some return to the religion of the Prophet, and a relaxing of secularism; but the Khalifate has not been restored, and it is hard to tell how much the younger generation is accepting the religion of its forefathers.

8. What I said on pages 231–2 about Judaism has been amply confirmed by a book recently published in New York.

9. That the vital age of religious creativity lies in the past must be admitted by any who study the facts, But a time will come when the equally vital age of scientific discovery which we associate with Darwin, Marx, Huxley, Thomson, Rutherford, Jung, and Freud, will in its turn also lie in the past. Yet in both cases these ages of creativity have left behind them permanent contributions to human life which go on fructifying and proliferating, and which will doubtless continue to do so, for an unforeseeable period.

10. The real question which we all of us have to face sooner or later

is: 'Which to choose, some form of humanism or some form of religion?' Does man achieve best the purpose for which he exists by turning in on himself and remaining the sole artist of his own life, or does he achieve it best by linking his efforts with those of the Self-Existent, and letting the latter use him? This *could* be a false antithesis: for as a famous Jew once put it: 'Brethren, work out your own salvation with fear and trembling, for it is God that worketh in you both to will and to do of his good pleasure.'

If the period 800 BC to 300 AD is appropriately called by Karl Jaspers The Axial Age, it may well be that the present scientific revolution is bringing mankind to a second Axial Age, even more drastic than the first one.

NOTE TO THE 1969 REPRINT

This edition and its immediate predecessor contain twelve new illustrations. It is hoped that these may prove acceptable to readers, for none have appeared so far since the blocks of those in the first edition (of 1941) wore out. Most of them are from new pictures.

The seventh edition had its type reset, and owing to circumstances beyond the author's control it unfortunately contained a number of errors which were not in the sixth edition. It is hoped that these have now all been corrected, and that the present text will be found to be a perfect one. My best thanks are due to Miss Susan Clark, a graduate of the University of Reading, for valuable help in making the corrections.

To avoid disrupting the text of the bibliography, the names of a few additional books have been added at the end of it, on page 319.

During the past twelve months there have been several events of importance, which it seems appropriate to record in a book concerned with the study of the religions of the world. First of all, five separate services of spiritual affirmation have been held, in which representatives of all the religions of the British Commonwealth of Nations and of Asia as a whole consented to take part. These were held respectively in Westminster Abbey, in the churches of St Mary-le-Bow, Cheapside, and St Martin-in-the-Fields (and at one of the latter H.R.H. Prince Philip was present); in the University Church of Great St Mary at Cambridge; and finally in the Guildhall of the City of London, at which Her Majesty the Queen was present. Secondly, the Divinity Faculty of the University of Cambridge has at last decided to include an Introduction to the Comparative Study of Religion as one of the optional subjects in the second part of the Theological Tripos, and this decision has been endorsed by the General Board of Studies, taking effect from October 1968.

CONTENTS

LIST OF PLATES

1. Australian aboriginals performing the initiation of a boy.

2. Stonehenge from the air. Perhaps the best-known example of a circular open-air sanctuary of a type widely distributed in the world, the exact use of which, however, is unknown.

3. Saivite sadhu (devotee of the god Siva).

4. A Krishna festival at the (new) Birla temple in Delhi. The latter was built by a wealthy friend of Mr Gandhi, with a view to drawing into a central sanctuary most of the various Indian religious groups.

5. A group of Shinto priests.

6. The admission of a girl to the Parsee (Zoroastrian) faith, performed by Mobeds (Parsee priests).

7. Procession of a Buddhist relic to a shrine at Sanchi. The bearer is U Nu, late Prime Minister of Burma. Mr Nehru is to be seen in the crowd.

8. Entrance to the Temple of Heaven at Peking.

9. Statue of Confucius from a Chinese temple dedicated to his honour.

10. Yemenite Jews keeping Seder (Passover).

11. The Kaaba at Mecca during the Haj.

12. The statue of Christ over the altar in St Saviour's Church, Eltham, SE London. Virtually a modern representation, drawn from the well-known Negro spiritual 'He's Got the Whole World in His Hands'.

'Many roads Thou hast fashioned: all of them lead to the light.'
(Kipling: Hymn to Mithras, in *Puck of Pook's Hill*.)

'He who is not against us is for us.'
(Jesus of Nazareth, in the Gospel of Mark.)

'It will greatly ease the missionary situation, and lift a burden from not a few consciences, if it is firmly established that it is *our* God who is dimly perceived by the fetish-worshippers, *our* God who hears prayers on the trembling lips of the non-Christian fatherless and widow, *our* God who receives psalms of faith addressed in ignorant sincerity to different beings.'
(The Reverend Godfrey Phillips, Professor at Selly Oak College, University of Birmingham.)

'The love of God is more precious and to be esteemed than the respect of the nobleman.'
(Teaching of Amen-em-Apt, 1400 B.C.)

'As knowledge of God is as necessary for true living as is the act of breathing for the body . . . I cannot do anything without breathing. But it may well be that I shall breathe all the better, and consequently walk, run, row, eat, think and speak better if I take some breathing exercises. This analogy is not exact because Divinity is much *more* than a mere breathing exercise – but it does set us on the right line. Communion with Deity is, or should be, the integrating period, the time when all our knowledge and all our experience are brought together and given their place in one integrated whole.'
(From the report of the first lecture delivered at Oxford by the late Manchester Reader in Religious Education.)

COMPARATIVE RELIGION

CHAPTER I

Introducing Religion

IMAGINE a visitor from Mars making a tour of the earth. In most countries he would see prominent buildings of one pattern or another, and would find on examination that they were neither factories, nor offices, nor places of entertainment. Indeed they appeared to exist as assembly-halls for the performance of actions which seemed to have no *direct* bearing upon the conduct of life. Some of them were on occasion used as schools, yet the teachers in them did not appear to be instructing the young in arithmetic, or in handicrafts, or even primarily in reading and writing, or physical culture. Our visitor would be puzzled. What, he would say, is this strange non-utilitarian activity, presenting such variation in type, which is spread all over the planet? In some countries it is uniform, but in others it varies from north to south, and there is one type, associated with buildings bearing a symbol †, which seems to overlap, and another, associated with the symbol (, which equally overlaps. In one country the buildings are some of them crowded at intervals in the usual way, but others are in ruins, or are obviously not being employed for the usual purpose. Yet even here there seem to be some non-utilitarian activities, associated with big open-air parades, or processions, or speeches, or visits to the tomb of a special individual. In another country a decade ago, while the buildings still existed they were for the time less frequented, their place being taken again by open-air parades accompanied by ceremonial and singing, and the display of the sign 卐.* Then

* This was obviously written before 1946.

again there are in many countries large and small communal dwellings which are apparently neither colleges nor schools nor hotels nor mental hospitals, but which are occupied exclusively by persons of the same sex, wearing a uniform livery, yet obviously not soldiers of any sort. Our visitor would seek a synthetic explanation of these activities.

Something like the above has been written before, and the intelligent reader will notice at once that it contains a fallacy. If the visitor from Mars were sufficiently like ourselves to be able to communicate with us in conversation, and to study our institutions with sympathy, he would need no explanation of our so-called non-utilitarian activities. But if he were at least as unlike us as, let us say, an ant is, he would fail to see that the activities were non-utilitarian, and might suppose that they had some strange bearing upon our political organization or banking, or perhaps that we were ruminants, and chewed the cud in this way; or again, he might be so unlike us that everything we did conveyed to him no meaning at all.

Anyhow, it is quite evident that, leaving Mars out of account, the ordinary earth-dweller, living in an age of transition, would very much like to clear his mind as to the history, place and value of religion in human affairs. There are any number of questions that he would wish to ask, such as: 'How did religion begin?' 'What function does it really perform in life?' 'Why were some types of religion, in which no one to-day believes, once so very much alive, and over so long a period?' 'Why are certain types of religion so obstinately conservative?' 'Is there any precedent for the revolutionary changes which seem at present to be overtaking traditional forms of belief and practice?' 'Can we, from a survey of the faiths of the world, derive any helpful forecast for the future?'

It will be the object of this small book not necessarily to answer all such questions in an exhaustive manner, but to help the enquirer upon the road to finding answers for himself.

Most large works on the subject, such for example as Sir James Frazer's *Golden Bough* and Dr A. B. Cook's *Zeus*, necessarily partake of the nature of 'jungle-books' – that is to say, they are so intricate in their design and so richly replete with details as to overwhelm the ordinary reader. There is therefore some excuse for presenting a short synopsis of a vast subject, which will enable the beginner to see the wood as well as the individual trees, and prepare him for more advanced study.

'Religion' is a European word, and it is a European convention which has led to its employment as a general term to embrace certain human interests all the world over. In Latin it was usually spelt 'rel(l)igio', and from very early times scholars have been divided as to its basic meaning. Of Roman writers Cicero held that it came from a root 'leg-', meaning 'to take up, gather, count, or observe', i.e. 'to observe the signs of a Divine communication or "to read the omens"'. Servius, on the other hand, held that it came from another root, 'lig-', 'to bind', so that 'religio' meant 'a relationship', i.e. 'a communion between the human and the Super-Human'. Subsequently it seems to have carried both meanings, for St Augustine the Great uses it in both senses. It is, however, most likely that the earlier one (whether or not we dislike it) was the original, since it is the exact counterpart of a Greek word (*paratērēsis*) which means 'the scrupulous observation of omens and the performance of ritual'. Most significantly the historical Jesus is reported as saying 'the Kingdom of God cometh not with *paratērēsis*', which may mean, 'not by looking for omens will you discern its approach', or 'not by ritual observance will you bring it nearer'. He adds 'the Kingdom of God is *entos humôn*', which may be interpreted as 'already realized in your midst', or as 'realized inwardly, and not by outward ceremonies'. Both make equally good sense.

For most Europeans, at any rate, 'religion' has come to

mean a fixed relationship between the human self and some non-human entity, the Sacred, the Supernatural, the Self-Existent, the Absolute, or simply, 'God'. From Suez eastward, however, such a relationship seems as often as not to be described or describable in terms of movement, as a 'Way'. Thus we have the *hodos*, or way, of the Pharisees. Early Christianity in the Book of Acts is called 'that Way'; Buddhism is described as 'the noble eight-fold Path'; and Japanese nationalist *religion* (if we must use the European label) is called Shinto, 'the Way of the Gods': while Communist Russia, true to her semi-Oriental ancestry, has for the time being rejected Theism (or rather the European term 'religion') in favour of surrender to the Dialectical Process – which is again a 'Way'. Confucius' message is called by him 'The Way'.

And this is a very commendable alternative, since, East or West, human beings have to go on living, and they feel instinctively that living, even in danger or discomfort, is in some way or other worth while; and the path they choose to follow is bound to be conditioned by their general belief about the relationship which they bear to the Whole of their environment, as well as by the attitude of the latter towards them. If therefore we continue to use the generic term 'religion' to describe the various species of a certain world-wide phenomenon, we must remember that the activities we observe are the expression of beliefs in some existing relationship between (let us call it) Deity and human beings, while if we are not Western Europeans, and are concerned with Process rather than with a Person (some Westerners are, too), let us recall that a 'way' is not simply meandering, but implies direction, and therefore relation to a goal or purpose. It is arguable that such purpose implies a Directive Mind, though not necessarily one of the human order. But here we are concerned not with argument, but with a record of facts, and a history and comparison of beliefs and opinions.

A modern writer has reminded us of the distinction between 'having a religion', and 'being religious'. The former state is unfortunately commoner than the latter, and we may compare the relationship of the two to that prevailing between the rich parvenu who collects beautiful things without understanding them, and the individual who, however poor, has been trained to love and perceive the significance of beauty.

Yet the possessor of a beautiful thing may learn to value it, and so perhaps it is better to have an imperfect appreciation of religion or to be religious in an imperfect way than to be wholly irreligious, since the essential function of religion is to integrate life. Such integration varies in quality not only in accordance with the goodness or badness of the religion accepted (and there is undoubtedly bad religion as well as good), but it also varies with the sincerity and whole-heartedness displayed by the individual in surrendering to it. The force of this has been observed by the anthropologists, who have noted in their field-work that where contacts with Europeans, whether traders, government officials or missionaries, have broken down the religious system of a so-called primitive people without replacing it by one at least equally satisfying, the life of that people becomes impoverished, and is in peril of falling to pieces. Conversely the psychologist observes about genuinely religious persons a certain unification of personality which is apparently unattainable without the essence of religion, and if he is engaged in psycho-analysis, and discovers in his patient a belief which has integrating value, he refrains from disturbing it (even if it seems to him personally untenable) for fear of damaging instead of healing.

Mr Hanbury-Tracy's description of his Tibetan friends conveys the same impression. 'On the whole,' he says, 'their theocratic system works well, and produces millions of happy individuals, who love their religion with a whole-hearted devotion, and are quite willing to be dominated by their Buddhist monks and itinerant ascetics. They have not the religious excitability of Islam, but the quiet trust in religion as a background to every act in daily life.' I seem to have read something like this about the religion of the pre-revolution moujiks in Russia; but it did not prevent Lenin and his comrades from thinking it 'opium', and smashing it up accordingly. I observe, however, that surrender to the Dialectic Process partakes of the essential nature of religion (partly of the Moslem, partly of the Buddhist type), and that its integration of life is genuine. We have, therefore, even in this case, an example of what Professor Hocking has called 'radical displacement', the discontinuous substitution of one religion for another.

Integration, or the unifying of personality, may occur as the result of centring one's self upon one or more of a number of different things. The character and quality of the integration will differ according to the object of interest. In 1916 an army chaplain wrote, 'The religion of the lorry-driver must be his lorry'. Equally, we might say, the religion of the lover may well be his sweetheart ('Anthea, who may command him anything'). The pursuit of truth for its own sake without regard for its actual commercial utility, by way of scientific research, may be undertaken with such passion as to integrate the life of the scientist. Some have made the accumulation of wealth, or the collection of pewter, or the acquisition of power over other men's lives, or their own personal safety, a consuming passion or a steadfast purpose, and these things have then become their gods. Another potent integrating force is fear. Sometimes religions are classified into those which affirm the world, those which escape the world and those which seek to transform the world. Yet as often as not the personality is unified around a dominant interest which is purely local. The prophet is inclined to call such a restricted interest an 'idol', in the sense of being an inferior god, or a 'no-god'. But an 'idol', strictly speaking, is an *eidôlon*, or image and symbol, and where the reality is hard to describe, such a symbol, whether mental, verbal or physical, may be a justifiable aid to concentration, provided that the mind is not content to settle on it, but to see through it and beyond it, and to reckon it as at best inadequate. The American chapel-deacon who said that he mentally visualized Deity as 'an oblong blur', was hardly in happier case than the Englishman who protested that his modernist vicar was always inviting him to worship 'a Scotch mist'. But we do not feel satisfied that the alternative to naïve idolatry is that of the Babu who said to Professor Hopkins: 'My wife, being imperfectly devil-upped, worships hare image. I, being perfectly devil-upped, worship myself.' We should perhaps prefer the spirit of the Indian sage Sankara (eighth century A.D.), who cried:

O Lord, pardon my three sins.
I have in contemplation clothed in form Thee who art formless:
I have in praise described Thee who art ineffable:
And in visiting temples I have ignored Thine omnipresence.

But in considering the effect of integration upon character we ought to be careful always to take the best examples: the finest specimens of Moslem piety; such men in India as Tagore; and among European Christians a Catholic saint like Charles de Foucauld, or a Protestant hero like Albert Schweitzer.

NOTE

It is humbling to find, as we study, that even false ideas, if believed in with sincerity, can be of service in the integration of the individual. Hence the danger of fraudulent religions arising, which obviously succeed by ministering to the integration of the credulous: while truth and error are often mingled without conscious insincerity, perhaps owing to emotional acquiescence, and without any attempt at rational enquiry. The pursuit of truth is vitally necessary in choosing one's creed, otherwise one tends to select what one likes; though the importance of this is not invariably recognized.

CHAPTER II

How our subject came to be studied

THIS will be a short chapter, and may be omitted on the first reading. But some students at any rate will like to know the past history of the scientific study of religion.

The impulse to catalogue the world and reduce it to a simple formula, however we may choose to explain it, seems to be European. It began, one supposes, with the Greeks, and if Alexander the Great had not died prematurely, we might have had from the pen of Aristotle a comparison of East and West, based on collected data. As it is, there is no real synthetic account of religions until the seventeenth century A.D. The scrappy information contained in the travellers' tales of Ctesias consists of little more than extravagant and misleading fables. Cicero, Plutarch and Sallustius write mostly about the nature and relations of the divinities known to the Graeco-Roman world, though in defining theocrasia, and in discussing the pros and cons of belief, they (and especially Plutarch) do make a beginning in the matter of theory. Early Christian apologists like Aristides recount their interpretation of the relationship between pagan, Jewish, and Christian beliefs; but, whatever we may think about the correctness of their assertions, they are in spirit, of course, propagandists and advocates. As we shall see later, the Christian claim made it necessary for its supporters to define their attitude towards non-Christian beliefs. This is first indicated in Paul's Epistle to the Romans (chapter i, verses 19 to end). Clement of Alexandria (c. A.D. 202) shows some slight knowledge of Buddhism, and Greek influences are strong in certain phases of Hindu and Buddhist art. There are parallels, as we shall notice, between Greek, Indian and Chinese thought, but this may be due to zoning, or the concurrent appearance of similar ideas in different places (according as we accept or reject diffusionist theories about the spread of culture). There is no conscious or acknowledged indebtedness. The influence of Neo-Platonist mystical technique was mediated through the translation of the pseudo-Dionysian writings from Syria to Ireland. We do not glean much information from the reports of the Franciscan friars who visited China for evangelistic purposes, and the travel-records of men like Marco Polo, though interesting, are not scientifically reliable. The early Renaissance cardinal, Nicholas of Cusa, suggested a federation of religions. But it is not until the end of the reign of Elizabeth that a treatise appears which makes any genuine attempt at a synoptic view of religious phenomena.

Lord Herbert of Cherbury, who was 22 years of age when the virgin queen died, and who ended his earthly career in 1648 (the year of the Peace of Westphalia), may claim to have initiated in this country the comparative study of religion. He holds no consistent position, but examines sympathetically the various opinions of his day, starting from very much the same position as Descartes, i.e. from a critical examination of his own processes of cognition. He is specially noteworthy for his assertion that religion is the chief distinguishing mark of man as a species, and that there are no real atheists, but only so-called atheists, who object to the false and inappropriate attributes which are assigned to Deity, and will rather have no God than one who is unworthy of belief: but he is also deserving of notice for his attempt at a scientific definition of religion which is summed up in five propositions:

    1. There is a Supreme *Numen*, possessing eleven attributes, i.e. it is blessed, self-existent, first cause, the energy and purpose of all things, eternal, good, just, wise, infinite, omnipotent and free.

2. It is man's duty to worship this Supreme Being.

3. Virtue and piety form the vital part of such worship.

4. Sin against this *Numen* must be repented of, and reparation made for it.

5. The world is morally governed. That is to say, in the future life man receives the due reward of his deeds.

Herbert is excusably misled by his Reformation tradition into attributing much early religion to the deliberate imposture of venal priesthoods, and his information about non-Christian faiths is naturally scanty and superficial, but he at least attempts to systematize his knowledge. Theorizing of a similar kind is to be found in the writings of John Locke (1632–1704), who is a typical product of seventeenth-century learning in this country, was elected from Westminster School to a scholarship at Christ Church, Oxford and is famous for his *Essay on the Human Understanding* and for his *Letters on Toleration*, written with special reference to the persecution of Protestants in France. It likewise appears in the essay by Anthony Collins, *A Discourse of Free-thinking*, published in 1715, which contains an interesting reference to early Anglican missionary activity (recently begun by the S.P.G. in 1699). The eighteenth-century Deists, with their penchant for 'natural religion', laid considerable stress upon what they believed to be a common residuum discoverable in all non-Christian faiths, and the Chinese in particular are described as 'their pets'.*

Travel and colonization from the time of Prince Henry the Navigator of Portugal onwards opened up large tracts of the world to Europeans, and made accessible to them much detailed information hitherto hidden. But observation, comment, and reflection seem to have travelled by a one-way

* See E. R. Hughes' recent account of the influence of Confucius upon Leibniz, Voltaire, and Rousseau, through their reading a Jesuit translation of his works, published in 1687 at Paris under the title: *Confucius Sinarum Philosophus*.

route until the present day. Whether actuated by Christian propagandist motives or scientific zeal, it is the Europeans who have until lately engaged in these activities. The *Lettres Persanes* composed by Montesquieu and the *Letters of John Chinaman* by Lowes Dickinson belong to the world of fiction, and have no counterpart in fact until the present age, when with the publication of Professor Mukerjee's work on mysticism, Professor Radhakrishnan's *Eastern Religions and Western Thought*, and the Khwajah Kamaluddin's treatise on Christianity and Islam (written from the Ahmadiyya Moslem stand-point), we get the beginnings of a new type of literature, which has been picturesquely described as a 'counter-attack from the east'. Unfortunately these latter works betray a tendentiousness almost as marked as that occurring in some which have been written from the Christian standpoint. (But it *is* true, as a friend said to me the other day, that Christians have discovered the great Eastern religions not only for themselves but for orientals, who have not always set as high a value upon them as we have!)

In between, however, we have a wealth of literature, showing the ever-growing interest which the study of the history of religion creates.

The first really systematic phenomenologists appear on the continent of Europe, Benjamin Constant in France, and Christoph Meiners* in Germany. The latter, who pursued his investigations at Göttingen, is thus described by Professor van der Leeuw: 'Not only does he attempt a classification . . . in which fetishism, worship of the dead and of stars and images, sacrifice, purifications, fasts, prayer, festivals, mourning customs, &c., are discussed in an orderly manner . . . He wishes to discover what is essential in religion, and in doing this he does not halt at the frontier formed by the antithesis between heathen religions and Christianity: all religions, he says, may

* Meiners was for a time an attaché at the German Embassy in London, about 1805.

possess as many unique features as they please; it is neverthe-less certain that each religion resembles others in many more respects than those wherein it differs from them ... Nor are finer distinctions lacking: that a people is poly- or mono-theistic of itself proves nothing: if one God is worshipped in the polytheistic way, the monotheism is not true and genuine.'

The age of the 'Aufklärung' (rationalistic enlightenment) in Germany was encyclopaedic in its methods, and in one sense began well. It was, however, succeeded by the age of Roman-ticism, and this, in its threefold aspect of romantic philosophy, romantic philology and romantic positivism, somewhat hin-dered the advance of scientific method by subjecting three quite proper departments of study to certain pre-conceived theories: (1) that all specific religious manifestations are symbols of a primordial revelation, (2) that the study of language will unearth the life of nature symbolized in religious concepts, (3) that religion is the voice of humanity speaking, though unfortunately, as van der Leeuw says, the positivists think it to have spoken falsely.

Subsequently this over-weight of theory was somewhat thrown off, and new and better empirical methods of historical and scientific study were adopted, the pioneers being Usener, Dieterich and Hackmann, and above all Chantepie de la Saus-saye, whose textbook on the history of religion, first pub-lished in 1887, marked the beginning of a new epoch, more especially since he assigned a wide scope to psychology.

Tribute should be paid at this point to Professor Friedrich Max Müller (1823–1900) a typical product of central Euro-pean scholarship, who eventually took up his residence at Oxford between 1854 and 1876 and worked there. He was mainly a Sanskrit expert, and a great Indologist, who knew the holy literature of India very well. But it was he who initiated and carried through most of the way the publication of the monumental series, Sacred Books of the East, and, as a sincere but liberal-minded Christian, stimulated others to explore what not only Hinduism but other non-Christian faiths might have to contribute to the spiritual riches of the world. His influence is traceable in the writings of many Victorians, notably Tennyson and Bishop Westcott. De la Saussaye's work was re-edited in 1925 by Bertholet and Lehmann, and remains still one of the most useful handbooks on the whole subject, though already even this newer edition grows increasingly out of date. A wealth of literature has poured forth since then, notably the great German encyclopaedia, *Die Religion in Geschichte und Gegenwart*, of which the first edition was completed on the eve of the outbreak of war in 1914, and the second edition in 1927 (the same year as the appearance of the *Encyclopaedia of Islam*), and the great British *Encyclopaedia of Religion and Ethics*, edited in Dr Hastings, first published in 1908. It is the fashion in certain Christian circles today to disparage the work of the religio-historical school, chiefly on account of its supposed neglect to take account of the specific genius of Christianity as Revelation; and this may to some extent be justified from the works of its members, who tend in many cases to estimate Christianity from what they say about it rather than from what is says about itself (which unfortunately is what some Christians tend to do in regard to Hinduism and Buddhism). But in fairness it must be pointed out that one of the most learned and judicious of the experts in the comparison of religions, Dr Nathan Söderblom, formerly Professor at Leipzig, and subsequently Archbishop of Upsala (*d.* 1931), was quite free from this sort of bias, and that his own faith and influence were all the stronger in consequence.

No doubt the study has its dangers. It may sink to the level of collecting dead insects or pressed flowers, which in the process lose all their colour and reality. Collecting religions is no better. The only tolerable way of engaging in the work is to let one's self be enthralled by man's ceaseless quest for

something supernatural and eternal which the ordinary life
of this world will never give him, and to try to put one's self
into the place of those who are obviously enthusiasts for a
religion which is not one's own. Comparison is possible only
when we know enough facts to make it, and until then it is
premature. Most of the work done in this book must be to
prepare folk for coming to know such facts as will enable them
to make comparisons with justice and fairness.

Classification is inevitable, but it cannot by itself tell us all
we want to know.

A natural distinction may well be drawn between (1) religions which are still living and expanding; (2) religions which
though still alive are stationary, stagnant or contracting; (3)
religions which have ceased to live. Islam is an obvious example of the first class, Judaism of the second, Manichaeism of
the third. Yet, although this looks an easy classification, it
needs to be remembered that a religion which is dead in one
area may be alive in another, and that a religion which appears
to be dead everywhere may exist under another label in a
number of places. Graeco-Roman polytheism may be defunct
in Europe, but much of its equivalent may be found in parts
of India. Primitive animism may be extinct in Britain, save for
a few local underground survivals in superstition and folk-
lore; but it is very much alive in parts of Assam, Borneo and
Polynesia. Roman state-worship has its counterpart in the
modern leader-cultus, and, until recently, in the Mikado-worship of Japan. Mediterranean Catholicism, in its desire to be
all things to all men, has taken into its hospitable lap items
which properly belong to Mediterranean ethnic religion,
and the latter thus survives under a Christian veneer, and
is not really a thing of the past (as for example in Sicily,
where as recently as thirty years ago torch-races, surviving
from the ancient cult of Dionysus, were still run by naked
kourētes in connexion with the *festa* of a certain saint,

though perhaps not strictly approved of by local ecclesiastics).*

A further important distinction may also be drawn between religious beliefs which appear to be as close approximations to truth as are humanly possible, and beliefs which are suitable or convenient to those who hold them. It is unfortunately the case that both nations and individuals are inclined to adopt the latter rather than the former, and that truth has sometimes to be coated with an institutional husk in order to render it palatable. This is of course the stock argument for Catholicism, and it would appear that it was Gandhiji's argument for much popular Hinduism. But what we observe will be misjudged and misunderstood if this not borne in mind. Prophetic religion is a very high creed for the masses; and just as Christian missionaries have often tried to accommodate themselves to their flocks, so (as we shall see) even Mohammed was led to resort to unscrupulous dodges in order to coax the Arabian tribes inside his rigid transcendental monotheistic system. The alternatives to such compromises are either iconoclastic revolution, or patient and rather depressingly slow permeation, in which the revolution comes to individuals one at a time, rather than to a whole community which is suddenly jolted *en masse* out of the ethnic into the prophetic groove. (The reader may, if he likes, at this point, turn to the Epilogue, and see what sort of comparisons and classifications have so far been tried.)

To those who fear that a great war may see the destruction of the noblest religion, and that its study may soon become merely a branch of archaeology, may be said: Military aggres-

* The late Mr J. C. Lawson, of Pembroke College, Cambridge, published in 1910 the results of an extensive personal enquiry into the survivals of Hellenic mythology and folk-lore in modern Greece. These were rather striking as well as copious. For instance, the cult of the goddess Demeter has become the reverence of a female saint Demetria (no historical character). Helios becomes Elias. (The story of the latter's apotheosis has always looked suspiciously like a fragment of a sun-myth.) Charon becomes Charos, the angel of death; and so on.

sion and non-moral violence are no new things in the world. They were known to the earliest dwellers in the river-valley civilizations. They are commonplaces in the Old Testament. They were familiar to Zarathustra, Buddha and Confucius, as much as to Jesus or Augustine the Great, to Bernard, Francis, Luther or John Wesley. That they are to many in our generation more of a scandal and a terror than they were to our forefathers is no mark of their impending triumph, but rather a hopeful sign of increased sensitiveness to man's wicked and carnal misuse of his divinely-bestowed freedom. So does humanity progress. So may the predatory types of humanity discredit and destroy themselves. *Sic itur ad astra.*

Yet there is no innate tendency in man to progress. He may equally remain stationary, or deteriorate. Even in chipping flint artefacts, it is well known that deterioration in technique is evident as between the Acheulean and Mousterian periods.

The art of propaganda in war-time was known and practised by the Assyrians in *c.* 800 B.C., as may be seen from the story of Rabshakeh (in II Kings xviii), who is quite as scurrilous and plausible as the little lame Spielmann of the Third Reich.

Those who study the history of religion in general and of Christianity in particular will often come across phases when they will be compelled to exclaim: 'This is not so high a level as that reached (say) two centuries ago.'

The following passage occurred in a broadcast by Dr I. A. Richards during October 1947:

'Here is a very odd thing. In literature the best in each kind comes first, comes suddenly and never comes again. This is a disturbing, uncomfortable, unacceptable idea to people who take their doctrine of evolution over-simply. But I think it must be admitted to be true. Of the very greatest things in each sort of literature, the masterpiece is unprecedented, unique, never challenged or approached henceforth.'

Is not something like this true in the sphere of religion?

CHAPTER III

New Materials

THE exciting thing about the last thirty years is the vast mass of fresh facts which have become available for the study of the history and comparison of religions. The pile of data is almost daily being added to, in ways both small and great. The story of man's quest for the Sacred, and of the alleged action of the Sacred upon man is of profound interest, since each individual has but a short span to spend on earth, and is naturally much concerned to know how best to live an integrated and honourable life, and to pass on the knowledge and art of it to his children. Thus it seems right to make as much as possible of this new material accessible to the public. Some of it will be found of pathetic, nay of tragic, interest. Some is inspiring, some repellent. The limit of our research has not yet been reached, and therefore a perfect map of man's religious development cannot even now be constructed; but so much more is known both in outline and detail than a quarter of a century ago, that a fairly stable provisional account can already be given. Most of us, however, who are engaged in studying the material are not in any vast hurry to complete our reconstruction. We want still more data, and for these we turn to the archaeologist and the anthropologist, as well as to the missionary and the student of texts and documents, and also to the laboratory-workers in psychology.

To take the latter first, we may expect to learn a good deal about the processes connected with Hebrew prophecy and Arabian divination from the line of study now being pursued by such enthusiasts as Rhine and Tyrrell,* with their extended investigations into the distribution and intensity of E.S.P. (extra-sensory perception and P.K., psycho-kinesis, known together as 'psi capacities'). These investigations have so far been applied only to Europeans. They should be applied with equal care and patience to Asiatics of various types: the more recent researches of Rhine in America upon P.K. may perhaps have some bearing upon the problem of miracles. Inquiries into visualization were first made seriously by Francis Galton, and his results have been available in print for a good many years: but much more research is now being done in this direction, notably in the matter of what is called eidetic imagery, or the tendency for visual images to persist or be reproduced after the external cause of them has been removed, and much more still remains to be done. We may note also the suggestive comments of Sigmund Freud and Sante de Sanctis on the phenomenon of *latency*, especially in conversion, as accounting for the precise appearance, disappearance or recurrence of certain religious beliefs and practices.

Turning to the anthropologist and archaeologist, whose work dovetails, we find that their chief contribution lies in helping us gradually to realize the horizontal diffusion of various religious ideas and practices with which we are becoming familiar. In the nineteenth century, when travellers found some familiar cultural phenomenon also present in a distant part of Africa or Asia, such as a creation- or flood-story, or sacrificial or sacramental ritual, they were prone to assume that it had got there through European or Christian influence, perhaps at a fairly recent date. We are now beginning to realize that such diffusions, though common in the case of pieces of applied science such as the petrol engine, or of clothing such

* J. B. Rhine, *New Frontiers of the Mind* (A106) and *The Reach of the Mind* (A319), Pelican Books; G. N. M. Tyrrell, *The Personality of Man*, Pelican Book (A165).

as felt hats, or even in the case of missionary-borne religions,
are not necessarily recent, but may well be of considerable antiquity, and perhaps not even diffusions at all. When we find in
fact similar but widely separated magical and religious practices, these may either be remnants of a widely extended zone
of custom which existed in the remote past, or else concurrent
developments due to the working of the human intellect in a
similar fashion in different places without any borrowing or
contact. But the former is the more likely explanation, and the
diffusion in question probably took place from some single
spot long centuries ago.

When I visited the British Empire Exhibition held at Wem-
bley in 1924, I was taken to see a dance performed by three
Tibetans. It was of a type enacted frequently, I believe, on the
frontiers of north India, and probably a fairly common form
of entertainment in such places as the bazaar at Simla, but it
was originally a piece of sympathetic magic, danced by hunters
to persuade some mysterious Power to send animals to be
killed for food, and the dancers wore masks surmounted by
the antlers of deer. Judge my astonishment when a year or two
later I saw a Scandinavian reindeer folk-dance of a very similar
character, and last year was sent a cutting of a photograph
from a daily paper, showing an almost identical dance being
performed (in England this time) in the street of Abbot's
Bromley, Staffs, the antlers used being stored between times in
the village church. Obviously all three dances had in the beginning a similar origin, whatever later significance they may
have come to possess, and some of the cave-paintings in the
Pyrenees (e.g. Teyjat and the Trois Frères cavern) are of such
a character as to render it likely that dances of this sort were
held as far back as between 20,000 and 12,000 B.C. The truth is
that even in the old Palaeolithic a huge culture area extended
from the Thames to the Cape, from the Atlantic to the Indies –
nearly half the world, with the same Chelleo-Acheulean

industry throughout; and this unity passes on to later periods.

Again, it is somewhat staggering to find that in Sumeria in the fifth millennium before Christ it was the custom for expectant mothers to invoke a female divinity, Ishtar, with votive offerings, and to record favours granted, by placing tablets on the temple walls inscribed with expressions of thanksgiving, and that it is still the fashion in Paris, Milan and even Berlin, for the Blessed Virgin to be invoked and thanked in this way, while in the Far East the goddess Kwanyin is the centre of a similar cultus.

We are also learning how religious ideas and practices as well as arts and crafts have in the past travelled along trade routes and the paths of military expeditions, quite as much as they do today.* Thus the cult of Mithras, originating in Iran, penetrated to the hills of the Scottish border, whither it was brought by soldiers in the garrison of the Roman wall. The Greek physician, Hecataeus, of the age of Alexander the Great, appears to have travelled as far east as the Punjab, and as far west as Gaul, and he refers to a megalithic temple of Apollo (? sun-worship) in an island off the coast of Gaul, which is generally supposed to have been Stonehenge. (Of course it may have been Avebury,† which is much older, and was larger.) But one of the curious features of Stonehenge is that it was probably erected by builders who were acquainted with a trick of dovetailing stones together by a tenon, which we

---

* See the connexion between Alfred the Great and the Nestorian Christians of India, recorded on page 141.

† The evidence suggests that Avebury was made by Beaker folk of the early Bronze Age, but that Stonehenge is of the early Iron Age. The test recently devised, of examining snail-shells found in samples of earth taken from the ditch and post-holes, is said to prove that the climate at the time of the building of Stonehenge cannot have been earlier than that prevailing in the fifth century B.C. Professor Grahame Clark considers that the work may belong to two different periods.

now know to have been in use among Greek temple-builders. This is not the only example of Greek art influencing Bronze-age or early Iron-age Britain: the golden coins of the British kings prior to the Roman occupation are decorated with a horse-design copied from the *staters* of Philip of Macedon. And this leads one to refer to another notable example of a zone of religious custom, i.e. the erection of great stones for cultus of various sorts, which is still being practised by certain hill-tribes in India to this day, but is found to extend from China to Ireland. The menhirs of Exmoor and the North Riding of Yorkshire (not to mention the megaliths of Brittany and Cornwall) are arranged in a manner almost identical with those of the Khasis and Nagas of Assam. One very ingenious etymological theory makes the name of the god Apollo connect with the word 'pella', which is a Greek synonym for the better-known word 'lithos', a stone, and 'pella' is by Grimm's law the same as the German 'Fels', a rock. We have actual record of the connexion of Apollo with certain menhirs. Thus both Apollo and the Jupiter Lapis of the Romans were probably either ancestral- or nature-spirits associated with megaliths. Stone circles are connected quite as much with open-air sky-worship as with the burial and cult of the dead, and it is remarkable that they are distributed over an area ranging from the British Isles to Peking, and including Africa, Italy, Scandinavia, Persia, Arabia and the North-west frontier of India. Stone-circles, avenues and menhirs are by no means all of the same age, any more than Gothic churches are. The practice of making them may well have prevailed through several millennia; and the most highly developed circle, the well-known white-marble Altar of Heaven at Peking, was erected as recently as 1889. Recent investigations have shown that the stone circle is related to the wood circle. There may well have been many woodhenges to one Stonehenge. And this leads to the further reflection that the 'place of worship' tends to develop out of natural surroundings which become stylized. Thus the grove is conventionalized into a circle of posts, and the posts become megalithic uprights. Similarly the camp-fire, hearth or cremation pyre becomes conventionalized into the altar of burnt sacrifice; and the chief's house, often little more than a hut with a porch and a stockade, into the temple of the god. The mountain or hill-top becomes (especially in less hilly countries) the artificial mountain, whether ziggurat, teocalli or bamah; and on these lines the 'arborescent look of lofty Gothic aisles' may well prove to be a real reminiscence of central European forests, a Tannenwald frozen into stone.

Much light has lately been thrown upon the dance as an expression of meaning, and upon its liturgical significance in Hebrew and even in Christian worship. It used to be thought that the Seville cathedral dance three times a year was an isolated phenomenon, but Miss Alford's investigations have lately revealed that such dances were known throughout the Iberian peninsula. The Seville dance is recorded as far back as 1508, but must actually be much older. There was another at Toledo. As recently as 1932 at Braga there was a morris dance called 'the dance of King David'. And another, actually in church, took place at Pedrogão Pequeno till 1875. At Zumarraga till recently there was a sword-dance in front of the high altar. At Oñate sword-dancers performed in front of the Host. In pays d'Arbérone at several places a troupe of dancers performed on the feast of Corpus Christi – after the elevation of the Host. And so on. But not only in Iberia. Down to the nineteenth century the villagers of Batsford and Wishford had the right to dance in Salisbury Cathedral, and the apprentices of York claimed a similar right in the Minster on Shrove Tuesday! Up to sixty years ago York apprentices each received on Shrove Tuesday a shilling and a half-holiday, the latter no doubt in connexion with the dance. For a further account of such dances see Violet Alford, *Pyrenean Festivals*; Christina Hole, *English Customs and Usage*.

New texts and documents are rapidly getting into print, some of them only, it is true, in a form accessible to experts, such as the Ras Shamra tablets (1929 and onwards), and the various early Babylonian texts, e.g. the Tammuz liturgy editied by Witzel, and the Ishtar liturgy, edited by Langdon; but others in popular translations, such as the 'Wisdom of the East' series, Sir Wallis Budge's edition of Egyptian wisdom-literature, the Everyman edition of selected Indian books, and *The Bible of the World*, a large corpus of religious documents of all kinds, published in England and the United States. A somewhat similar collection, made by Lehmann and Haas, appeared a few years back, for those who can read German; but most of the works mentioned above provide English translations, and many of these are putting out of date versions which appeared in the nineteenth century. The work of the Pali Text Society is beyond praise, and the latest additions to its series of translations of Buddhist works, executed by the late Lord Chalmers and Miss I. B. Horner, are of the greatest value for our knowledge of early Buddhism, and fit admirably on to the work of Mrs Rhys Davids, which is still the subject of keen controversy, and which has led us to recast our views of the original teaching of Gotama, very much as the work of Dr Schweitzer has led us to reconsider the original teaching of Jesus of Nazareth.

Dr Guillaume has lately collected and set in order a mass of information about divination, prophecy and second sight among the Arabs and others, which sheds considerable light upon the technique of Hebrew prophecy, his quotations from Ibn Khaldun, al Ghazâli and Maimonides being of special value. Most striking, indeed, and most modernistic is the theory of Maimonides that the strange symbols referred to by the Hebrew prophets, such as the visions of candlesticks, horses and mountains in Zechariah, the scroll of Ezekiel, the wall made by a plumb-line seen by Amos, the beasts of Daniel and the seething pot of Jeremiah, were all of them seen in a dream or vision, and perceived as to their meaning when the dreamer awoke. Thus does Maimonides attribute a sort of Freudian technique to these ancient seers, and one cannot but wonder whether perhaps he is right.

In 1928 I had the privilege of laying before the University Theological Society in Cambridge a series of data regarding the localization of the Divine Presence in food, especially passages from the Jesuit Fr Acosta's description of the Mexican cultus of the god Vitziputzli, which threw fresh light upon the controversy then raging with regard to Eucharistic cultus. More recently much fresh information has become available regarding the use of so-called sacred books in the various religions, which compels us to revise the generalizations current in the middle of the nineteenth century.

At this very moment a new monograph is appearing from the pen of Professor E. E. Evans-Pritchard dealing with the primitive Nuer people of the Southern Sudan, which is of great interest to all students, whether concerned with Old Testament studies or with Comparative Religion.

And so the materials go on being accumulated and interpreted with considerable speed. The pace is so hot that no really up-to-date list of them is possible.

The position, in fact, with regard to religions will soon tend to resemble that prevailing in the world of science, i.e. the initiative will pass from the memorizing to the analytical part of the intelligence (see Crowther, vol. 1, pp. 143-4). The enormous mass of interesting data will get sorted and catalogued, and then some comparatively young men will astonish us, and flutter the hearts of conservatives in all denominations, by seeing what it all means. Already a number of disturbing inferences are bring drawn.

CHAPTER IV

The Beginnings

How did religion start? – If we could answer that rightly, we might, so some think, the better forecast its ultimate future. This is by no means certain, since ugly embryos often grow into handsome adults; still it would be more satisfying to our curiosity if we could arrive at a clear explanation. As it is, we are able only to infer the remote past from the researches of archaeologists and pre-historians, and the vestigial remains existing among so-called primitive races which are still lagging behind in the Stone age, or perhaps in some case have deteriorated and reverted to earlier and otherwise discarded modes of living and thinking.

One fact at any rate is certain, namely that the problems with which religious beliefs and practices seek to deal were not created by those practices, but are, so to speak, the raw material upon which religion has to work. There would seem to be four of these,* and they are obviously inter-related.

1. The self or ego.
2. The world or the environment of the self, including other selves.

* Another writer whom I cannot now trace has made a similar, but slightly different, division. He says that there are three things which we cognize, but which rise completely above all possible sense-experience (for checking by pointer-readings). These three are: (i) Self-existence; (ii) unpredictability or indeterminism; (iii) continuance of a certain element within the self which can have further experiences beyond bodily death. These are the same (as will be seen) as Kant's God, freedom and immortality!

3. The Self-Existent, variously conceived, but felt and even dreaded, long before It is the object of thought.

4. Valuable objects, again variously conceived.

Each of these four is a problem in itself, but to dismiss religion as resulting from an illusion due to misperception is to misunderstand it entirely. Attempts have been made in the name of religion to show one or more of the four to be illusory, but not all four at once. Hindus may affirm that the self, the world and human values are unreal, and that the sole existent is Brahma, who is beyond good and evil. Jains may reject the third item if defined as a unitary transcendent being, and say that the only realities are finite selves and moral values. But religion as previously defined is not reducible to the error of compensatory projection or fantasy-weaving. The four items mentioned above are recognized by all normal human beings, and no one can, without impoverishment of life, for long evade the attempt to construct such an integration of life as will provide an adjustment to these four categories. All at some time seek a working belief which will answer the questions: What am I? – What is this 'myself' of which I seem to be aware? – What is this world of environment? – What does it mean? – What is it for? – What is my relation to it? – What is death? – What is the nature of that which is beyond my control, and indeed beyond the control of any of my fellow-mortals? – Is there not a Something or Somebody Permanent and Abiding amid the change and decay which I see all around me and in which I share? – And again, in some few exceptionally gifted individuals among my fellow human beings do I not seem to discern shadows and symbols of the nature of that Deep Reality? – Do I not find in them and in the depths of my being a Super-Human Imperative speaking? – Finally, I find myself setting values upon the various objects around me. Sometimes it is merely a matter of food, warmth, rest or shelter. At another it is a matter of the storage of crops or water, or the procuring of hunting-weapons. Or it may be human leadership, or physical desirability, or a special kind of character or human quality which I come to prize. But in leisure moments I find myself questioning life, and asking, Why should anything be worth anything? – Why these values? – And what do they imply? – Is there an ascending scale? – (I find myself ready to inconvenience myself almost to a ridiculous extent for the sake of some of them.) And, further, are those which I hold dearest, and for which I am ready to risk life itself, guaranteed by the Self-Existent reality which I cannot control, or does the Latter mock me, and exhibit hostility or indifference to the vital choices I make? – Is it or is it not the case that this Reality sometimes seems to call upon me from above or within to hazard all for the sake of some apparently quite intangible thing? – And do I not sometimes feel myself guilty of a certain failure in respect of my loyalty to such intangibles, though at other times I may gird at myself for being such a quixotic fool? – What is this sense of uneasiness, of thwartedness, of lack of attainment, which besets me?

The realist stateman is inclined to say that so far no satisfying answers have been forthcoming to any of these questions. One such modern has written: 'How can this rubbish-pile of errors be considered as containing evidence of truth?' and another, while declaring that the great questions still remain unsolved, would invite us to remember that our primitive forefathers, though desperately uncomfortable, still had a blind instinct that life was somehow worth going on with (otherwise we should not be here), and that therefore we in our modern misery and uncertainty may pin our faith upon the same natural instinct. This is rather like the Yorkshireman returning late from a party, and saying, 'Ah doan't knaw wheer Ahm goan, but *still* Ahm on ma wey'.

While sympathizing with such individuals, I should hardly

have thought it worth while to write a book about the history of religions if I did not think we were getting anywhere at all. It must be confessed freely that all the answers orginally given to the questions arrayed above have not been good ones, nor does the survival value which some of them possess testify to their adequacy. People often tend to believe what they like, rather than what they need, what suits them rather than what is probably correct. At the same time, just as any answer which ignores or outrages any one of the four categories with which we started is unlikely to be true, even if it cannot be otherwise proved false, so any answer which honestly attempts to deal justly with any of the four categories must be held likely to contain at least something of the truth about it.

And so we will make a start with what seems discoverable about the earliest forms of religious life among the lower cultures.

We shall be concerned at first with very humble and rudimentary matters. Man's spiritual life, like his body, emerges out of the dust. It is no belittlement of the genius of Shakespeare, Bach or Darwin, to recognize that in the embryonic stage the foetus which afterwards grew into the boldily shrine of each mighty personality passed through a stage when it was endowed with a tail and gill-slits. Hence we must not be shocked or dismayed if we find that the loftiest types of prophecy, sacramental worship or mystical vision have developed out of crude and even unattractive beginnings. It is not what a thing may be traced back to that is significant, but what it grows into and ultimately becomes. 'It is not fair to ask for beauty in a seed, even though some seeds *are* beautiful.'

We have no cetain knowledge of the religious practices of any sub-human anthropoids whose existence may be fairly well assumed somewhere between the apes and the true men. It is, however, known that chimpanzees exhibit great unhappiness if banished or separated from their fellows, and the

Chillingham wild cattle have a curious way of outlawing individual beasts who have apparently committed a breach of some rule or convention of the herd. These look like rudimentary forms of the sense of sin and of its punishment. Again, many of the members of sub-human species have a rudimentary sense of awe and 'spookiness'. Dr Oman tells a story of a horse he was riding in the Highlands which showed signs of this 'primal numinous awe'. Certainly aninals are conscious of a very real uneasiness in the presence of the death of one of their own kind. None of them, however, make any pretence of burying their dead ceremonially.* The first recorded examples of the latter come from the age of the so-called Neanderthal men, some fifty to one hundred thousand years B.C.

Piecing together such information as archaeology and anthropology are able to provide, what kind of adjustment to the four categories mentioned above do we seem to discern in the lowest cultures?

1. *The Self or Ego.* – The main points seem to be the conception of the self, in its composition, and as related to dreams, death and ghosts.

Most Westerns today analyse themselves into body and soul, But other earlier races made a different subdivision, and even believed in a plurality of souls. The Iroquois Indians had six words for non-bodily elements, and the Haida Indians of British Columbia distinguish mind, ghost and disembodied spirit, but have also two words for an embodied spirit, while in China, New Guinea, Indonesia, etc., the belief that man has two souls is widespread. Some Melanesians believe an individual to have as many as seven souls, while Egyptian thought distinguished five soul-elements, and it is probable that the

---

* It has been suggested that rabbits and badgers co-operate to bury corpses of dead badgers 'ceremonially', but Mr Seth-Smith informs me that the evidence is insufficient to establish this as a fact.

Romans possessed plural notions as well. St Paul speaks of body, soul and spirit. On the other hand, the possession of multiple souls is balanced by the notion of 'soul-less men'. Not all human beings are credited with souls capable of being separated from the body; and this explains the reservation that immortality is at first in many cases (for example in Egypt and in China) an aristocratic privilege. Only the big chiefs and warriors have a spirit that goes on living in another world. This is perhaps an early form of what later speculative theologians have come to call 'conditional immortality'.

The belief in a continuant spirit is derived largely from the phenomena of dreams, since it is held (e.g. by the Lengua Indians of South America) that the separable spirit for a time leaves the body and wanders freely about, enjoying experiences of its own. At the same time some form of continuance seems to have been demanded by the consciousness of the most primitive man as he stood by a grave-side, and put into the tomb food and utensils for the use of the dead. We can picture him as saying, like Goethe: 'Do you think a coffin can impose on me?' Physical phenomena such as are today under investigation were obviously known from the earliest times, and visions of dying or deceased persons, possibly subjective, may have given rise to belief in ghosts.

2. *The World, including Other Selves*. – It is not a far cry from humans to non-humans, and the gap between them which seems to exist not only among many Christians but especially among Mediterranean peoples (whether Christian or not matters little) is not nearly so marked elsewhere. The early attitude seems to imply a possible relationship between the human and the non-human, and to think one's self descended from a honey-ant, a witchetty-grub or a crocodile does not feel incongruous for a certain type of primitive mind. A Papuan included the crested dove, the black cockatoo and even a particular iguana as members of his tribe. African folk-tales

convey the impression that men and animals are members of one family. The domestic animals in the west of Europe certainly are so regarded. Hence the practice in Holland of announcing the death of the farmer to his cattle or bees. It is not that the status of man is depressed, but that the status of animals is higher than in the Hebrew scriptures. To Hebrews man is the lord of creation, ordained to have dominion over non-human organic life, and in this respect the Franciscan attitude – 'our sisters the birds' – is not Hebraic. The gospels are perhaps neutral in this matter, and St Francis doubtless derives his friendliness towards animals and birds from eastern mysticism entering the Christian church through the writings of pseudo-Dionysius, so that we have here an element akin more to what is found in India, than to European tradition. Mr Gandhi defended cow-protection on the score that it symbolized the unity between the human and the sub-human creation; and if a Western had been inclined to call this defence mere rationalization, and to deplore the effects of the practice itself, Gandhi might very well have replied with a twinkle – 'What about dog-protection in England?'

Early man would seem to have drawn but little distinction between himself and his animal, bird and reptile cousins, and this is the obvious explanation not only of what is called totemism (or the allocation of a possibly non-human ancestor to a tribal group or sub-group), but also of the belief in transmigration of souls, which would certainly have been repugnant to anyone holding Hebraic views. It is thought that transmigration doctrine in India is the legacy of the non-Aryans, since in the earliest strata of the Vedas there is no mention of it, nor does it figure in European Nordic mythologies. It is said to have occurred in Druidism, but this may be due to some infiltration westward along the Mediterranean from the Near East, which certainly knew the doctrine (as it was taught by Pythagoras in Italy), or, alternatively, it may have been a survival

from the very early culture which preceded the peopling of
the Mediterranean lands by dark whites. In India, therefore,
it need not have been an introduction by the early Dravidians,
but perhaps a legacy of the australoid aborigines who preceded
them, and who may have passed it on to the invaders.

When we leave the sub-human creation and come to man
himself, it is clear that the reverence for departed spirits plays
a very large part in early conceptions of the Sacred. Some
Polynesian tribes have club-houses where objects symbolizing
ancestors are preserved, and there is really not much essential
difference between these and the rooms in Chinese houses
where ancestral tablets are preserved. What, however, is not
so clear is the precise amount of 'worship' which is offered
to ancestors. Is it more than a mere compliment to a deceased
human being, or is it a gesture of real adoration towards the
Divine which is present in every man? The latter seems to
contain a strong element of probability in it, since the reverence for animals which has been labelled 'theriolatry' is almost
certainly a gesture not to the individual animal but to the
manifestation of the terrifying or powerful Sacred which it
displays.

Initiation appears on the surface largely a social rather than
a religious matter. It concerns the transition from immaturity
to adult membership of the tribe, and its ceremonies (*rites de
passage*) celebrate the solemnity of that transition, toughen the
individual, and are associated with the imparting of tribal traditions and the necessary erudition of an adult member of the
tribe. A good deal, however, has been made of the social
aspect of religion – in other words, the treatment of the group
itself as the Sacred – and those who virtually maintain that the
first deity was the tribe (the word *en masse* so to speak) see in
initiation the most religious of all acts, i.e. the attainment by
the growing boy or girl of self-consciousness as a member of
the sacred unit. But this is certainly not the whole story.

Religion has not one root but several, and, as we shall see in a moment, there are many peoples in an extremely early stage of development whose Sacred Object is not the personification of the tribe, nor even derived from such a personification. Initiation, therefore, sometimes involves the attainment of an adult relationship to a Transcendent Sacred as well as to a Sacred Community, though it may well be that such a Transcendent Being is not very nobly conceived, but may be merely a totemic super-animal, a large natural object, or the personification of a heavenly body, or simply a glorified ancestor. What is perhaps the common property of all initiations is the sense that man as he is is not his true self. For whatever purpose, to attain full efficiency he must be born again, and at initiation the boy or girl sometimes actually takes a new name altogether, and gives up being called by the old name – an episode not entirely unknown even to us, since children at school often drop their infantile pet names, and adults promoted to high dignity give up the use of one Christian name and bring into use another to mark the attainment of office; while kings and bishops have official names which they do not necessarily use in private life.

3. *The Self-Existent*. – Here we arrive at the basic problem. The controversy still rages as to whether the earliest known conception of It in the savage mind was (*a*) animatism or (*b*) monotheism. In any case It soon becomes pluralistic. To avert suspicion of bias, the various positions had best be stated. The evolutionists, though differing as to details, are on the whole agreed as to the main outline. They see man at his lowest stage of thought incapable of imagining a personal deity, however local or diminutive. This is the stage of *animatism*, belief in a vague, potent, terrifying, inscrutable Force, which manifests Itself in varying degrees and with unequal potency in all types of phenomena, meteorites, bull-roarers, rocks, trees, waterfalls, lightning, wild beasts, blood, eclipses, old men, women

in certain conditions of the sexual life, epileptics and so on. Though largely inarticulate, this is a sort of primitive pantheistic monism, which gradually changes to personalism of a pluralistic sort, and to the belief in a vast number of tricksy and capricious spirits large and small. This passes on to polytheism, and polytheism in turn gives way to a unified thought, either pantheistic, theistic or even deistic. At the opposite extreme from this explanation stands that of the anti-evolutionist, who says that man, even in his earliest stages, is able to grasp the idea of one good God, and has grasped it; and that naïve animism, polydaemonism, polytheism, as well as their rejection by philosophic monists, pluralists, materialists and so on, are all instances of decline from an original pure faith, which it was the mission of Hebrews and Christians to restore to mankind. The defence of this latter thesis is not entirely desperate, for the simple reason that there is a residuum of evidence, when all is said and done, for the prevalence among some of the pygmy and other very backward peoples of a kind of naïve monotheism; while among polydaemonistic savages are often to be found traces of what is called belief in a 'high god', apparently the vestigial remains of the same sort of naïve monotheism; but this 'high god' is quite in the background, and is so much of a *roi fainéant* that nobody addresses any worship to him (or her – for the high god is not necessarily of the male sex).

Between the evolutionist and the anti-evolutionist stand those who, on the evidence at present available, cannot make up their minds, and feel bound to suspend judgement. The evolutionist theory seems to them a little too tidy to be true; and yet they feel that the truth is probably something resembling it. The anti-evolutionist theory seems to them plainly biased by the (at least sub-conscious) wish to prove Genesis I literally correct; and yet the enormous pile of evidence collected by Fr Schmidt of Vienna has not been properly digested by such anthropologists as are devoid of pro-Biblical bias. Something, one supposes, must depend upon whether the pygmies are survivals of a generation of human beings bearing the same relationship to later types as that borne by the hipparion to the normal-sized horse, or whether they are just local varieties, or diminutives of a normal sized species, in which case their beliefs need not be of profound antiquity or significance.

So there the matter remains. Perhaps the general primitiveness of animatism will eventually be established to the satisfaction of even the most hide-bound conservatives, with the proviso that here and there human beings may have jumped intermediary stages, showing transilience in the spiritual as well as in the biological sphere, and have arrived at a naïve monotheism not very different from that of a good many simple Christians. Even so, such monotheism has not proved anything like as dynamic as that of the greater Hebrew prophets, of some Christians, of Zarathustra, or even of Mohammed. The value of any monotheism seems to depend on the extent to which Deity is conceived as being not only transcendent but responsive and disposed to take the initiative, so that quasi-personal relations can exist between Deity and humanity. Where such are absent, the 'high god', whether in the higher Hinduism or in primitive Australia, is, as we have said already, a *roi fainéant*, and receives no worship.

The sense of the Self-Existent is held by Fr Erich Przywara to derive from three sources, or rather three main lines of experience: (1) distance, (2) depths of the soul, (3) stream of process; and since all these three forms of experience are from the very first possible, even if the inarticulate primitive is incapable of describing them in explicit terms, it is not easy to rule out the possibility of concurrent types having existed from the very beginning of human society (as Dr Paul Radin maintains), though primitive gregariousness will naturally tend to make the third type of experience more frequent than the other two at a very early period. The communal hut is not a comfortable nursery-garden for prophets or mystics. Actually it was believed by Professor Elliot Smith that the earliest attempt at the conception of a personal deity was probably that of the Great Mother, the personification of fertile maternity,* as we find it among the Aurignacians of (say) 15,000 B.C. and later in an almost identical form among the neolithic and early bronze-age Mediterranean peoples of Crete, Malta, &c. In South America there are some 'matrilinear' Indians who worshipped a single deity of the 'Great Mother' type till they came in contact with Europeans, and then developed into polydaemonism.

Yet whatever form experience of the Self-Existent may take, it produces an attitude of relationship to a 'Thou', whether that 'Thou' be a vague force, the Whole Universe, a glorified ancestor, the personification of a heavenly body or a unique High God. This attitude is reflected from very early times in (i) what is called 'sacrifice', and in (ii) the sense of there being things to be done or not to be done.

(i) Sacrifice, as a common feature of most religions, needs some explanation. It is generally held to involve the dedication of an object to Deity, and then its destruction, either by killing, burning or pouring out; but this does not quite cover all forms of delivery into the keeping of the god, since in some cases the object dedicated is merely left in the precinct of the dwelling-place of the god, and then afterwards consumed by priest or people. Five motives for sacrifice have been suggested: adoration, thanksgiving, bargaining, propitiation or peace-offering and expiation or reparation; the last two being closely allied. Sacrifice is sometimes disinterested, but it is usually animated by the mixed desire so well expressed in the early Victorian schoolboy's letter to his parents, 'Gratitude,

* See p. 58.

duty and a view to future advantages compel me to address you'. As a small compliment to capricious daemons, we may note the pots of honey sacrificed by the pygmies of Mount Elgon to forest spirits, and 'the good piece', a small bit of food thrown over the left shoulder by the Sussex yokel, to appease some forgotten godling, worshipped or feared by his remote ancestors.

One dominant motive is the desire to keep the divinity in question alive. 'Gods die from lack of nourishment.' The destruction or delivery of the offerings is not to be thought of in terms of death but of life. The object is to feed the god, that he or she may go on presiding over human destinies, and should there also be a communion meal upon the sacrificial elements, to enable the communicants to share in the life of the god, who has already taken up the offering into union with himself.

Yet though bred of humble and even selfish origins, sacrifice is capable of developing into the noblest of all religious acts – the utter self-abandonment of the worshipper to the purpose of the Self-Existent Being, and the continuous reparation for one's inadequate devotion to the service of a Deity, with whom, to use a very human expression, one has fallen in love. Perhaps the very simplest form of the rite is the adoration of a vague power, concrete in some awe-inspiring or potent object. Readers of the Bible will have been puzzled to hear of folk in Mesopotamia who 'burned incense unto their drag-net or hook'. But to offer sacrifice to a tool or machine is a well-recognized practice in India, where on a certain day in the year, the festival of Ayudah Puja, it is the custom for most Hindus to do sacrifice (or puja) with incense or flowers, or even a kid, to the tools of their profession. The sacrifice of a bullock has been offered to a motor-cycle, and of a sheep to the machinery in a factory!

Perhaps the bargain type of sacrifice is the one which we

encounter most freely, especially in the pages of the Greek classics. Readers may be familiar with the burlesques of such ceremonies which occur in the plays of Aristophanes, who treats priests with as little esteem as that with which the average British playwright treats the typical stage curate. Peithetairos in the 'Birds', for example, builds a city in the clouds, and so cuts off the smoke of the sacrifices from the gods, who begin to feel starved, and send an embassy to arrange a treaty with the new republic. But the founder of the city is a typical anticlerical, and drives away a priest who wants to come in and perform a liturgical act. Or again, there is the well-known Platonic dialogue, 'Euthyphro', in which Socrates is represented as asking 'But what is the object of sacrifice? Does it really have any effect? And in any case what sort of deities are those which have to be haggled with, and whom we even try to cheat by substituting a cheap offering for a more expensive one, in the hope that they won't notice the difference?' It is hardly surprising to find that the Hebrew prophets are just as unsparing in their denunciations of this type of cultus (Micah 6 and Psalm 50 will serve as good enough illustrations). The gods of the nations are but 'eidola', symbols – or projections (?), but it is the Lord who made the heavens, and He needs no sacrifice except that of moral personality. Yet the great mass of mankind is very difficult to shift from its precautionary attitude to the great Unknown. It still prefers to err on the safe side, and to make sure that the fierce anger of an irascible spirit whose benevolence it doubts is mollified. We can never get very far away from the caustic conclusion of Professor Leuba that God is approached mainly in order to be made use of – as so many human beings are by their inferiors. Nevertheless, it would be cruelly unjust to ignore the improvement in the conception of sacrifice which accompanies the enhancement of the character of the god worshipped. Psalm 40, especially as interpreted in the Epistle to the Hebrews, shows that Deity as conceived in Judaeo-Christian thought is to be worthily worshipped only by the total surrender of one's self to his ethical commands – even though they may involve a painful death or a suffering life. The wrath of this God is not the capricious temper of Zeus, who in a moment of petulance may drop a thunderbolt on one of his own temples, nor is it the vengeance of Yahweh, who destroys the sinner in the act of sinning, but the holy anger of Him who loves the sinner in spite of his offences, and who, though the latter may be sundered from Him by his sin, works unceasingly to win him back again. And finally we reach the conception of self-sacrifice which is set forth in the Prayer of Oblation in the Anglican Communion office, where the inadequacy of the worshippers is made up for by their self-identification with the perfect sacrifice of God. To this there is said to be some analogy in the Buddhist imitation of the human Gotama as a means of satisfying the requirements of the Inexorable Universe or Absolute, whose self-expression is the Buddha-nature.

(ii) The sense of 'to be done or not to be done' is usually labelled 'taboo', a Polynesian word meaning 'strongly marked', and so 'forbidden'. At first the things forbidden are sometimes (not always) to our thinking rather strange. One can understand a corpse (possibly plague-stricken) being taboo. But it is not obvious why a piece of ground touched by a new-born infant should be. Yet taboos are not always irrational. They are the germ of a reasonable belief in an absolute standard of right and wrong; and the queer ways in which this sense at first expresses itself are no disparagement of the later and more developed belief. At the same time, in what is sometimes called the pre-logical phase of human behaviour, the connexion between cause and effect is not easily detected, since it is not so much absence of logic as the result of inferences from phenomena which we ourselves have long abandoned. For instance, the Mikado's clothes were taboo, because the Mikado was believed to be of divine descent. But it is better to have some sense of restraint in the presence of Self-Existent Being than none at all, and even if the commandment for a girl is only 'thou shalt not look at a bull-roarer', that is a trifle better than having no commandment, since the bull-roarer, like the 'cat' in the game of 'tip-cat', symbolizes an object in the face of which the woman must act with caution and restraint; and so we have the beginnings of moral purity.

Thus taboos, sacrificial ceremonies and myths are the religious toys or models which are played with by the race in its childhood, but which are not idle things, since they prepare it for the more serious business of adult spiritual life, just as the bricks and dolls of boys and girls prepare them for handicraft and motherhood. No useful purpose can be served by treating 'the sacraments of simple folk' with contempt.

4. *Values.* – The earliest valued thing is food. It becomes plain that the provision of food is not entirely in the hands of the hunter, collector or agriculturalist. There is an uncontrolled Power beyond him which he has to court or obey if he wishes to supply his needs. 'No man can succeed in life alone, and he cannot get the help he needs from men.' Hence ceremonial arises, concerned with the establishment of relations with that Power. Among the Todas of South India and the Bunyoro of Central Africa the important item is milk, and the function of the priest or priest-king is to perform such rites as will secure the supply of milk, and prevent it from going sour. Much of this seems magical, but we must remember that the word magic is usable in two different senses for which we really need separate words. It may either mean (*a*) meaningless ceremonial or (*b*) ceremonial intended to force Deity to serve one's own private purpose. Perhaps Lord Raglan is right in saying that most magic is religious practice that has lost its theology. It is not until man becomes fairly secure in possession of his bodily needs, and stable in his dwelling-place, that

he can begin to speculate as to whether there are not values of a less obvious sort which should be preserved, such as honour in battle, duty to parents, and in general what are called 'the imponderables'. It is only with what we shall describe as the golden age that we get the passage from lower to higher, from anthropocentric to theocentric religion.

Much of the life of early man was communal, and on the level of the barrack-room. It lacked privacy. Hence the adjustment to the four categories had to be achieved in a communal atmosphere. There was not much chance for anyone to have a religion of the type associated with the definition of Professor A. N. Whitehead – 'What a man does with his own solitariness'. Whether he lived in a cave or a barrack-house such as those found among the Dyaks of Borneo or the Amazonian Indians of the Matto Grosso, or whether, as in certain cases, especially in large parts of Africa, the hut accommodated only a small family unit, there was at any rate only one main room, similar to the kitchen of a British working-man, and everything happened there. There was no chance of being alone indoors.

But we have to take account of certain great changes in the organization of human society. Two of these have occurred in our own time: the coal and the petrol revolutions. Others came much earlier, at long intervals. One of the first was the discovery of how to store food for the next year, or for the winter or rainy season; another was the discovery that it was possible to save seeds or roots and plant again, and so to increase the amount of food. Then came the breeding and domestication of animals, whether for slaughter or transport. These led to vast increases in population, and so to swarming, raids, migration and colonization. Another discovery was how to make fire, another was the use of metals, and yet another the use of wheeled transport. At first there were only hunters and fishers, people living from hand to mouth, or collecting.

Then came farmers in villages and townships by the great rivers, along valleys or streams, on the banks of lakes or lagoons, and among the delta swamps. These communities were not isolated, but developed trade and marketing; and leisure arose, partly from the discovery or belief that certain days were unlucky or taboo for working (so that people as it were 'institutionalized their fear', especially of the moon), partly from the consideration that you cannot do the same things all the year round, so that when ploughing or sowing is completed there is a gap in activities. Thus sacred days arose, and were marked by emotional displays or by acts of sympathetic magic, such as jumping to make the corn grow (this survives in the Good Friday skipping on Parker's Piece, Cambridge), or egg rolling, or the playing of tip-cat at the same season – to promote fertility. Lunar restrictions led to a lunar calendar. In ancient Egypt one-fifth of the year was made up of sacred days on which work was prohibited, and Republican Rome had one-third of the days in the year which were *dies nefasti*. In these and other ways the energy of the adult population became locked up, and accumulated as a surplus. The animals did not appear in order to be killed, bad weather postponed an expedition, or it may be one was compelled to wait for the breaking-up of the frost or the drying-up of the rains, or again the days grew shorter as the season waned. Hence dancing by the light of the fire, development of arts and crafts, telling of traditional folk-tales, drama, and the art and ritual, i.e. processions, sacrifices and dances, which express the pent-up expectation of a thing greatly desired and long delayed. Then also there would be ceremonies connected with marriage, birth or growing-up, and lastly funeral rites, especially mourning, and ceremonies directed to propitiating the spirit of the dead person, or to 'showing him respect'. In all these ways it is easy to see how the institutions of early religion built themselves up, and became elaborated.

But perhaps we ought to rate as one of the greatest revolutions the growth of privacy in dwellings, following of course the preliminary discovery of how to make permanent houses as distinct from temporary shelters, or mere wind-breaks. The logical extreme of this growth of privacy, and also perhaps a protest against the communal dwelling, is the retirement of individuals into complete solitude. This began, one supposes, by elderly people finding the noise of the young folk and the crowd in the hut getting on their nerves, or perhaps by the old people themselves becoming tiresome to their younger relatives, and so being pushed out into the jungle. But the tendency is to advance the age of retirement into the working years, and so the solitary thinker and seer arrive on the scene. But individualism in the hut-dwelling is not simply a question of age; it may also be one of abnormality. The lunatic and the prophetic soul alike do not fit very well into a communal atmosphere, and sometimes the boundary between the two is not very clearly defined. A Siberian shaman among the Tungus who divines or tell fortunes may be an epileptic or neurotic – or even a drunkard, who in his potations has his tongue loosed. The prophet is often a queer opinionated fellow. But these abnormal personalities, however awkward as members of a community, are sometimes useful – like 'the bee-boy who is not quite right in his head' but has second sight, like his mother, and 'can do anything with bees'. So although they may get expelled into solitude, or wander away, they are still consulted – and feared, as being peculiar, and drodsome, and possibly in touch with the Sacred. And so we get the development of 'sacred men'. Neither Ezekiel, nor Anthony of Egypt, nor George Fox would have been thought a 'good mixer', but these men were rare geniuses, and in religion, pioneers. One gathers that in pagan as distinct from Moslem Africa individualism in religion is unknown, for the religious life goes in rhythms of communal activity, and no religious action can be performed by the individual apart from his social unit, the tribe. We shall see that this stage in India gives way to an immense exaltation of the solitary life, and so to the curious reversal which Schweitzer has called 'world- and life-negation', with the complete abandonment of the social order. This arises apparently from a surfeit of the world and its routine, due it may be to high temperatures, or to a sense of frustration or disillusionment, or to a sort of obsession with the Self-Existent, 'To noughten all that is made for to have and to hold God whyche is not made,' as Lady Julian of Norwich puts it. Integration then becomes almost anti-social. Beside the growth of sacred times and of sacred persons (who differentiate into the prophet and the priest), we also get the growth of sacred spaces, which, as has already been observed, arise from the stereotyping of the natural, so that the sanctuaries are artificial developments of spots where numinous experience has taken place. This sanctity extends even into the world of imagination and the unseen, so that there come to be 'countries of the soul', places like Valhalla, the Elysian Fields, She'ol, and the Pure Land of Suhāvati Buddhism. Such celestial realms are conceived by man at quite an early stage of his mental life, and are referred to in the most ancient Egyptian texts, and also in the beliefs of the Solomon Islanders.

Communion meals (sacred occasions) begin with the crude notion of eating the deity. Thus the Tariano tribes of the Upper Amazon literally eat the flesh and drink the blood of their chieftains by cremating their bodies, mixing the ashes with native alcohol made from the manioc root and then consuming it ceremonially. But the localization of the Divine Presence in food goes far beyond the crudity of a cannibal feast, in which the victim is the incarnation of the god, and even far beyond that of a glorified Christmas dinner. It is no disparagement of the Christian Eucharist to recall how it has grown out of very humble origins, and how communion meals of some sort or another are world-wide among agricultural peoples. The author cannot repeat here in full what he has written elsewhere on the subject, and must refer readers to it, but it is permissible to quote one passage from the Jesuit account of the Peruvian August festival, in which a maize loaf was broken up and eaten: 'Four sheep were offered . . . and the priest had the sancu (the loaf) on great plates of gold, and he sprinkled it with the blood of the sheep . . . and then the high priest said in a loud voice, so that all might hear: Take heed how you eat this sancu; for he who eats it in sin, and with a double will and heart, is seen by our father the Sun, who will punish him with grievous troubles. But he who with a single heart partakes of it, to him the Sun and the Thunder will show favour, and will grant children, and happy years and abundance, and all that he requires. Then they all rose up to partake, first making a solemn vow, before eating the sancu, in which they promised never to be traitors to their lord the Ynca, on pain of receiving condemnation and trouble. The priest of the Sun then took what he could on three fingers, put it into his mouth, and then returned to his seat. In this order and in this manner of taking the oath all the tribes rose up and thus all partook, down to the little children . . . They took it with such care that no particle was allowed to fall to the ground, this being looked upon as a great sin.' Similar accounts come from Lithuania, Athens and Tartary.

No doubt we ought also to take some account here at this point of the development of the use of images (sacred emblems). Fuller treatment of this is best to be found in Mr Edwyn Bevan's lectures on Symbolism, but a few plain points may here be noted. Imageless cultus characterizes equally the lowest and the highest stages of religion (that is, if we call them lowest and highest, and not simply two different stages, as indeed I think we must do, using the word highest not in the sense of 'final' but of 'most highly developed'). We

have seen that figurines may be early – as early as the Aurigna-
cian period. Toy thinks that the image comes in with the
approach of the agricultural stage, but it is not easy to see why
this should be, unless we see its genesis in the Kern-baby – the
idol representing the spirit of vegetation. Anyhow, idols are
not on a wide scale anthropomorphic at an early date, and the
Venuses of Brassempouy and Willemdorf may not be goddesses at all, but models of human beings made for purposes
of sympathetic magic. In 1943 Mr A. L. Armstrong discovered another of these female figurines in Pit 15 at the
prehistoric flint-mining site of Grimes Graves in Suffolk.
The image (which is in appearance rather like a miniature
of Epstein's Genesis), was found on a pedestal at the entrance
to an underground gallery, and near it were several cult-
objects, a cup and the remains of a (? sacrificial) fire. The
estimated date is early neolithic, and the idea seems to have
been the invocation of a fertility goddess of the underworld
to supply a good quantity of flint! The commonest early
images, both small and large, are mere lumps of stone or wood
with no particular shaping, unless it be that they resemble
some part of the human anatomy. In India it is worth recording that an image is an object of religious devotion only after
it has been 'quickened', i.e. consecrated by a Brahmin priest,
so that the Divinity concerned can be said to have 'taken it up
into union with himself', and so to have made the idol 'an
effectual sign'. This necessary condition once led to a curious
controversy at a railway goods-office in India, where freight
was being levied upon some (literal) household gods that were
being moved by train, and the official urged that if they could
not be proved to have been 'quickened', they would have
to be charged for as furniture. As idols, they might have been
entitled to a free pass!

CHAPTER V

Gods many and Lords many

ANYONE who has visited (let us say) the British Museum, or the archaeological galleries at the Louvre, or the Musée Guimet cannot fail to have been impressed by the ease with which the great nations of antiquity accepted the supposition that the world in which they lived was dominated by a plurality of beings of human or even bestial character, framed on a scale larger than the normal. The impression is toned down by the reflection that except in out-of-the-way places in Asia or Africa that sort of belief is now dead. Yet such is far from being the case. The time-lag in human development may have left pluralism surviving in savage parts of Africa and the Dutch Indies, but it is also very much alive in more important countries, Japan and India. Political nationalism may in both cases be bolstering it up, but politicians could not long succeed in such a venture, if there were not something inherent in human nature which found satisfaction in what we usually call 'polytheism'. Let us try to discover what that 'something' is. Why was it that the ancient Sumerians could credit the existence of deities who, though terrifying, were yet human beings writ large? How could Egyptians for a period equal in length to that which separates us from the reign of Alexander the Great (nearly 2,500 years) have been to all appearances perfectly satisfied with a view of the universe which made it rather like a colossal game of chess, with no players, but only pieces of varying magnitudes, moving about of their own initiative, and treating humanity as pawns? Why is it that Indian students who visit this country may wear

European clothes and attend lectures on biochemistry, and yet keep a compartment in their lives where they sacrifice marigolds and rice to the image of a goddess? This goddess, Sarasvati, is consort of Brahma the creator, and though originally a river-deity, is now associated with wisdom and learning.

We may even go a step nearer home, and ask, Why is it that many Roman Catholics so much prefer to address their devotions to a variety of saints, and to erect in their churches a multiplicity of altars, rather than to adopt the centralized simplicity of the Protestant Reformation?

One obvious answer is that a pluralistic view of the Sacred is much more congenial to some peoples than to others. It is not necessarily a matter of race, but of traditional culture. The tendency to form a unitary conception of Reality is much more deeply rooted in some cultural groups than in others. It cannot even be attributed wholly to economic causes, since pluralism is just as prevalent in one sort of society as in another, and may descend through generations as the traditional view of the Sacred, even though the economic structure of that society may undergo radical alteration during the interval.

This, however, hardly explains why the existence of the various divinities should have been believed in at all; for no one can really have supposed that they had been seen by anybody. (Even here we must not be too sweeping in our denials.) The belief in the existence of a plurality of Powers (sometimes conflicting and not always pleasant or benevolent) is actually being supported by the evidence of people's experience. Things happen which are thought to be explicable only on the assumption that these Powers exist and are capable of interfering in the course of human affairs. Now, in the worship of these Powers, the presiding priest or intermediary was accustomed to put on certain insignia or vestments. When thus robed he was not merely believed to be the representative of the deity in question; he *was* the deity for all practical purposes. People who were not necessarily credulous fools were really satisfied, it is clear, that when they had gazed upon a vested image or vested priest they had seen the god at least sacramentally. This is the only satisfactory explanation of the statement put by Apuleius into the mouth of his hero Lucius ('I saw the gods of the upper and lower worlds and adored them close at hand'), and also of the statement in Exodus xxiv 9 ('They saw the God of Israel; and there was under his feet as it were a paved work of sapphire stone, and as it were the very heaven for clearness. And upon the nobles of the children of Israel he laid not his hand: and they beheld God, and did eat and drink').

There is in the Sinai Peninsula a sanctuary called Serabit, where stand the ruins of a considerable temple. Turquoise in large quantities is quarried in the neighbourhood, and is known to have been used in the adornment of the temple. We may well have here then, in Exodus 24, a naïve account of something actually seen by Semitic worshippers at a Sinaitic sanctuary. It seems certain that in the temple areas all over the Near East at this time there were adyta or inner sanctuaries where Epiphanies of the various deities were from time to time staged by the officials of those sanctuaries, and that the worshippers were satisfied by these representations. There was no actual trickery or deception. The sophisticated worshipper regarded what he saw as sacramental of the Unseen, of the existence whereof he could have no doubt. Foucart suggests that the idols in Egypt began by being sacraments, but ended by being symbols.

But what, we ask, was the Unseen in each case? It does not seem to have been a Transcendent Deity such as we find described in Isaiah 40, but a real projection or personification or some Power, hostile, dangerous, sinister or friendly and benevolent, but at any rate felt to be operant in real life. Or again, it might be the concrete presentation of some ideal. Thus

Athena was obviously the projection of the minds of the citizens of Athens. At first a female fertility divinity, she becomes the personification of the ideal of the civic life. Similarly Mars among a race of soldier-farmers was the projection of their war-like impulses, the personification of their ideal, and so the Power that presided over and guided their campaigns. Lord Raglan indeed holds that 'the gods' are always the product of ritual actions releasing pent-up emotion, and that myth is simply the official story which explains the ritual. Thus the gods of the myths never were real persons or deified heroes. This perhaps goes too far. Most think that Euhemerus was at least in some cases correct. (See page 111.)

Another way of regarding the plurality of deities was that of theocrasia, fusion or identification. There might be many local names, but one divinity. Or there might be many localized activities, but only one active god. Thus in the Vedas we read (*Rig Veda*, i. 164.46):

> They call it Indra, Mitra, Varuna, and Agni,
> And also heavenly, beauteous-winged Garutman;
> The Real is One, though sages name it variously,
> They call it Agni, Yama, Matarisvan

and in the *Golden Ass* of Apuleius the goddess Isis is represented as saying, 'I am she whose godhead, single in essence, but of many forms, with varied rites and under many names, the whole earth reveres', and giving ten titles under which she is worshipped in ten different countries. Cicero (*de Nat. Deor.*, xxviii) declares that Deity, who is different in every part of Nature, appears as the earth under the name of Ceres, as the sea under that of Neptune, and so on. Plutarch, who is plainly a monotheist at heart, says much the same.

It is not to be supposed that everyone in Greece, Rome or Egypt thought about the gods in the same way; but from a consideration of the various ways of regarding the local or national divinities, and from living instances in India, China and Japan, we can begin to gain some idea of what it felt like to live in Babylonia, Egypt or Greece at a time when polytheism reigned supreme. It is not of course easy to put ourselves into the emotional or mental attitude of their peoples, but we can make some progress towards a sympathetic understanding. Yet if the divinities were fictitious, how, we ask, was it possible for people to continue believing in them for so long? Let us be careful what we say. The symbolic manifestations, no doubt, had sometimes an element of fiction about them. But no one could deny the personal experience of unseen and apparently conflicting Powers, most of them capricious, but for that reason all the more to be propitiated and bargained with. The staged epiphanies were therefore of secondary importance. What mattered was that the Powers themselves existed. Yet not all manifestations were fictitious. The sun, moon, stars were obviously potent in action. Was not life dependent upon the sun's rays? Did not the moon seem in some way connected with tides, and her phases of visibility and disappearance to run concurrently with certain human and seasonal rhythms? It was not unnatural to suppose that the lesser luminaries had also their part to play in influencing the lives of human beings. Again, the Mississippi is not the first instance of 'Ol' Man Ribber', for the Nile, the Ganges, and the Tiber have all been personified and worshipped.

Pluralism is thus partly the product of the rich diversity of life. The Hebrew poet in the book of Job describes the hippopotamus as 'the chief of the ways of El', where El is the Supreme Being. But the pious Egyptian regarded the female hippopotamus as the localized symbolic manifestation of Ta-Urt, a sort of female fertility deity, domestic in interests and presiding over childbirth, but by no means supreme.

Let one suppose that what we are describing was a series of sudden inventions. There is no point at which someone

says, 'I will be an animist', or 'I will be a polytheist', just as
one says 'I will be a Communist – or a Fascist'. The very
labels themselves are modern. There is much to be said for
Dr Paul Radin's theory that in nearly every human community where chance mating took place and a general average
of life was maintained there would have been found the germs
of most varieties of thought about the Self-Existent. Some
individuals prefer a pluralist, others a unitary conception of
reality; some are temperamentally materialist, agnostic or
atheist, others are *dévots* or *scrupuleux*. Where the woman is
the stronger partner, matriarchy develops, and Deity is conceived as the Great Mother. Where the man dominates the
situation, rule is patriarchal, and Deity is the Old Man in the
Sky, or the Great Chieftain. Communities of each sort are
sometimes found near one another, and cultural conditions,
quite as much as breed, determine which is to prevail, though
a particular unit of the human race distributed over a wide
area may stick to one type of culture, and so to one sort of
religion. And again, the federating of members of two different groups, either by marriage, conquest, colonization or
alliance by treaty, may lead to the multiplication of gods,
since marriage or politics may involve the enlargement of the
national or tribal pantheon, and taking over an area of land
meant taking over duties to its celestial as well as to its terrestrial population.

We have already dealt with the unfinished investigation
into the problem of primitive monotheism. What we can
now say with some certainty is that by the time the urban
communities have developed in the great river valleys, religious belief has invested the world with a plurality of deities.
The process began in the villages and among tribes in a pre-
urban condition, so that the partitioning of the world among
celestial overlords goes back a long way.

We now know something, mostly of an external character,

about the early cults of the Indus and Ganges valleys, and of the Yellow River in China, and a good deal more about the religion of the Euphrates-Tigris area, the Nile valley and the valley of the Orontes. In the case of the last three it is surprising how many of the data bear a relationship to what is familiar to readers of the Old Testament. Keys to an understanding of the so-called Mosaic code and kindred material are found many millennia before Christ among the Sumerians. Egyptian and Babylonian books of proverbial philosophy remind us of Hebrew wisdom literature, and the more recently unearthed tablets of Ras Shamra, between Aleppo and the coast of the Mediterranean, reveal the nature of the pre-prophetic Canaanite religion, the origin of Hebrew nature-festivals, and (quite incidentally) the fact that the demon Baal-zeboul, mentioned by Christ in his speech in Luke xi. 18 and elsewhere in the gospels, was formerly an ethnic deity of the underworld in pre-Hebraic Palestine, and that the spelling in the Greek text is the correct one, as against the spelling in the Syriac and Vulgate, Beel-zebub.

MESOPOTAMIA

There is reason to believe that there was a vast chain of pre- or proto-historic cultures stretching from Central Asia to the plateau of Iran and thence to Syria and Egypt long before 4000 B.C., and that the Sumerians themselves entered Mesopotamia before 5000 B.C. Both they and the founders of the Indus valley civilization may have been descendants of a common stock of people dwelling in the neighbourhood of what is now called Baluchistan, since figurines found in Sumeria and at Mohenjodaro show a similar type of feature, and this is reproduced today among inhabitants of the district between Iran and the Punjab. (It has been suggested by Sir Denis Bray that a pocket of these ancient peoples may survive among the Brahuis, near Quetta.) The Sumerians were probably the first founders of the city state as an institution. They had a written language which they inscribed upon thin clay tablets, and each city had its own god and temple, so that the importance of a state or its monarch influenced the status of its god. With the beginnings of astronomy (or rather, astrology) we have the worship of various heavenly bodies, who are believed to control the fortunes of earth-dwellers. These gods are mostly therefore nature-deities, though we also get the personification of the social organism and the deification of rulers and chieftains. Enlil, the god of the city of Nippur, presided over the earth, while the great goddess Ishtar (Ashtaroth to the Zidonians and Astarte to the Greeks), specially worshipped at Uruk, was the patroness of fertility and love. A tendency appears to group gods and to grade them in hierarchies, and also to fuse them together, in so far as they resemble one another. The first federation or empire was founded by the high-priest of Uruk, and a merger of city-states was apparently accompanied by a merger of celestial beings. The Sumerians were probably in their original state dwellers in a mountainous region, and their gods were often mountain-deities, or at any rate, being often personifications of heavenly bodies, it was considered proper to worship them in temples as near to the sky as possible. Hence when the Mesopotamian plain was colonized by these people it became necessary to erect artificial mountains or high-places, and these are known as ziggurats. They were also houses for the god and the local ruler (his earthly vice-regent), and places of burial. Typical of such a sacred citadel is the temple of the moon-god at Ur, which has been recently excavated. These ziggurats had external ladder-like stairways, and it has been suggested that their appearance when thronged with worshippers, or rather with sacred ministers in vestments, may have been the origin of the symbolism of Jacob's dream at Bethel. (The relation of this type of temple to the teocallis of Central America is a puzzle. There is no evidence at all of colonization via the Persian Gulf, nor any apparent connexion between Mexico and Mesopotamia. It would seem, therefore, as though we have here simply two independent examples of architects trying to invent an artificial mountain for purposes of cultus.) For details of the polytheistic religion of Sumeria readers may well be referred to the works of Sir Charles Woolley. The gods of Mesopotamia were *grands seigneurs*, and the temples were essentially their palaces, They were fed with abundant sacrifices, sometimes human, but mostly, by a process of substitution, animal. In the long centuries these temples became the repositories of crafts and learning of all sorts, and, although most of the religion strikes us today as magical and man-centred, it has had a profound influence upon institutional religion and liturgical worship ever since. It is in these temples that we first find the practice of set liturgical devotions, of hymns or psalms not entirely unlike the Hebrew psalms, and of the use of music of a sort, both vocal and instrumental.

But we have to reckon with many political vicissitudes in such a long period, ranging from 5000 to about 483 B.C. Somewhere about three or four thousand years before Christ we find the Sumerians conquered by a Semitic invader by name Sargon, the leader of a people called Akkadians. He founded an empire known as the kingdom of Sumer and Akkad, which endured for about two centuries. Then came a second wave of Semites, who made their headquarters at a small town called Babylon, and these newcomers, under their king Hammurabi, in the course of the next century became masters of the whole country. Hammurabi as a legislator developed the Sumerian codes of his predecessors, and his famous laws resemble those of the Pentateuch in certain details. A third wave of Semitic invasion brought in the people who made the city of Asshur on the upper Tigris their centre of government, and who are known in consequence as Assyrians. Babylon suffered many vicissitudes. About 1926 B.C. it was conquered and held by the Hittites, an Armenoid people who established a state to the north of Mesopotamia, and between 1746 and 1169 it was taken and ruled by the Kassites, who were probably an early wave of proto-Nordics. The Mitanni, who are also prominent at this time, were in like manner an Armenoid people ruled by a proto-Nordic horse-breeding aristocracy, and it is significant that their gods had names very similar to those found in the Vedas of India. About 1100 B.C. the Assyrians themselves conquered Babylon and reigned there for some 400 years. Then in the eighth century B.C. there arose another Sargon, who was probably responsible for the deportation of the ten tribes of the northern Hebrew kingdom. The Assyrian empire continued for another 150 years, and then a coalition between a new Semitic people, the Chaldeans, and two Aryan (or rather Nordic) nations from the north, the Medes and the Persians, ended in its downfall, with the capture of the imperial city of Nineveh in 606. It is of course probable that the Medes and Persians were non-Nordic to a great extent, like the Mitanni, but that they were ruled by a Nordic aristocracy. The new Chaldean empire, better known as the second Babylonian empire, lasted under Nebuchadnezzar the Great and his descendants until 539 B.C. It was then followed by the conquest of the country by Cyrus the Persian, and after 299 years of Persian rule by the conquest of the whole country by the Greek king, Alexander the Great.

The object of the above brief historical survey is to show how large a number of waves of different peoples passed over this great Mesopotamian plain, and what a variety of influences contributed, in consequnce, to the development of its polytheism. This consequent hybridization renders any contact of the Hebrews with this region of immense importance for a proper estimate of the religious beliefs and practices of the latter, and nothing is more noteworthy than the contrast between the treatment of the myths of Babylonia by its own inhabitants and their treatment by Hebrew writers. The first chapter of Genesis has been described as a monotheistic poem composed in a Babylonian slum by a Hebrew evacuee, but it is in sharp contrast to the non-moral pluralistic tales of Babylonia proper. The same remarks apply to the flood-story, with its hero Ut-Napishtim – the Babylonian Noah – and even to the story of the righteous sufferer, Tabi-utul-bel (seventh century B.C.), a tale of the same *genre* as the book of Job, though not necessarily its lineal ancestor. But it will be noticed that the hybridization includes the influence of proto-Nordics, and it is coming to be thought that the effect of the Kassite and Mitannic contacts was to bring in from the central Asiatic plains a conception of deity which may have arisen among certain groups of proto-Nordic nomads, in which there was at least the monolatrous worship of a high-god under a non-anthropomorphic guise. Dr Frankfort's finely-illustrated volume upon Mesopotamian seals has shown to the public one striking fact – namely, that, whereas the ordinary seals of the Mesopotamian region have figures of gods which are either theriomorphic or anthropomorphic, the seals of the Mitanni eschew any such pictorial imagery, and show either a solar disc or some other symbol on the top of a pillar. It is known that these Mitanni contributed a queen to Egypt, and may even have intermarried with the Davidic dynasty of the Hebrews, and it is at least a curious coincidence that the reforming king of Egypt, Ikhnaten, of whom we shall have to speak elsewhere, was the grandson of a Mitannic princess.

To sum up, it has been pointed out more than once that there is as great a distance chronologically between Sargon the First and Alexander the Great as there is between Alexander the Great and the present day, and that, long before Sargon the First, people had been living in cities under Sumerian rule, practising religion and cultivating the soil for as long again, so

that it is not unfair to say that half the duration of human civilization, and the keys to all its chief institutions are to be found
before Sargon the First. This may well be true, but the time had
not yet come, nor the place, for the great religious revolutions
which will be related in the next chapter, and these rendered
the massive polytheisms of the great river-valleys completely
obsolete, even though the latter took their revenge by stamping
upon the worship of the newly-conceived god of the prophets,
philosophers and seers the patterns of the older pluralistic worship, which invoked sometimes as many as twenty-three divinities, and also believed in a variety of daemons or bad sacred.

EGYPT

The story of Egypt is not unlike that of Mesopotamia. There
is the same great river-valley affording food to a large population, and there is the same blending of the human species,
caused by very early incursions from the south-west, and later
influences coming in from the north. The basic population, of
a reddish-brown skin, and typically Mediterranean features,
which overran the primitive Libyan inhabitants, is blended
with immigrants of Armenoid, Semitic and even negroid
stock. From the period of the old kingdom to the Roman conquest in 30 B.C. there are some 3000 years, and the history can
be divided into nine periods, comprising a Semitic occupation
from 2540 to 1850 B.C., which is preceded and followed by
Egyptian dynasties; an Ethiopian occupation, which is in its
turn ovethrown by the Assyrians, Babylonians and Persians,
followed by the rule of Alexander and his Ptolemaic successors; and finally the incorporation of Egypt into the Roman
empire. It will thus be seen that the country had an independent life of its own for only two out of the nine epochs, and that
after 1100 B.C. it became merely a province in other empires.
The religion of Egypt is, therefore, no more a single faith than
that of India. It is a group or federation of a number of cults,

and the presence of a variety of deities represented in animal, bird or reptile form suggests the incorporation of totem animals among the objects worshipped. But the two great divinities are the Sun and the Nile, and life in its many forms seems to have been the chief interest, so that the worship of the heavenly bodies, and pre-eminently (in the most ancient times) of the sky, is the dominant feature. The worship of Rē comes later, and later still that of Amen and Osiris. Reminiscences of a benevolent king mingled with myths about fertility and agriculture seem to make up the story of Osiris, who is not only a type of the divine sovereign described by Frazer in *The Golden Bough* (who has to ascend the throne by killing his predecessor and is himself killed in turn when he has performed his part, thus carrying on the transmission of divine life to the dynasty and the fields of his own country), but is also in his turn the president of the court of the gods which tries human souls at a last judgement. A good brief account of these Egyptian deities is to be found in the manual by the late Mr A. W. Shorter. Once more, polytheism bequeaths a legacy to subsequent religion. The personality of Isis, the queen consort of Osiris, with her little son Horus seated on her knee, has passed on into that of the Queen of Heaven of popular Mediterranean Catholicism. The last judgement continues to be depicted in Byzantine Christian art, and so in the medieval wall-paintings of English village churches (e.g. Barton near Cambridge), with the same symbolism as in Egypt – the soul being weighed in a pair of huge scales, though in Christian art these are manipulated by the archangel Michael, not, as in Egypt, by an inferior divinity, Thoth.

It is interesting to compare the ground-plans of the Mesopotamian, Egyptian, and Indian temples, and to ask how the basilica type with an altar or group of altars at one end gradually developed, and so paved the way for the plan of the European Christian cathedral.

The pluralistic beliefs, ceremonies and legends of early dynastic Egypt differ little in fundamentals from those of Mesopotamia. What is perhaps more interesting to us today than this bevy of strange deities is the certain knowledge which has come to us in the last few years, that during the centuries a susbstantial amount of moral philosophy developed in Egypt, and that the papyri in which this has been preserved to us have now been edited with enough care to enable English-speaking readers to appreciate it. We have thus a series of documents, believed to be more or less datable, and ranging from the Teaching of Kagemna, which is approximately 2980–2900 B.C., to the teaching of Amen-em Apt, which is thought to date from the eighteenth dynasty – i.e. 1500–1360 B.C. Between the two occur at least three other books of moral precepts. All of these except the one by Amen-em Apt are purely prudential, and simply give good advice as to how to succeed in life. They commend virtue not only because it is the best policy, but because it leads to emoluments, promotion and physical well-being; but they say nothing about conduct as a duty towards God. When, however, we come to Amen-em Apt we find both these elements referred to, and also apparently the lofty idea that virtue is its own reward. One of his aphorisms runs: 'Better is a beggar who is in the hand of God that the rich who are safely housed in a dwelling,' and another: 'Truth is the great bearer of God. He gives it to the man who loves him.' Still more curious is it that to this Egyptian sage 'the gods' as such do not count. He speaks of 'God' or 'the God', and the implication is that he is either a monotheist or at least monolatrous in his habits. If he is (as is supposed) of the eighteenth dynasty, he must be contemporary with the movement initiated by the king Amenhotep IV, to which we shall refer later on. Thus it appears that in Egypt at a period much earlier than that of the great Hebrew prophets there were stirrings of spirit which look like the beginnings of a moral monotheism, though their influence may well have been limited, and though the country as a whole remained polytheistic.

Other defunct polytheisms are being reconstructed for us by the work of archaeologists in Crete, Malta, the Balearic Isles, Etruscan Italy, Greece (Mycenae) and Anatolia, as well as in the New World. The Cretans, who presumably were of much the same physical type as the Portuguese, worshipped, above other minor divinities, a goddess carrying a snake in each hand (of whom we believe we have a number of figurines), and it is significant that not only has the modern Portuguese villager been seen by Mr Rodney Gallop to somersault over the horns of cattle, just as his Minoan forebears did, but that he still pays his chief devotions to the Queen of Heaven (now of course Mary the Mother of God) rather than to God the Father or Christ the King. The religion of the Etruscans, like Etruscan script, is still something of a problem. These curious Venetian-red people are thought by some to have sprung from Lydia in Asia Minor, but how they developed in Lydia, and at what date they colonized Italy, we do not know. On the whole their religious outlook seems to have stressed the fearsomeness and cruelty of Nature and of departed spirits. There is no little resemblance, both culturally and physically, between them and the head-hunting Dyaks of Borneo, and the custom of hepa-toscopy, or the taking of omens from the liver, accompanied by the use of a kind of map of the organ in question, is common to both, but is of course found in Sumeria, which lies between them. Professor Conway has drawn attention to the grossness of the Etruscan symbolism and to its pictorial imagery of infernal torments. Yet it had also a materialistic conception of Paradise. There was an elaborately graded poly-theism, but also ancestor-worship, and a cult of the dead.

CENTRAL AMERICA

The religious phenomena of Central America are still under consideration, and in the history of prophetic religion are not perhaps of vital importance. Yet, for the sake of completeness, they must be referred to, and in any real survey or interpretation of pluralism, perhaps a little more in detail, as being less well known to Europeans.

The population in these parts of the world, prior to the European invasions of the Renaissance period, appears to have been descended from colonists who crossed from the direction of Asia and Polynesia into the Americas by way of a now partially submerged land-bridge from the north-west. In Mexico and the Yucatan area there would seem to have been (from the evidence of sculptured monuments) two distinct breeds of inhabitant – the lower classes and the ruling aristocracy. Both types still exist among the Indian population, and can be identified. The former has a broad, rather flat face, with thick lips and a *retroussé* nose, and is perhaps rather like the Eskimo. The latter has a Roman nose, prominent lips and a curiously sloping forehead. The ruling people occupied this country about 2000 B.C., but did not reach the zenith of their development till much later. When the Spaniards discovered their country these people were emerging from barbarism, and were in a curiously mixed condition. On the one hand they had little if any knowledge of metals, and no literature, but on the other hand they possessed a high technique in the use and carving of stone, a singularly elaborate system of chronology and calculation, together with observation of the heavenly bodies and a rich though fierce cultus of natural forces.

It is hazardous to draw comparisons and discover analogies between the cultures of Central American peoples and those of Egypt and Mesopotamia. Whatever remote connexion may have at some time existed between the megalithic cultures of Europe and the middle East and those of the New World, the latter have developed in such great isolation that the connexion cannot with any certainty be determined. The Maya chronological cycle is unlike any other known; while almost nothing about these people suggests any Eurasiatic influence. Of course we do not know what geological changes have occurred in the direction of the Pacific, which have resulted in the peculiar island-character of so much of its western area. There has certainly been much submergence.

The religion which we get, therefore, in Central America is an almost perfect example of a Nature-worship isolated from other influences, and stabilized on the basis of a conception of Nature which makes it simply the sum-total of non-human hostile forces. There seems no element of kindliness in it. There is nowhere, as in India, a doctrine of *ahimsa* or non-violence, and no idea of a deity who is the embodiment or projection of the gentle and benevolent friend. In this respect the Central Americans resembled the Etruscans. There is no need to give in an introductory book a complete list of the numerous deities, with all their attributes and interests. Whether one deals with Tezcatlipoca, the wind god, with Huitzilopochtli, the Mexican Mars, or with Mictlan, the Aztec Pluto, it is the same story; the gods need to be propitiated and fed with the life of human victims. The pantheon enumerated by Spence contains at least twenty-eight divinities, and of these all are personifications either of natural forces, of heavenly bodies or of human activities. Sun-worship was the most popular and perhaps considered the most necessary cultus throughout Mexico. It is said that the early Mayas did not sacrifice human beings, and that the custom is the result of the hybridization of stocks which has already been noted. This may be so, but at any rate one or other of the component elements in the Central American population must take the blame for having practised this barbarity. Sometimes it was children who were immolated, sometimes prisoners of war. 'Blood,' says Spence, 'was the favourite offering to the sun, and in the *pinturas* he is depicted as licking up the gore of the victims with his long tongue-like rays. The sun must eat if he is to be sustained, and terrible was the ritual which provided for his subsistence.'

Much United States money has been lavished upon the repair of the ancient monuments of the Isthmian regions, and in Mexico in recent years great attempts have been made, in a spirit of nationalism, to revive some of the ancient pageantry connected with the worship of the heavenly bodies (without human sacrifices of course). The processions and dances have shown great splendour, and bear some analogy to the revival of the old Germanic rituals by the National Socialists of Central Europe.

There is an allegation by Prescott (*Conquest of Mexico*, 1st ed., vol. i, pp. 148 ff.) that Nezahualcoyotl, King of Tezcuco, at a date long before that of the Conquistadors, built a temple to 'the Unknown God, Cause of Causes', in which no bloody sacrifices were offered. The authority for this is a certain Father Vega, but it is impossible to check the accuracy of his rendering in Spanish of the ancient Tezcucan chronicles. The apparent combination of St Paul and St Thomas Aquinas leaves one suspicious. If he were correct, we should have an important piece of evidence from Central America for a reforming monotheism similar to that of Amenhotep IV in Egypt.

This monotheism of the fifteenth-century A.D. Tezcucan king, Nezahualcoyotl, is, however, confirmed in the chronicles of the Spanish-Mexican writer of the sixteenth century, Ixtlilxochitl, who had access to ancient Tezcucan records, and was himself of Tezcucan descent. See Vaillant, *The Aztecs of Mexico*, 1941, mentioned in the bibliography.

GREEKS AND ROMANS

In a short book it is plainly impossible to give a complete account of Greek and Roman religion, since neither now survives in its original form, and both must therefore be of less interest to readers than systems which are actually alive today. But since both immediately preceded the rise of Christianity, and both in their course present us with analogies to events in India, it is necessary to say at least something about them.

The temperaments of Greeks and Romans were very different, and the genius of the two peoples is proverbially dissimilar. Yet both grew to maturity in peninsulas in which there was invasion from the north, followed by hybridization between the invaders and a southern dark race which they overcame. We naturally remember India again, though the areas involved are much smaller and less heterogeneous, and the political developments were different. The fact is that we must in this connexion give up thinking in terms of Europe and Asia, and learn to think of the impact of Nordics upon non-Nordics, or at any rate of the impact of Alpo-Nordics upon non-Nordics, an impact extending from Ireland to Calcutta, and perhaps even to Mongolia. We must also think of the age of philosophy as succeeding to that of naïve religion in a number of widely separated spots, and by no means simultaneously, the time-lag being considerable, and the process recurring whenever a new period of naïve religious piety has exhausted itself. It is indeed possible that in communities as well as individuals there has of necessity to be an alternation between the intellectual and the emotional approach to Deity, and that in neither direction can mankind expect to progress beyond certain limits. In the last resort choice has to be made between certain well-defined attitudes, such as are described in this volume. As Keyserling once put it: 'The foci of the ellipse are beginning to fuse into the centre of the circle, and Man to-day stands in the shoes of all possible ideals'.

Greek religion is usually held to divide into five stages: a primitive period of Aegean religion; an Olympian or classical stage: a philosophical period marked by the decline of Olympianism and the collapse of the city-state; a revival of piety due to failure of nerve and the decline of optimism about human nature, leading to a series of religions of redemption or salvation out of the world; and finally in the fourth century A.D. a brief but artificial revival of polytheism, ending in its collapse before the spread of Christianity. Of these periods the most important are the third and fourth, and there are some scholars who would classify Christianity as one of the series of redemption-cults of the fourth period. It was, indeed, in such a guise that Christianity first spread, but it cannot be described on those lines without leaving out certain Hebraic elements which were also an essential part of it, and without ignoring its extraordinary success in superseding every single one of its fellow-competitors. Comparative students will naturally be interested in the study of Ionian Greek and Indian philosophical theologies placed side by side. How much trade-routes led to a commerce in ideas we cannot tell, but the appearance of Pythagoras in the Greek colony in Italy, and the strange points of contact between elements in Indian Upanishadic, and Greek metaphysical thought are striking, if inexplicable, as will be seen when the next two chapters are studied. The probability exists that the connexion between India and Hellas came by way of Persia. The Ionian doctor Hecataeus, who was at the Persian Court of Susa, was possibly the type of Ionian Greek who brought back to the Aegean world knowledge from the Punjab. The Medes who conquered the Persians and combined themselves with them were ruled by Nordics of the same type as the fair element among the Greeks. The Greek empire of Alexander was only a second edition of the Medo-Persian empire, ruled by Nordics of Macedonian birth. In both cases the subject-peoples were very largely non-Nordic. The one realm went westward from the East, the other eastward from the West, and in both cases a Nordic king became orientalized in style. The clash between Greeks and Medo-Persians in the days of Xerxes was thus rather like a clash between British and Germans, and the absorption of Lydia and Ionia by the Persian Empire was not unlike the swallowing up of smaller European states by Germany and Russia. It is at any rate certain that India knew the Greek Ionians as Yâvanas as early as the period when North-West India was under Persian rule. There is great agreement between Upanishadic doctrine and that of the Eleatics, Xenophanes and Parmenides, and again between the Samkhya and the views of Empedocles and Anaxagoras. Iamblichus, the biographer of Pythagoras, tells us that he travelled widely, studying the teachings of the Egyptians, Mesopotamians and Brahmins, and there is a curious story related by Strabo of an Indian king, Porus, who in 20 B.C. sent an embassy to Athens which included a Sadhu, who in a fit of fanaticism burnt himself to death there. This incident is believed by some to be referred to by St Paul in 1 Corinthians xiii. 3.

Roman religion is difficult to detach entirely from its Greek counterpart, since there were early Greek colonies in Italy, and, with the political expansion of Rome in the Mediterranean, Greek territory became acquired by her, Greek literature influenced Roman, and Greek fashions were copied. The Romans were essentially a practical people (highlanders of the Italian uplands, a hybrid product of mid-European and Mediterranean stocks), and excelled in administration, but they were not original thinkers, or given to speculation. Hence they borrowed freely from their neighbours, and came not only to identify their Roman divinities (some of them Etruscan) with the gods and goddesses of Greece, but to adapt the speculative writings of Greeks for Roman readers. This is done, for example, by Cicero in his treatise *De Natura Deorum* (concerning the Nature of the Gods). On the whole Roman polytheism remained longer in a pre-anthropomorphic condition than Greek. Recent research tends to show that both shared a similar tendency (formerly thought specially Roman) to personify qualities, aspects of activities of life. Indeed, this tendency is equally discoverable in Egypt, and it is sometimes said that to conceive of Deity as anthropomorphic is not easy, and that it is a relatively difficult feat of the human mind. Be that as it may, the tendency to deify qualities or activities lasts longer in Roman religion than elsewhere, and by the intense sub-division of such *numina*, as they are called, their total number is greatly increased, so that a small deity or godling, male or female, or even hermaphrodite, appears to be in charge of every detail of agriculture or home-life. There was even a female principal called Cloacina who presided over sanitation and drains! The natural reaction against this appears to be the sense of the perceived activity of a single Deity at specific points in the course of events, such as the crisis of a battle, the birth of an heir and so on. It is therefore deduced by Altheim that the most marked feature of Roman religious experience is the sense of the discontinuous intervention of Deity in the history of individuals or of peoples. If this is so, it forms a most important link between Hebrew and Roman thought and temperament, and may account not only for the ease with which a firmly based historical Christianity spread in the Roman world, but also for the form in which it spread (sanctioned after 381 by imperial decree) – i.e. as a religion with a creed containing a date, 'sub Pontio Pilato', and with an intense insistence upon the historical reality of the Founder, as distinct from legend, myth, and ghostly or unreal appearance. Hebrew and Roman temperaments are quite different from that prevailing in India, where, as we shall see, there is little interest or confidence in the significance of the historical course of events. No Hindu sacred book, except perhaps the Ramayana (which is the rule-proving exception), contains a story, and an Indian would see no justification for treating the tale (for example) of St Paul's shipwreck in the Book of Acts as edifying matter for inclusion in a lectionary of scriptures for public reading. Later Roman religion was much concerned with the cultus of the Emperor or of Dea Roma. Horace speaks of Augustus as an incarnation of Apollo. But Tiberius, if we may believe Tacitus, rejected divine honours. Other Emperors, if not worshipped during their life-time, at least achieved apotheosis after death.

The pluralism of both Greece and Rome is so much a commonplace that it needs no emphasis, but it is perhaps worth pointing out that the highest peak in the artistic development of each religion immediately preceded its rapid decline. This is a sharp lesson for official clergy. No elaboration or enrichment of details of worship will avail to secure any religion against abandonment or decay, if its doctrines are found unsatisfying by the intelligentsia, and its downfall may come just when institutionally it seems at its zenith. It may well retain the support of the peasantry or the half-educated, but it will inevitably lose the allegiance of the first-rate minds. Even if it endure for a long period, it will do so more as a picturesque institution than as a vital expression of belief.

The names of the chief divinities are familiar to most people, but it needs to be remembered that they were not all accepted simultaneously by the Greeks. Zeus seems originally to have been simply the sky, not yet anthropomorphically conceived. Zeus the sky-king comes later. The altar of Olympian Zeus at Pergamum had neither temple nor statue. Apollo is later than the Great Mother, and Dionysus is later still, his cult having entered by way of Thrace (or, as some think, from Egypt, by way of Crete) long after the chief Olympians had been installed as objects of worship. Indeed the Dionysus-cult is almost like a piece of missionary expansion, since the god is not native to Hellas. The myth woven about him told how he was the son of Zeus and a mortal woman, Semele, by whom he was virgin-born (as touching an earthly father). In the Cretan version of the story he is called Zagreus, and is the son of Zeus and Persephone. The child was murdered by the Titans, who devoured his body, and from them the earth-dwellers are descended. Zeus restored him to life by a miracle. The human race was, therefore, believed to inherit a kind of original sin or ancestral guilt, and from this one could be freed by initiation into the mysteries of Dionysus. Whatever one may think about the sources of such a nature-myth, it is perfectly plain that it formed a good ground-work for the conversion of Levantines to the Christian faith, since the dogmas of Incarnation, Sin and Redemption are foreshadowed in it, and Jesus of Nazareth is a much more compelling figure (if only because genuinely historical) than the vague legendary figure of the son of Zeus. It is said that there was an important temple of Dionysus at Tarsus, the birthplace of St Paul, and it is certainly the case that one of the early Christian apologists refers to the resemblances, however superficial, between the legend of Dionysus and the Gospel story.

The fourth phase of Graeco-Roman religion has attracted much attention in recent years. Initiation is, as we have seen, a very ancient episode in human life, especially that which takes place at puberty. It is not surprising that to the ancient Greeks science, art, philosophy and also religion were equally regarded as incapable of being 'taught' to the public. There had to be initiation into professional secrets and mysteries. (Something like this has survived in University degree-taking ceremonies even to the present day. A teacher who has not been initiated by taking a degree may know his job, but it is thought that he is more likely to be an ignorant quack.) The religious mysteries are fairly well of a pattern. Release is sought from the uneasiness which besets life, and especially from the perishable nature of things earthly, and it comes to be believed that by identifying one's self with the experiences of some semi-supernatural being one can achieve conquest over death and freedom from evanescence. Professor Magnien has recorded a copious list of mysteries in various parts of the Near and Middle East (Isis, Adonis, Artemis, Cybele, Hecate and so on), followed by sixteen specially Greek ones, including the not originally Greek mystery of Dionysus referred to above, and in particular he gives twenty-two places, besides Eleusis, where the mysteries of Demeter and Persephone were celebrated. The myths, of course, varied in detail, though there was usually a dying and resurrection somewhere in the centre. The technique also varied, but the psychological effect aimed at was much the same in all cases. Blessedness is achieved not by straight thinking but by obedient acceptance of doctrine, which is administered by a sort of spoon-feeding. The knowledge so administered is occult rather than rational. After a series of instructions the candidate is called upon to submit to a performance of ritual which makes one think of a masonic ceremony. He is veiled and perhaps stripped; he may be washed with water, sprinkled with blood* or plastered with some white substance like china clay; he has to put on special new vestments; hands are laid on him; versicles and responses are said; in some cases a symbolical meal is eaten by him; finally in a blaze of light he is vouchsafed a vision representing one or more of the divinities concerned. There seems no doubt that these rites did provide what is vulgarly called a 'delivery of the goods'. They did cause to descend upon people, in proportion to their suggestibility, a sense of peace

* Mrs Herbert Best records that a ceremony almost exactly like the ancient 'taurobolium', or washing with bull's blood, is still practised at Katsina, in West Africa, at the anointing of a new ruler.

and liberation. It is hard otherwise to account for their popularity, or for the readiness to pay fees for participating in them. They certainly set a standard pattern to which any future religion of redemption, escape or deliverance had inevitably for many centuries to conform, up to the time when individualism as we see it in Luther proceeded to short-circuit the technical paraphernalia, and to make it both cheaper and easier to achieve peace and certitude *sola fide*, by faith alone, without the intervention of initiating officials and their rather expensive ceremonies. The truth of the Christian religion is neither impaired by the admission that it spread as a mystery religion, nor established merely by showing that its initiations were psychologically efficacious. What is at any rate indisputable is that it was the successful competitor for the allegiance of the Mediterranean world. To some extent, perhaps, it succeeded by taking over elements from rival systems. But it certainly came to occupy the ground because of its high, simple and attractive doctrine of God, its fresh Hebraic ethical monotheism; and also because its cult-hero was a real and recent historical character, not a vague and remote half-legendary figure. It is not certain that any other of the various religions could have established itself as an international movement. Had the Christian movement been seriously checked, we should not necessarily have had a Mithraic world – i.e. a world in which the Persian cult-hero Mithras was the prevailing object of worship. For Mithraism was essentially a man's religion. There was, says Professor Nock, less chance if anything of the Roman Empire turning Mithraic than of seventeenth-century England turning Quaker. Both Mithraism and Quakerism were essentially minority movements. Mithraism also varied from the standard pattern in having no professional priesthood, but a series of grades, through which any man could pass, and no central death and rising again, but a chain of Divine actions, each of which was an event in the world's drama.

One important feature in later Greek history must by no means be overlooked. The conquests of Alexander were not simply of political significance. Legge has remarked that it appeared as though Alexander had set free the gods of the ancient world to wander from one end of his empire to the other, and it is indeed a fact that the idea of proselytizing now appears for the first time in the world's history. If we are not mistaken, a new element of the most momentous character owes its origin to the special conditions created by the Macedonian emperor. Buddhism must have been prevalent in India for nearly a century before Alexander; but it was not until after it became the religion of the state, in the reign of Asoka, that the policy of sending missionaries for its propagation to countries outside India was inaugurated; and Asoka was the grandson of the king Chandragupta who had talked with Alexander face to face. It would indeed seem as though there was some kind of magic which stimulated those who associated with the conquering Greeks to take a larger world-outlook than heretofore. Certainly it is a fact that from now onwards purely ethnic religion begins to be supplanted by religion organized internationally and opening its fellowship to all and sundry, without regard for their race or station. The possession of a *lingua franca*, in this case *koinê* Greek, made such a movement easier in the Mediterranean world, but this hardly accounts for the eastward spread of Buddhism, which we shall have to note in Chapters VII and VIII.

NORTHERN AND CENTRAL EUROPE

Although the pre-Christian religion of Northern and Central Europe is no longer a living thing, in spite of artificial attempts made here and there by the Nazis to revive it, it possesses for most of us a sentimental interest at least, since it was the faith of our remoter ancestors, and relics of it still survive in the shape of ruins or traditional customs. Probably, therefore, most people would like to know something about it. To give any useful information in a brief space, however, is not easy, since without considerably qualifying reservations it is hard to avoid inaccuracy, and our knowledge is often scrappy, and is in any case external.

First, as regards survivals. These are less rare than one might expect. We naturally look round for discarded idols – and not entirely in vain. Visitors to the city of Canterbury who take the trouble to inspect the excavations in the grounds of St Augustine's College will see at the west end of the foundations of the Saxon basilica an upright granite pillar. This is no fragment of a cross, but a typical menhir, as much a heathen emblem as the idols which St Patrick is reported to have overthrown at Tara. A similar stone is to be found at the west end of the parish church of Maentwrog in the vale of Festiniog, and has given its name to the village, for maen means stone, and Turog was a local heathen deity. Or again, there are the monstrous turf-cut images at Wilmington* in Sussex and Cerne Abbas in Dorset, should they be genuine.

When we turn to customs we encounter even less difficulty. The late Dr Haddon used to say with a chuckle that you could find almost all pre-Christian ceremonies except human sacrifice practised somewhere in the British Isles. You certainly could until recently, as the records of the Folk-lore Society can testify. For example, as late as the year 1853 in a Devon village on one of the spurs of Dartmoor it was still the custom for the lads of the village to go to a menhir in one of the neighbouring fields and to sacrifice a ram by cutting its throat and then burning it, after which there was a feast upon the roast carcase. Down to the year 1678 bulls were sacrificed upon the island of Inis Maree in honour of a local saint who was still called by some of the peasants 'the god Mourie', and was the

---

* Mrs Davidson seems lately to have established that this figure represents Odin.

local Celtic deity under a Christian veneer. Until recently (perhaps now no longer) a lamb used to be sacrificed at King's Teignton on Whit-Monday; and the story given in Stow's (late sixteenth-century) *Survey of the City of London* is now almost hackneyed, in which he tells of the reception of a fat buck at St Paul's Cathedral on 29th June each year by the Dean and Chapter, all of them wearing garlands of flowers on their heads, the buck being led with a fanfare of trumpets up to the high altar and there presented and blessed, and then afterwards killed and roasted to make a feast for the worthy ecclesiatics. (I once asked Dean Inge how he would like to revive this ceremony, which was obviously a survival from the pre-Christian period in London.) Baring-Gould is also quoted has having seen at Ditchling in Sussex during the nineteenth century a horse-sacrifice which was evidently the relic of a sacrifice to Odin.

Now let us consider the position a little more seriously. We are actually concerned with the religious beliefs and practices of five main groups of people:

    i. The pre-historic inhabitants.
    ii. Their immediate successors, the dark-white Iberians.
    iii. The round-headed Alpine stock, crossed with Nordics, and even here and there with Latins.
    iv. The genuine Nordics.
    v. In the east of Europe, the Slavs and Northern Mongols.

The first group is of course composite, and whether we talk about Aurignacians in the Plynlimmon moorland, or Prospectors on some part of the coast-line of Britain, it is idle to suppose that we can definitely point to their direct descendants or indicate survivals of their religion. All we can say is that it must have been more or less on the Tasmanian or Polynesian level, and that some odd fragments of it may have got transmitted to later groups.

The second group consists of Neolithic people, and whatever can be said about such in places like Corsica or in Southern Europe will apply to them in Britain. The third group is made up of successive waves of the people we call Celts. In this country much has been made in popular thought of what is called our Celtic inheritance. But what is it? We only too often overlook the effect of welding together stocks of varying antecedents within one island area. The Celts themselves are not a pure stock, but mostly the product of crossing between Alpines and Nordics. They come before us first as an expanding people dwelling beyond the Rhine in North and West Germany, whither they have migrated from the mountainous regions of the Alps and Carpathians, strongly blended with and dominated by Nordic and proto-Nordic stock. They pass westward over Gaul, drawing influences from the inhabitants of the lands they colonize, and then proceed in waves to Britain, where we know them as Brythons, Goidels, and so on. Once in this country they again enter into relations with the existing neolithic inhabitants, Iberian and pre-Iberian, and today, if we consider what are known as the two Celtic groups of languages, we find that their use is connected with folk who are very largely descendants of a rather dark, short population, and who are not themselves typical Celts, tall, red-haired or green-eyed. If, therefore, the original Celts were of this type, they must have transmitted their language to those whom they conquered and dominated, and these people must have accepted it, contributing a number of non-Celtic words, and intermarrying with their conquerors. What, then, happened to religion? The probability remains that there was a good deal of amalgamation. Since both parties had a purely ethnic cultus, there was no prophetic objection to borrowing and religious alliances. Thus the religion of the bronze-age 'ancient Britons' must have been a polytheism very similar to that known to have existed in Gaul before Caesar's conquests, in which pre-Celtic tradition was strongly preserved. The Druids were plainly the priesthood of the Celtic population of Gaul, Britain and Ireland. The Celtic invaders of Britain were the descendants of folk who had previously settled in the Marne area, and had there probably intermarried with the pre-Celtic population, producing there a hybrid culture in which the Druids played a most important part. When these people crossed into Iberian Britain they recognized there much which was already familiar to them by tradition, and this gave rise to the incorrect belief, quoted by Caesar, that Druidism originated in Britain. What is probably true is that the highly differentiated Druidical priesthood in Gaul, and subsequently in Britain, was the result of Celtic contacts with non-Celtic people. Thus the remains of non-Celtic neolithic religious rites are often wrongly called Druidical, because they were taken over and used by Druids, who, however, did not necessarily originate them. The word 'Druid' itself is not so much a proper name as a title, like priest or prophet; and in one ancient writing Christ himself is called 'God's Druid'.

The British population now received at the Roman occupation additional elements, both by occasional intermarriage between Latins and others who came either as government officials or as members of the Roman army, and by the introduction of specially Roman *numina* as objects of worship, and in places the cult of Mithras. Finally there followed the spread of the Christian religion, relics of which survive in the Brito-Roman churches of St Pancras and St Martin at Canterbury, and of St Mary-in-the-Castle at Dover.

The fourth group appears at the end of 350 years of Roman occupation, in the shape of a series of waves of more distinctly Nordic polytheists, Anglo-Saxons, Jutes and Danes. These had a special mythology, which was about 1938 the subject of most sympathetic study in Central and Northern Europe, and the discussion of which then filled to overflowing the journals for the scientific elucidation of the pre-Christian faiths of the world, to the exclusion of almost everything else. The Teutonic peoples are the western expansion of the Nordic stock which had its origin either in south Russia or perhaps on the shores of the Baltic, and which, as we shall see in Chapter VII, expanded eastward so as to create the important 'Aryan' element in the population of north India. In Western Europe it constitutes four sections: the western, comprising the Anglo-Saxons and Jutes, the southern, comprising the Saxons, Frisians, Franks and Alamanni, the northern, comprising the Scandinavians, and the eastern, comprising the Goths, Vandals, Burgundians and Lombards. The earliest period in the history of these peoples of which we have clear knowledge shows them as possessing features of a relatively complex culture. Their work in bronze and gold is of a high order. Among their religious symbols occur the double axe, which is characteristic of ancient Crete, and also the solar disc, both seeming to betoken a penetration of ideas from the Mediterranean as far as Scandinavia in the bronze age. This conjecture is further strengthened by the comparison of the Runic alphabet of Scandinavia with ancient scripts in the Near East, and also by the recent discovery of a sort of Teutonic eschatological prophecy which bears considerable likeness to a similar Pehlevi writing in Persia.

Evidence as to the earlier customs and beliefs of these people is thought to be accessible in the famous treatise, the *Germania* of Tacitus. We may doubt the accuracy of Tacitus' information, but at the same time we cannot help recognizing that some of the practices to which he refers correspond to similar ones which are known to have existed among our immediate forefathers. The Teutonic peoples were polytheists of much the same type as the invaders of India. The two most important Nature-deities were Wodan or Odin and Donar or Thor. The former appears as the god of war, the protector of warriors, who gathers those who fall in battle to the dwelling-place of the elect – Valhalla – whither they are conducted by attendant maidens or Valkyries. (We remember how Hitler at Hindenburg's funeral ended his oration by saying: 'Go then, dead field-marshal, to Valhalla!') Wodan is not inconceivably a German chieftain who has undergone apotheosis, and been exalted into a god. His name is connected with a root which also appears in Sanskrit, and in Latin, in the word *vates* or prophet, suggesting someone who is filled with a wave of supernatural inspiration or force. Wodan himself from his throne rules what are called the nine worlds. He appears on earth sometimes as the wild hunter, with his eight-footed steed, Sleipnir, accompanied by a noisy rout, sometimes as a one-eyed man with a broad-brimmed hat and accompanied by ravens, in which guise he is the god of wisdom and of spells. The conception of Wodan as the All-Father and king of the gods may be a later development, and even attributable to Christian influences. Some of his features seem to have been transferred to St Michael, St Martin and St Nicholas in German legends. The worship of Wodan demanded bloody sacrifices, and with it is also connected the drinking of mead, which, like the *soma* of the Eastern Nordics, is thought to bestow divine wisdom. Donar, or Thor, is the good and encouraging deity who is represented as riding through the air in a chariot drawn by two rams. The oak is sacred to him. His weapon is the famous hammer Miollnir, with which he conquers the powers opposed to him. We hear also of Frey, a god of fertility and peace. It is obvious that some of the names of our days of the week are taken from the names of these gods. Much has been made of the familiarity alleged to have prevailed between the average Teuton and his god. The phrase 'the beloved friend Thor' is taken as typical, and is contrasted with the sense of awe and dread with which deities in other countries were regarded. The scale of virtues commended as being pleasing to Deity is also different from that prevailing among (let us say) Mediterranean Christians. Honour and self-respect and courage are praised, but humility, pity and loving-kindness are less esteemed.

The fifth and last group of Europeans with which we are here concerned hardly enters into the purview of Englishmen, but it very greatly concerns the inhabitants of Germany. The Slavs are a wave of the great Alpo-Carpathian group, but they are not its most effective members. They tend to be dark-haired, pale-skinned, dreamy and imaginative.* They are, therefore, inclined to fall into the hands of folk stronger than themselves, and it is a curious fact that in early days they were so often harried by slave-raiders and sold as bondsmen that their racial name became a common noun: 'slave.' The Slavs have a high birth-rate, and so a great tendency to expansion, and this takes place by infiltration rather than by conquest. Where the Slavs have engaged in wars it has usually been because they were organized, egged on and led by some other people, either Asiatic or Teuton. There are two groups of Slavs, the Northern, comprising the Russians, the Czechs, the Slovaks and the Poles, the Southern, comprising the Serbo-Croatians and the Balkan peoples. But in most cases the ruling class has been non-Slavonic, and in the case of the early Russians and Poles it was almost certainly Norse or Scandinavian. The religion of the early Slavonic peoples seems to have been a pluralistic Nature-religion. The names of the deities are known. Svarog was the god of fire, and Dazbog was the sun-god. Perun was the sky-god. A medieval chronicler says of the early Prussians: 'They vainly worshipped all creatures as god, to wit, sun, moon, and stars, thunder and lightning, birds and four-footed beasts. They had also sacred woods, fields, and streams.' It is thus

---

* This may once have been true; but we may fitly ask whether it adequately describes the Polish airmen and Tito's patriots of the war of liberation.

evident that there was nothing distinctively noteworthy about early Slavonic religion.

Upon all these various peoples came the impact of three distinct types of Christianity: that of the Celtiberian Romano-British people of Ireland and western Scotland, that of the Italian-Gallican Christians and that of the Byzantine Church. The pre-Christian religion wilted rapidly, and although some of it was driven underground and became in many cases a witch-cult, while some survived under a Christian veneer, in the main it suffered radical displacement. At the same time it is only honest to recognize that in certain respects it was the displacement of one superstition by another, and this is true not only of Britain but of Scandinavia and the main continent. Boniface, although he hewed down the sacred tree of Thor at Geismar, carried miracle-working relics with him, and a recently edited book of prayers from the early Scandinavian church is virtually a manual of Christian magic and charms. Doubtless the standard varied, and noble spiritual figures like those of Bede and Alphege were not uncommon. But that the Christianity of the dark ages in Europe was a paganized Christianity can scarcely be denied. The cults of Jesus as a magician and miracle-worker, and of the saints, replaced the worship of the gods. Yet the Hebraic background of the Christian religion always involved the possibility of people holding a unitary and ethical conception of reality, and the Anglo-Saxon homilies contain a pretty pure type of Christian teaching.

PLURALISM IN GENERAL

A few more general remarks upon pluralism in religion may not at this stage be out of place.

First of all, if readers will look at the table on pages 94–95, they will see that although some types of divinity attract attention in one part of the world more than another, the general similarity between the various groups of gods is well-marked,

Locality	Title or sphere of influence	Sun-God	Messenger of the gods	Moon-god	Luck deity	Earth-mother or father	Goddess of fertility and birth	God of alcoholic drink	God or goddess of death and of the underworld	God of travellers	God of agriculture	God of hunting	Rain-god or Water-god	Fire-god	War-god	Light-god	Sky-god
China																	M
Celts of Britain		M			M	M	F F		M M F		M[7] M				M F		
Celts of Gaul							F				M M F				F M		
Etruria		M F	F				F F	M							M		M
Egypt		M		M		F	F F		M[5]								M F
Greeks		M	M			F	F		M F						M		M
Irish Celts							M F								F		
Indians, N. America																	
Indians, S. America			F														
Japan		F			P M F	M	F			M	M				M	M	
Indians, Costa Rica				M													
Navaho Indians																	
Caribs						F											
Mexico		S		F					M	M			M	M F F M	M	M	
Peru		M			M	F											
Zuñi Indians																	
Iroquois Indians																	
Romans			M								M				M		
Scandinavia		M					F		F		M				M		
Sumeria		M[4][5]	M	F	F	M	F M[1]		F		M[4]		M[1]	M F	M[1]		
Surians (Ras Shamra)									M								
Iran (pre-Zarathustra)		M				F									M	M	
Germanic tribes		M			F	F	F[2]		F						M		M
Vedic India		M	M			F		M					M	M	M P	M	M

M = male deity.   S = singular.
F = female deity.   P = plural.
H = Hermaphrodite Deified culture-heroes (explicable on Euhemeristic lines) are almost uni[versal]
T = Triad

N.B.—Many local variants of these existed. Thus among the
    No attempt is made to record the various totem-deit[ies]

TABLE (NOT EXHAUSTIVE) TO S[HOW]

Spring-god or goddess	Wind-god	Storm-god	River-god	Dawn-gods	Goddess of truth	High god	Destructive nature	Benevolent nature	God of craftsmanship	Bad sacred, or personification of evil	Thunder-god	Sea-god	Creator-god	God of Love (sex)	Twin deities	God or goddess of mind or wisdom	God of healing	Deified women who have died in childbirth
			F			M			M			M	M			M		
											M						M	
		F	F	F	F	M M[5]	M			M M		M	M	F		F		
		F M	F							M				F		F	M	
	M	M	M						M	M	M	M				M	M	
			M							M		M						
												M	M	M		M	M	
												M	M					
														H				
M	M															F	M	F
			M								M		M[5]					
				M														
M[3]			M S				T			M M	M M	M M[3]		M F	X X	M S[3]	M F	
		M	M								M	M				M		
									M				M[5]					
									M				M					
M M									M		M	M	M[5]					
M P			F S			M	M F	M	M	M	M		M	M[6]	X	M F		F

[1] The same deity – Nergal.
[2] Also of navigation.
[3] Wind and wisdom (Odin).
[4] This god, Ninib, was a solar deity who presided over agriculture and war.
[5] With a consort, quite often (Egypt, Greece and Peru) a sister.
[6] Post-vedic.
[7] A Chinese general deified.

are a number of different war-gods and earth-mothers.
nifications of sub-human life.

VARIETIES OF POLYTHEISM

and that though the form of the pantheon may in part be due to diffusion, yet the similarity of materials and interests with which man had to reckon is in itself quite enough to produce similar objects of worship.

Second, it is said that the ability to conceive gods in man's own image was a relatively late and difficult achievement, and we have already seen that the early Roman *numina* were qualities rather than persons. Polytheism is therefore a sign of a pluralistic tendency, but not necessarily of anthropomorphism. The development of anthropomorphic deities in Greece was plainly a humanizing of the natural, rather than a degradation of the supernatural, and at first polytheism seemed to solve the problems of the Greeks better than monotheism did. Third, it is not by any means fair to charge pluralism with evil results. No doubt it had its limitations, and gave only a temporary advantage, but there can be no reasonable doubt that there was something about it which helped on the advance of civilization, making deity to be no longer shapeless, or brutish (at any rate after the gods came to be conceived in human form), but at least approximating to the standard of some exceptionally able human beings. This, of course, was not an advantage if the human beings in question were of the Sultanic type such as figure in the Arabian Nights Entertainments! Polytheism also gave a greater freedom of mind, and encouraged men to adventure; and when the fusion or alliance of deities occurred it made for the formation of composite states. There appears also to have been some connexion between pluralistic religion and the development of private property. But without superseding pluralism through theocrasia, it was never possible to make it into a theological system, and as soon as men began to try, or started to theorize, it was seen to be irrational, and the Greeks criticized it to death. It is a sure mark of polytheism that it has no ideas beyond civilization, and no quarrel with it. It can create a state, but it then becomes shut up in it as the

*Chart to illustrate some of the creative activities of religion,
correlated with other events*

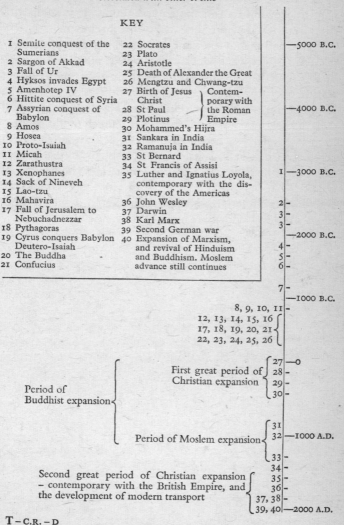

KEY

1 Semite conquest of the Sumerians
2 Sargon of Akkad
3 Fall of Ur
4 Hyksos invades Egypt
5 Amenhotep IV
6 Hittite conquest of Syria
7 Assyrian conquest of Babylon
8 Amos
9 Hosea
10 Proto-Isaiah
11 Micah
12 Zarathustra
13 Xenophanes
14 Sack of Nineveh
15 Lao-tzu
16 Mahavira
17 Fall of Jerusalem to Nebuchadnezzar
18 Pythagoras
19 Cyrus conquers Babylon Deutero-Isaiah
20 The Buddha
21 Confucius

22 Socrates
23 Plato
24 Aristotle
25 Death of Alexander the Great
26 Mengtzu and Chwang-tzu
27 Birth of Jesus Christ ⎫
28 St Paul   ⎬ Contemporary with the Roman Empire
29 Plotinus   ⎭
30 Mohammed's Hijra
31 Sankara in India
32 Ramanuja in India
33 St Bernard
34 St Francis of Assisi
35 Luther and Ignatius Loyola, contemporary with the discovery of the Americas
36 John Wesley
37 Darwin
38 Karl Marx
39 Second German war
40 Expansion of Marxism, and revival of Hinduism and Buddhism. Moslem advance still continues

—5000 B.C.

—4000 B.C.

1 —3000 B.C.

2 -
3 -
3 -
—2000 B.C.
4 -
5 -
6 -

7 -
—1000 B.C.

8, 9, 10, 11 -

12, 13, 14, 15, 16 ⎱
17, 18, 19, 20, 21 ⎰
22, 23, 24, 25, 26

27 —0
28 -
First great period of Christian expansion ⎰ 29 -
30 -

Period of Buddhist expansion

31 -
Period of Moslem expansion ⎰ 32 —1000 A.D.

33 -
34 -
Second great period of Christian expansion 35 -
– contemporary with the British Empire, and 36 -
the development of modern transport 37, 38 -
39, 40 —2000 A.D.

state religion, just as Shinto is in Japan. It is unable to lift it up or to preserve it from corruption, by setting up an independent standard beyond that of the natural. Ethnic it is, and, with all its beauty and picturesqueness, ethnic it remains.

Beside polytheism we must set something which is closely related to it, i.e. what Hocking has called 'plural belonging'. In this case the worshippers affect more than one religious system, and visit temples of different faiths quite freely. The phenomenon is well known in China, but may be found all over the East; and it is not unknown in a much modified form even in England, where a zealous *dévote* may attend both parish church and also Spiritualist or Christian Science or even theosophist meetings. In a certain northern parish (typical of others) all women may belong to the Mothers' Union and attend monthly services in the parish church, while at other times worshipping in all manner of conventicles.

CHAPTER VI

The Golden Age of Religious Creativity

IF we make a graph of the spiritual activities of the human race as history reveals them to us, and plot the principal items between 5000 B.C. and A.D. 1940, we cannot help being struck by the density of the points recorded as occurring round about a certain period. A glance at the diagram will enable the reader to verify this. We are unable to say that the various events so recorded have many common factors, nor can we distinguish any actual evolutionary chain connecting them. The most we can say is that within the scope of about eight or nine centuries all the chief varieties of solution for the deeper problems of humanity emerged. It would seem that in some way or other the time was ripe for their appearance. But having once appeared, they do not lead on to any others. Under various titles the same various solutions recur, with perhaps slight variations in form. Hence the task for us and for our successors upon the planet is not so much to discover a new religion or to receive a new revelation, as to decide which of the various alternatives propounded we shall ourselves adopt.

In the centre of the group of emergents occurs the rise of the Christian movement. Its dominant feature is an absolute claim as an Act of God, rendering it unique and 'once-for-all' as a revelation. The scientific observer is bound to say, however, that he is compelled to treat it historically as part of a group of movements, and to place it in series, relating to it other phenomena in spite of its claim to uniqueness. He will be truly scientific, nevertheless, only if he allows it to speak for itself, and, instead of suppressing or belittling its claim, sets on record the account it professes to give both of itself and also of its neighbours and apparent rivals. Only in this way can its claims be fairly judged beside those of other faiths. Only in this way can anyone hope to discover whether these claims are justifiable, and also whether the various other faiths can be related to it in such a way as to do justice to their pretensions, while preserving the special claim which Christianity makes.

It is a commonplace with specialists in the history of religion that somewhere within the region of 800 B.C. there passed over the populations of this planet a stirring of the mind, which, while it left large tracts of humanity comparatively uninfluenced, produced in a number of different spots on the earth's surface prophetic individuals who created a series of new starting-points for human living and thinking. Three chief aims stand out: to know the world, to know ourselves and to know the meaning and purpose of the Whole – aims concerned with science, society and spirit. Science and society were the concern chiefly of the Ionian Greeks and their cousins in Hellas and Alexandria, and after their time the study declined for many centuries, until the renascence of Greek learning in the sixteenth century in Europe led to a rekindling of the fire, although sparks of it had continued to glow here and there in the medieval monasteries. Since then it has burned steadily up to a year or two ago. But wherever men and women were not settled in convention and traditional habit, the contemplation of the Whole, and diverse ways of relating mankind to It, are the dominant interests of the entire period from 800 B.C. to A.D. 300, dubbed by Karl Jaspers, the Swiss existentialist, 'the Axial Era'.*

In Persia Zarathustra appears – an isolated prophet who achieves only a temporary success. In India, as we shall see, there were immense changes, and many seers and thinkers. In Greece the scientific did not succeed in swamping the philo-

* See final paragraph on p. 7.

sophical-theological interest, and popular polytheism was discarded for new conceptions of Deity – Platonic, Aristotelian, Stoic or Epicurean, which have remained classic interpretations, and have aided in shaping the thought of the Western world ever since. In China the sages undermined the pluralistic religion of its bronze age, and carried their meditations in directions not unlike those of the Greeks. In Palestine a wholly unique series of intuitional religious leaders battled for a complete break with ethnic religion, and the struggle ended in almost complete success for their cause, and in the emergence of a small Jewish national church-community, pledged to a spiritual monotheism in some features resembling that of Zarathustra, not entirely discarding the paraphernalia of temple, priest and sacrifice, but sufficiently pregnant with great new ideas to be able to give birth to the momentous Christian movement, the classic development of which perhaps ends with its achievement of toleration under Constantine in 313.

PERSIA

It is of great importance to distinguish carefully between the original person and work of Zarathustra and the more or less fictitious character and achievements of 'Zoroaster the Magian'. The Magians known to the Greeks, and referred to by Herodotus, Plato, Strabo and Plutarch, were not orthodox followers of the Persian prophet. They were the priests of certain religious colonies established in the west of Iran during the age of the Achaemenides, from Mesopotamia to the Aegean, and existing there up to the Christian epoch. These emigrants, severed from the area where the reforms of Zarathustra had prevailed, escaped a large measure of his influence, and only partially adopted his doctrines, remaining faithful to much of the earlier Nature-Religion of Iran. Their adopted language was Aramaean, and they became incapable of reading the Avesta, or collection of Zoroastrian sacred writings, of which they may not even have possessed copies. They interested themselves in astrology, and were as different from the proper Zoroastrians as the Alexandrian Jews were from those of Palestine.

To understand the peculiar significance of Zarathustra we must, therefore, go back to those sections of his reputed writings which are indubitably genuine.

Professor Herzfeld thinks that we now have three safe dates for the much-disputed history of Iranian religion.

> (1) c. 520 B.C.; the recognition by Darius (at the beginning of his reign) of Zarathustra's monotheistic community, and the consequent cessation of 'daivayasnian' polytheism.
>
> (2) 485 B.C.; a rebellion of the followers of the old religion, which was superficially suppressed by Xerxes, who attempted to effect by force the general acceptance – not realized by Darius – of Zoroastrian Ahuramazda-worship. This attempt was bound to fail from the beginning.
>
> (3) 404 B.C.; the official re-establishment by Artaxerxes II of the original polytheistic religion, by means of a compromise, which is reflected in the later (liturgical) literature of Zoroastrianism, and which preserved the name and patronage of the original prophet, but with concessions to the very system that he sought to reform.

Persia, or more properly Iran, contains two main ethnic groups, apart from smaller infiltrations. These are respectively the Tajik, who are the original inhabitants (and comprise mainly people similar to the Dravidians of India, together with here and there a sub-stratum of older ulotrichous stock), and the descendants of the proto-Nordic invaders from the Eurasian steppes, who are the Medes and Persians proper.

Five Gathas or songs are claimed as genuine compositions of Zarathustra himself. They are certainly written in early Persian, and from them we can glean a few (but very few) facts about the circumstances of the prophet's life. He seems to have emerged at a time when there was acute tension between the Iranians proper and some non-Nordic nomads, Turanians or early Mongols, from central Asia. These marauders were, like the ancestors of the Tajik Persians, polytheists, and were continually raiding the Persian territory and carrying off its cattle. Zarathustra seems to have begun as the champion of the oppressed owners of the cattle and to have appealed to his one good God to deliver his people out of the enemy's hand, urging them on the other side to be more faithful to Ahuramazda, and to give up lower forms of 'daeva-worship'. It is clear, however, that the name of Ahuramazda is not his invention, since it occurs in an Assyrian inscription of a much earlier period. Zarathustra thus appears to be very much the same type of religious leader as Moses or Mohammed, and his endeavour seems to be to recall his people to a purer faith, to which they are in danger of becoming disloyal.

The Gathas in structure resemble the Upanishads of India (see page 128) – that is to say, that are miscellaneous collections of prayers, instructions and hymns, strung together without any special attempts at symmetry, and including casual references to Zarathustra's family, sayings attributed to him, and two fairly complete chapters on the nature of Deity. Added to these Gathas are many writings of a much later date, the whole forming a corpus known as the Zendavesta. As manifested in these later developments, Persian religion appears not so much polytheistic but definitely dualistic – a rare and almost unique example of the good and bad sacred not merely believed in simultaneously (that is common enough), but balanced against one another. It is a serious mistake to treat Zoroastrianism as though it had been of this pattern from the beginning. From the Gathas it is clear that the doctine of Zarathustra himself was a sublime and distinct monotheism, though below the Supreme Being are satellites or Amesha Spentas, who are of the nature of archangels, and, if not exactly creatures, are at any rate inferior divinities, and receive no worship. Later Persian religion also mentions the god Mithras as possessing almost equal honour with Ahuramazda. But it is fair to say that Zarathustra was as much a monotheist as the second Isaiah. When in later Zoroastrianism we find reference to the evil spirit Ahriman, we are in a different atmosphere. In the Gathas 'good mind' and 'evil mind' are possible or actual states of the individual, though the spirit of deceit and wickedness, personified as Druj, is opposed to Asha or righteousness. Against wickedness Zarathustra is unrelenting. He shows no sign of forgiveness, but is as militant as the Psalmist who says to God: 'Do not I hate them (the wicked) right sore, even as though they were mine enemies.' Yet man's life to him is in the main a good and precious thing, since it is in spite of dangers and temptations a responsible one, having as its avowed object the service of the One Supreme God in the conflict for good against evil. The Gathas contain the assertion of a future life and of a last judgement, as well as of the immortality of the soul. In the later portions of the Zendavesta occurs the idea of a divine-human saviour who will interpose to destroy the power of evil and establish a permanent commonwealth of righteousness upon earth. Thus, as will be seen, there is a good deal familiar as belief both to Jews and to Christians which is already present in Persian religious thought, and it is considered certain that the effect of the exile of the Jews in Babylonia at the time when that country was under Medo-Persian rule was to increase the content of their creed. Indeed, the legacy of Persian religion would appear to have been more momentous to the Jews than to the Persians themselves, and the latter perhaps would not have preserved for subsequent generations the actual teaching of their prophet, if they had not come to treat the Gathas enshrining it as written records of magical power – charms, in fact.

The life of Zarathustra was embroidered by later generations with honorific legend.* His mother miraculously conceived him when she was of the age of fifteen. All Nature rejoiced at his birth. Attempts were made to kill him by a Turanian prince, the Herod of the story. He retired into the mountains for meditation and was led by an archangel into the presence of God and received a revelation, and was thereafter tempted by Angra Mainyu, the Lord of Evil. Yet he has never been regarded as the incarnation of deity, but solely as the revered prophet. Persia having become in succession a Christian and then a Moslem country, there are not many today who claim to follow Zarathustra's teaching, but in Iran there are communities numbering several thousand in Yezd and Kirman, and about 100,000 in Bombay, who, as Parsis, are the descendants of Persian immigrants. At Mazar-al-Sherif, in Afghanistan, there were also reputed to be some; but Mrs Rosita Forbes on a recent visit could not discover any.

The somewhat hackneyed statement that later Zoroastrianism is definitely dualistic needs to be considered. It became current intellectual coin in the nineteenth century, owing largely to what Milman wrote about it in his *History of Christianity*, but it is now considered doubtful whether it really credits the power of evil with authority and status completely equivalent to those of the power of good. Real dualism may have been the creed of some very few philosophers, but it is doubtful whether it has ever exercised any popular influence. Present-day misfortunes are tempting some despairing souls to think that it may be a correct explanation of the Universe, but it should encourage such to reflect that never, even at the worst periods of past history, has any extensive acceptance of

* Dhalla, *Zoroastrian Theology*, p. 199. Zarathustra, he says, is a historical personage in the Gathas. In the later Avesta he is surrounded by an aureole. In the Pahlavi works his personality is enshrouded by miracles, and he becomes superhuman; but see p. 140 regarding this.

dualism occurred. Even polytheists have always cherished the conviction, or at least the hope, that the total forces of the good sacred were numerically, if not at least dynamically, superior to those of the bad sacred. Let us note further that humanity has in these matters generally managed to avoid confusing black with white. It has had as a rule some kind of standard, which is guaranteed by its 'good sacred', its beneficent deities. It may be doubted whether this 'good sacred' is supreme in the absolute sense, or merely 'powerful', thus providing only a measure and margin of security to the 'good'. Perhaps the man in the street has not always thought his position through; and certainly there are passages in the Old Testament which show that some of the earlier Hebrews at any rate could only visualize a Supreme Self-Existent Being who was the source of evil as well as good, of unpleasant as well as pleasant things.

EGYPT

The story of Zarathustra and his temporary reformation must remind some of the curious and oft-told story of the Egyptian king, Amenhotep IV, to which we must here make a brief reference. This extraordinary man, who appears to have ascended the throne of Egypt about 1375 B.C., was the grandson of a proto-Nordic princess of the race of the Mitanni, who had married the Pharaoh Thothmes IV.* The young king, neglecting the defence of his realm, devoted himself to a fundamental alteration of the balance of Egyptian religion. Although it thus became centred by him round the worship of the symbol of the solar disc, it was nearer to anything that can be called monotheism than any other form of belief and cultus prevailing in the Middle East at that time, though not so different from the Mosaic monotheism, which according to

---

* He had also two Mitannic stepmothers, the subsidiary wives of his father, Amenhotep III.

tradition, sprang up a little later. At any rate it was introduced deliberately into Thebes, where the king at his own expense built a new temple, but did not succeed in overcoming the opposition of the established priesthood. Finally he built himself a fresh capital and another great temple midway between Thebes and the sea, at the place which is now known as Tell-el-Amarna. Recent excavations have revealed how much the lay-out and arrangements of the new temples differed from those of the ordinary Egyptian sanctuary. The death of the reforming monarch led, however, to a violent reaction, and every effort was made by priests and people to efface the work of one who was evidently regarded as a heretic, and whose extravagant expenditure on religious novelties had left his frontiers unguarded and exposed to invasion.

We do not know how many Egyptians were affected by this strange effort of Amenhotep IV to change the course of the religious life of his subjects. He certainly converted some of them, and he introduced the word Aten as the title of the sun-god, instead of the usual one of Rē (though exactly how a sun-god becomes converted into the spiritual deity of an ethical monotheist still remains an unsolved mystery). He himself adopted the name of Ikhn-aten. The same name appears in the document called the teaching of Amen-em Apt, previously mentioned, and the inference is that the special form which we have seen that this moral instruction assumed may have been caused by the author's adoption of the new religion. Sir E. Wallis Budge on documentary evidence is disposed to date monotheism in Egypt earlier than Ikhn-aten. Breasted does the same. Indeed there are signs of it in some of the moral treatises, which may go back to the third or fourth millennium B.C. (cf. *Aten* with Hebrew *Adon*, lord). He was only a boy at the time of his accession, so that his reforms may have been instigated by his relatives. Still more striking, however, is the moral treatise associated with the name of Ani, the scribe who is said to have lived under the twenty-second dynasty, and therefore possibly about 925 B.C., even nearer to the time of the Hebrew prophets. Here we read: 'Noisy, vain repetitions are an abomination unto God. Pray thou thy prayer with a loving heart, all the words being hidden. He will do for thee all that is necessary for thy daily needs.' And again: 'When thou art making offerings to God, take good heed that thou doest not that which he holds in abomination.' The word used for 'God' in most of these passages is said to be *pā nêter*, which has the same significance as Il Allah to Moslems, i.e. the Almighty. The inference is that we have here again the beginnings of an ethical monotheism, not unlike that which developed later among the Hebrews. Was the sojourn of the latter in Egypt in any degree responsible for this?

GREECE

Events among the Greeks during this crucial period are almost as well known as those among the Hebrews, at any rate to those who have had a classical education; but in the case of the general reader this cannot always be assumed, and, therefore, a brief outline of them must be given. We take up the story where we left it in the previous chapter, and enlarge what was there said about the third stage of Greek religion. There are, it is well said, two streams of unification in Greek thought, the first poetical and popular, the second philosophical. In the plays of Aeschylus (*c.* 470 B.C.) there are whole passages which pre-suppose a faith that has crossed over the boundaries of monotheism. The earliest of the philosophical critics of whom we know anything is Xenophanes, who in 532 B.C. left Colophon in Ionia to settle in Sicily, and afterwards in South Italy. He was the founder of the Eleatic school (so called from its birth-place, Elea), and, although only fragments of his writings survive, as far as can be judged he proclaimed the existence of a single non-anthropomorphic deity.

His famous epigram, that if horses could speak they would certainly say that Deity was like a horse, has become a commonplace, and has been fruitful in producing other similar assertions, among them that embodied in an essay by Feuerbach (translated into English by Harriet Martineau), the gist of which is that man made gods in his own image; and also the familiar poem 'The Fish', by Rupert Brooke. But it is a mistake to treat Xenophanes as an actual forerunner of the projectionists. He was, in fact, much nearer in outlook to the great Hebrew prophets, especially deutero-Isaiah, and plainly believed in a real objective deity who was all sight, all hearing and all intelligence, yet akin to mortals in neither mind nor form. He attacked the cult of statues as images, and discredited the mythology occurring in the pages of Homer and Hesiod. From Xenophanes onwards criticism of religion enters into the general Greek attitude to life; but it would probably be a mistake to regard all the critics as actually anti-religious. Thus, although there are utterances of Heracleitus which are directed with acuteness against the outward forms of contemporary worship, it is not possible to say that Heracleitus aimed at the overthrow of all religion, however defined. Indeed it is Heracleitus with whom the doctrine of a Logos begins, and he oscillates between the two conceptions of self-existent Being, as personal and as impersonal. Anaxagoras, who was one of the two tutors of Pericles, is said by Plato (in the *Apologia of Socrates*) to have been accused of atheism. But *atheos* to the Greeks did not necessarily mean what it does to us – i.e. the rejection of any central deity, even of the super-personal, non-anthropomorphic type. It meant the rejection of the Olympian deities who could be flattered or wheedled. Thus Protagoras (*c.* 415 B.C.) says: 'In the matter of the gods I have not been able to attain the knowledge of their existence or non-existence, or of what form they are; for many things hinder the attainment of this knowledge, both the obscurity of the subject and the shortness of human life.' Protagoras, however, taught that the ultimate element in the universe was 'Nous', usually translated 'mind', which is unlimited, and has universal power. Whether he regarded Nous as in any sense personal cannot be determined, but he was probably as much a theist at bottom as the Chinese teacher Chu Hsi (see page 191), if J.P. Bruce's* estimate of the latter be accepted. But Diagoras, a contemporary of Protagoras, goes further. Rendered sceptical by his sufferings, he rejected the possibility of the existence of any deity, singular or plural, who could reward or protect virtue and confound wickedness. He is in fact completely modern, especially in his remarks about answers to petitionary prayer. When someone directed his attention to the votive tablets in a temple, erected by grateful survivors of shipwrecks, he replied: 'Those who were drowned did not put up tablets.' This kind of retort is just as formidable, whether one believes in the Christian God or in a plurality of (on the whole) benevolent gods and godlings.

The Socrates of the Platonic dialogues is certainly no follower of Diagoras, even though he is at times destructive in his criticisms. If he and his biographer were really in agreement, it must be plain that they stood on the brink of a moral monotheism. Plato uses 'God' and 'the gods' with rather casual alternation, and does not seem careful to assert a unitary conception of deity; but in his *Nomoi*, written when he was old, he seems to indicate a tendency towards belief in one God, and recommended that people who openly reject that belief shall be dealt with as bad citizens, and a danger to the State, and that they shall be admonished, imprisoned and even sentenced to death, if they are found incorrigible. He thus lays the foundation for the principle of persecution in all its forms – the forcible repression of all who reject the official ideology of

* Cf. article by the author in the Conference number of the *Modern Churchman* for 1950 on the whole question.

the sovereign State, from the penal laws against heretics and dissenters to the establishment of an Ogpu or Gestapo. Socrates is represented as affirming the existence of a daimôn* or inner guide of a divine character, but it is hardly clear whether this daimôn is the localized activity of the Supreme Being, or merely a familiar spirit, only a little higher in status than a guardian angel.

Not long after the time of Socrates comes Euhemerus (340 B.C.), with his notorious explanation of the gods as human beings who by might or cunning had persuaded men to accord them divine honours. This is so near to what was often the truth (in Babylonia, Egypt and under the Roman Empire) that it undoubtedly impressed many people, though it does not explain the sincere tendency of many to see in human beings of great virtue, beauty or holiness at least adumbrations of the Godhead in all its fullness. But Godhead is a neuter word. And so we find that in the long run the effect of Euhemerism was to encourage the de-personalizing of the idea of deity. 'The divine' (to theion) was believed to be a sublime principle or quality, manifesting itself in the lives of eminent persons. Thus the wheel went full circle, and men found themselves almost back at the pre-animistic interpretation of phenomena (sometimes called dynamism) where the chieftain is a warrior full of impersonal mana.

Aristotle (384–322) is perhaps a monotheist; but his interests are not religious, but man-centred, and his unmoved Mover is hardly a personal god so much as primordial Principle, and because It is perfect, It can have no knowledge, love or intercourse in respect of anything but Itself. Aristotle recognizes 'the gods', but they themselves seem subordinated to this primordial Principle. Epicurus (341–270) is even less encouraging,

---

* From Hesiod (c. 700 B.C.) to the Stoic period daimôn has a good meaning – 'beneficent guardian spirit'. (So Dr W. H. S. Jones of St Catherine's College.)

since the gods for him, even though they may exist, are entirely indifferent to human affairs.

But perhaps the nearest philosophic approach to monotheism comes in the system of the Stoics (so called from the painted porch or Stoa at Athens where they held their school for instruction). Here under Zeno (*c.* 360–264) and his immediate successor Chrysippus, there developed a real attempt at a sort of natural theology, in which Deity is the Universe, conceived, however, in various ways, first as fire, then as wind, then as Nature, Reason, Providence or Destiny. At first a kind of materialistic pantheism, Stoicism develops finally into an austere worship of a God who is transcendent as well as immanent, as is plain from the famous hymn of Cleanthes (331–232), in which the Supreme Principle is actually called 'Zeus'; but in its earlier stages it resembles much more the 'Religion without Revelation' of Professor Julian Huxley. Stoicism taught a kind of universal brotherhood – all are the citizens of One Great Commonwealth, and have the obligation of mutual service, yet more as a duty than from any motive of love* or goodwill, as in Christianity or Buddhism. The souls of all men, as fragments of the indestructible Universe, survive death, though not as individuals. But since nothing can happen to us but what is in the constitution and course of Nature, death is not to be feared. The chief aim of the ideal wise man should be to live according to Nature (so like what is taught by the followers of Lao-Tzu in China); and the highest virtue is *apatheia* – freedom from passion (so like inactive action and the passionless life as taught in India). There is no conception of progress towards a consummation, as in Hebrew and Christian teaching, but everything goes in an infinite series of cycles, and whatever providence or purpose Zeno thinks he can detect in the course of events, that course is of infinite duration. Much of what is in reality Stoicism found its way into Chris-

* But see p. 114.

tianity during the fourth and fifth centuries, and shaped the form and expression of Christian teaching. Thus Saint Ambrose wrote a treatise called *De Officiis*, more or less corresponding to a treatise of the same name written by Cicero, but, although it contains features which are distinctively Christian and based on the New Testament, it also includes much which is taken over with little modification from Stoic ethics. To this day many educated lay-folk, indeed, are Stoics rather than Christians, without knowing it; and it has been held permissible by some to regard Stoic doctrine as not logically unsuitable to serve as a foundation or background for a Christian structure of belief.

One is led to suspect that future generations will see in Stoicism less a late development of the Greek genius than an intrusion of a much more definitely oriental philosophical religion into the Graeco-Roman world. The most illustrious exponents of the Stoic creed were drawn from countries outside Greece proper, and, even though our acquaintance with their teaching is derived from Greek documents, it must be recognized that the founder was a Phoenician, and that other Stoic leaders came from Babylon, Tyre, Sidon, Carthage, Cilicia, Phrygia and Rhodes. Not a single Stoic of any fame was a native of Hellas proper. Zeno had something about him of the Hebrew prophet, and the stern, unbending and almost fanatical moralism of the leader and his disciples is in marked contrast to the light, almost reckless gaiety of the Greek spirit. Stoicism, it has been said, came to the rescue of a society where all the old sanctions had broken down under the pitiless and disintegrating criticism of Greek rationalistic philosphy, and supplied something in the nature of religion to an almost bankrupt world. But, although it impressed the conscience of this world, it was a creed of despair and acquiescence, and had no belief in Progress, or in Deity as Love; and so, even though Christianity largely absorbed its ethical terminology, it invested the terms used with new content and new values.

The age in which Christianity arose was indeed an age of moral reformation and desire for regeneration. The later Stoics, such as Epictetus and Marcus Aurelius, are earnest preachers of righteousness, and their writings contain many passages which resemble some of those in the Sermon on the Mount. But they contain others which fall far below the level of that world-famous utterance, and, although they inculcate benevolence of a sort, it is a different virtue from the *agapé* hymned by St Paul in I Cor. xiii. Marcus Aurelius does not exhibit the Christian quality of humble mindedness, and he and other Stoics hope for nothing that the world cannot give them, and advise no one to expect too much of life. Their rather melancholy fortitude has in recent years been revived by Dr Lippmann the humanist, with his doctrine of 'high religion', which is a republication of Stoicism, and is certainly one of the possible answers to the problems of life in every age.

It is only fair to give a few extracts from the chief Stoic writings which so much resemble those of the Christian apologists that they might almost be mistaken for passages taken out of the writings of the latter.

Seneca, who died in A.D. 65, wrote:

'No man is good without God.'

'God made the world because he is good; as the good never grudges anything good, He therefore made everything the best possible.'

'God has a fatherly mind towards good men and loves them stoutly; and, saith he, let them be harassed with toils, with pains, with losses, that they may gain true strength.'

'A holy spirit resides within us, the guardian and observer of our good and evil deeds.

Epictetus, who was in Rome in A.D. 75, wrote:

'The first thing to learn is that there is a God, that his knowledge pervades the whole universe, and that it extends not only to our acts but to our thoughts and feelings.'

'To have God for our maker and father and guardian, should not that emancipate us from all sadness and all fear?'

'When you have shut your door and darkened your room, say not to yourself that you are alone. God is in your room, and your attendant genius likewise. Think not that they need the light to see what you do.'

Yet similarity of language does not involve identity of thought. What the Stoic meant by *theos* was not what the Hellenistic Jew meant by the same word. The Stoic saw nothing profane in asserting that the wise man is the equal of Zeus. Moreover, the Stoic list of virtues commended was different from that of the Christian. Pity to the Stoic was a sign of weakness, and compassion a misuse of clemency. In place of sympathy he set *apatheia*, the control of the emotions. The wise man, it was said, ought to imitate the gods in relieving distress, but without experiencing any sentiments of compassion. Life was not to the Stoic a game to be played to the end, even if you seemed to be losing. Suicide was to him an act of sublime virtue, if your self-respect demanded it. Yet we must admit that the declaration 'all men are born free' was first made by a Stoic. It is always possible that later Stoics were influenced by Judaism and subsequently by Christianity. But even those who are of pre-Christian date must take the credit of having taught men to prize integrity, self-discipline and virtue, and to put God first, even if they were vague as to His attributes.

For those who can read German, by far the best modern book on Stoicism is *Die Stoa* by Dr Pohlenz, 2 vols, Leipzig.

CHAPTER VII

The Phenomenon of India

In this chapter and the next I propose to desert the general synoptic policy hitherto pursued, and to describe the course of religion in India, China and Japan by itself. I do so partly because so much more deserves to be known about it in English-speaking circles, partly because the problems and material which it presents are of almost unique interest. India in particular furnishes within its limits examples of every conceivable type of attempt at the solution of the religious problem, and at the same time forces us to consider data apart from which our own Western evaluation of that problem must be partial and even parochial. What is written here must of course be read in the light of the situation created by the setting up in 1947 of the new Moslem state of Pakistan, embracing its eastern and western provinces.

We are bound to begin with some facts about geography, population and race. India is about half the size of the United States of America, and has an area of about 1,573,107 square miles. It contains about one-fifth of the human race, and in an area half as large as Canada there are 35 times as many people. It also contains nearly threequarters of the inhabitants of the British Commonwealth of Nations, a somewhat staggering fact.

India, if we include an area taking in Baluchistan and Burma, is roughly as big as France, Spain, Italy and the third Reich taken together. Its population in the 1921 census was reckoned at 312 millions; and among these the various religions which

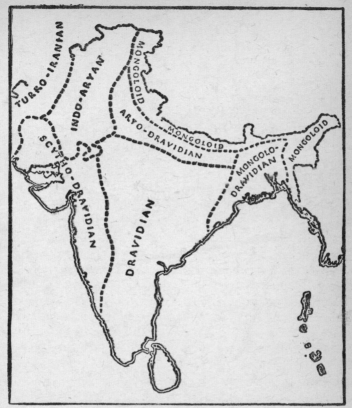

I. MAP OF INDIA — RACE DIVISIONS

we have to describe were represented in the following proportions:

Hindus	216 millions
Buddhists	11 millions
Moslems	68 millions
Animists	9 millions
Sikhs	3 millions
Jains	1 million

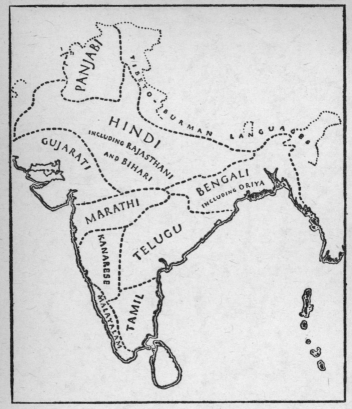

2. MAP OF INDIA — LANGUAGE DISTRIBUTION

Christians	4 millions
Parsis	101,800
Jews	21,000

(but the 1931 census showed 353 millions total population, and that of 1941 showed 406 millions,* with proportionate increases in each section).

* This figure includes the Dominion of India, Pakistan and Burma.

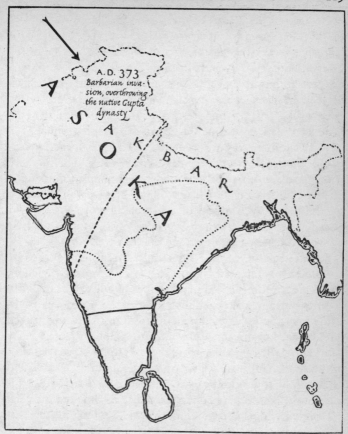

A.D. 373
Barbarian inva-
sion, overthrowing
the native Gupta
dynasty

- - -   Area of Yueh-Chi influence, A.D. 100
———   Boundary of Empire of Asoka, 272 B.C.
.... Boundary of Empire of Akbar the Great, A.D. 1550

3. MAP OF INDIA — THE KINGDOMS OF ASOKA AND OF AKBAR

A glance at the accompanying three maps will help to clari-
fy the situation. The first shows the main racial divisions, the
second the distribution of the main languages, the third the

boundaries of the realms of the Buddhist King Asoka and of the Moslem Mogul Emperors. The upper part of India contains two great river valleys, that of the Indus and that of the Ganges, both fed by waters from the immense wall of mountain which shuts them off from central Asia. Between the two lies a great plain, in area two and a half times the size of the British Isles. This was once the bed of an ancient sea, and as the waters receded, it became the centre of activities which have spread their interests far outside India. Today half the population of the whole country is massed in this area. The southern part of India, with a fairly homogeneous population, consists of a series of lesser river-valleys running east or west, bounded on the north by a group of arid uplands, the Vindhya or 'Divide', which, true to its name, has ever constituted a barrier between the life of the north and that of the south.

Scattered about in various small and diminishing groups are the oldest inhabitants of India, the so-called pre-Dravidians. These are mostly hill and jungle tribes of a low culture, with features often greatly resembling those of the Australian black-fellows. In the Indus valley there are signs of a much mixed population, Eurafrican, Alpine and Australoid, at a very early date. The earliest inhabitants are thought to have been negritos of the Andaman Island type, now surviving in the Kadars and Uralis of the forests in the extreme south of India. The Australoids came later. It may be supposed that at some remote period southern India was continuous with Ceylon and the East Indies, and that Australia was not then an island. But with the alteration in land-levels which must subsequently have taken place, India became a large self-contained unit, and henceforward could receive access of new populations only through the passes from the north-west, except where landings were effected on some part of the coast line.

This north-western gate of entry has provided India with all her most momentous immigrations, until the seaborne commerce of Europe brought new adventurers and finally new subjugators. But from the north-west came (1) the Dravidians, somewhere before 2000 B.C., (2) successive waves of Nordics (so-called Aryans), (3) Mongols, (4) Scythians and finally (5) Moslem Arabs.

The Dravidians were dark white, and probably represent an over-spilling of population eastward from somewhere in the direction of Baluchistan, though seaborne invasion is not an excluded hypothesis. They seem to have established a great civilization in the Indus valley at a date between 3250 and 2750 B.C., and to have spread southward as far as the extremity of what is now the island of Ceylon. Little at present is known about them in these early days, since the script found in the ruined cities of Mohenjodaro and Harappa has not yet been decoded: but they would appear to have been polytheists, and to have held certain types of horned cattle sacred, so that perhaps the beginnings of what is now known as cow-protection existed among them. Judging from statuettes which have been dug up, they seem to have recognized and reverenced the deity known in later times as Siva, and also a female vegetation divinity. Male figurines are rare, but there are signs of tree worship, of zoolatry, and of belief in nagas or snake-spirits (common in the India of today). Intermarriage with pre-Dravidians must have taken place, and today the resulting population covers most of that part of India which lies to the south of the Vindhya.

The first wave of Nordics is believed to have passed into India somewhere about 1700 B.C., but others followed in succession. These were people very much of the type of our Scandinavian forefathers, hard-fighting, heavy-drinking folk, with a certain contempt for the short dark races they conquered, since they called them Dasus or Dasyus, 'squat creatures' (very much as Hitler spoke of 'those dwarfs of Prague'). It is significant that in the epic of the Ramayana the monkeys led by Hanuman make league with King Rama, but these were in reality not so much anthropoids as 'lower' races. To a considerable extent these Nordics kept their race pure, and became the progenitors of the highest Hindu castes. But they were not entirely successful, since the Nordic, though pugnacious and aggressive, does not thrive in the tropics, and it is evident that quite a number of the invaders took to themselves Dravidian wives. Anyhow, in the course of a few centuries the religions and cultures of Nordics and Dravidians had become intermingled. The word 'Aryan' or 'Arya' is really an adjective, and means 'noble' or 'distinguished'. It is the same as the word which we now use for Persia, 'Iran', and this was the ancient name of that country after its colonization by Nordics, who with arrogant self-esteem seem to have applied it to themselves.

Map 1 will show that the south and centre of India contained the purest Dravida stocks, that in the west and middle north Nordics and Dravidians are intermarried, that in the north-west (the Indus valley) now occur the purest descendants of Nordic invaders, blended in the west-north-west with Turko-Mongol stock, and that in the north-east and along the slopes of the Himalayas there is a strong Mongolian element, with Dravidian crossings in the province of Bengal, producing the familiar Bengali type.

Map 3 will show what a barrier the Vindhya is to any invader or administrator. The great Buddhist king, Asoka, 272 B.C., did not succeed in controlling the south or Deccan, and the Moslem Emperor, Akbar, in the sixteenth century A.D. controlled much less.

It is estimated that the inhabitants of the Indian peninsula outnumber the Anglo-Saxon population of the world (even including the entire population of North America) in the proportion of three to two, and of these by far the larger proportion still live in village communities of a very conservative character, amid much poverty. The climate, except in the uplands, is tropical, and the supply of water in the sourthern portion depends, as is well known, upon the regularity with which the rain-clouds, travelling across the Arabian Sea, burst upon the line of mountains known as the Western Ghats.

These conditions have had much to do in determining the religious outlook of the inhabitants of India. Thus, the hybridization of certain well-defined human stocks in an enclosed area has been one influence. Another has been the tropical climate, accompanied by droughts, plagues, famines, floods and a feverish fecundity of organic life, all of which things have impressed on sensitive minds the extreme lavishness and ruthlessness of nature in some of her moods.

From the beginnings of the Nordic invasion (say, 1700 B.C.) up to the present day we get the following phases of religious development:

(1) The primitive period or prehistoric age, of which we know nothing save that it is not likely to have differed very much from the same stage in other parts of the world.

(2) The period of Dravidian invasion, of which again we know next to nothing, though excavations in the Indus valley have shown that about 2000 B.C. the latter contained an area of great city cultures ranging over a distance of 100 miles in length, and already very ancient.

(3) The so-called Vedic period of Nordic conquest and expansion, roughly from 1500 to 800 B.C. – 700 years.

(4) The Brahmanical epoch from 800 to 500 B.C., a period of 300 years, during which the development of the institutions of sacerdotal Hinduism is proceeding.

(5) The philosophical period, roughly 500 to 100 B.C. –

* For details of (1), (2) and (3) see Stuart Piggott, *Prehistoric India* (Pelican A205).

400 years, accompanied by the growth and expansion of Jainism and Buddhism.

(6) The Incarnation period, overlapping the previous one, running approximately from 200 B.C. to A.D. 500, and including the introduction of a certain amount of Syrian Christianity.

(7) The age of the Moslem invasions, A.D. 664–1206, leading on in the sixteenth century to the establishment of the Mogul Empire.

(8) The period of the Bhàkti saints, overlapping (7) and ranging from the thirteenth to the nineteenth centuries of our era.

(9) The age of European influence, beginning with the Portuguese colonizations in the later part of the fifteenth century and extending to the present day. This involves the re-introduction on a very wide scale of many types of Christianity, and latterly the influx of newer European thought-movements, such as nineteenth-century science and the doctrines of Marxian communism, as well as those of the nationalist religion of race and blood.

These phases do not obliterate one another as they succeed, but the present situation in India is the product of the successive waves, each of which has left some permanent mark and has influenced its successors and been modified by them. For example, the Nordic invasions did not impose an entirely new kind of polytheism, but merely overlaid what already existed with a number of additions. The divinities symbolized at Harappa and Mohenjodaro continued to find votaries, as well as the village gods of the subject peoples: but the great gods of the Vedic pantheon were added. Similarly, the Moslem invasion, while destroying the very anti-militarist culture of the Buddhist north, left the rather inaccessible south almost untouched, and eventually produced a hybrid religion – that of the Sikhs, which is a genuine blend of Hindu theism with Islam. Again the literature of the philosophical and Incarnation periods has persisted in its influence right up to the present time, so that the Upanishads and the great epics as well as the Gita and the Bhakti hymns give a cultural background for modern educated Indians, and mould the thought of such men as Tagore and Gandhi, though it is noticeable that Nehru and his associates are more influenced by the non-religious economic and political doctrines of modern Europe. And once again, the rise of Jainism, of Buddhism and of early Bhakti has profoundly influenced Hindu ethics ever since. It is safe to say that the emphasis upon *ahimsa* or non-violence, and the idea of *mettā*, or good-will, belong to the age when these great movements originated, but have continued unbroken to the present day. It is of the utmost significance that the answer given by them to the military problem is totally different from that given in the Gita. Buddhism, inculcating the virtue of *mettā*, says 'Do not fight or kill'. The Incarnation of Krishna, viewing vast armies drawn up ready for battle, says, 'Fight, so long as you understand what is happening', i.e. 'the Eternal slays not nor is It slain'.

It will now be necessary to say something about each of the periods in turn. The *first two* have already been sufficiently dealt with, but *period three* deserves rather more attention. We must put away the idea of one great single invasion, and regard the subjugation of the Dravida and Australoid peoples by the Nordic invaders as the result of a series of waves extending over many years. The polytheism of these northerners as expressed in their hymns is joyous and even rollicking, and much resembles that of the Vikings of Scandinavia. Brahma, the creator, has the elements of a 'high god'. The most popular god is Indra, who is the personification of the energy locked up in the thunder-storm. He is a genial hero, fond of liquor, and sometimes drunken (see *Rig-Veda*). Next in popularity is

Agni, the god of fire, who is essentially the friend of the home. But perhaps the grandest of all the so-called Vedic gods is Varuna, who is not simply the sky god, but in some of the hymns addressed to him almost approximates to the one god of prophetic Hebraism. The bad sacred is not conspicuous, but is represented by Rudra, who represents the ruthlessness of Nature. In the religious thought of this period there is no idea of transmigration or rebirth, but departed warriors are believed to go to a kind of Valhalla. The Vedic age shades into *period four*. In this the caste-system is seen taking shape, priesthood becomes differentiated, and sacred literature and rules of ceremonial accumulate. *Varna*, or caste, is not now thought to be an entirely Nordic invention in India. There are signs that it existed among the Dravida peoples, keeping them separate from the primitive tribes they conquered. Separation of priesthood from chieftainship is also Dravidian rather than Nordic. It is said that there were no temples in India before the Gupta period, about 320 B.C. and after the rise of Buddhism, and that the temple or divine-place type of cultus, though universal at a very early period in the Near and Middle East, begins later in India. This, if correct, would account for the apparent absence of temples at Mohenjodaro, though it is thought that dwellings for a company of priests, together with places for ceremonial lustration, have been excavated there. The ceremonies of the Nordic invaders of the Vedic period were performed in the open air, presumably round a fire, or at an altar under the open sky. *Period five* is typical of what has happened in many lands, i.e. the decline of the personalistic interpretation of life before the march of human reflection. It is to be seen in Greece, in China and in Catholic Europe. As elsewhere, it assumes alike the form of monistic and pluralistic philosophy. In order to understand it we must first gain some knowledge of Indian literature.

The sacred literature of India is very different from that of the Bible. To begin with, there is little interest in the course of events as such, and so there are no 'historical books', except the two epics. Then there is a less sharply defined canon. Yet the principle of the use of sacred literature is much the same as elsewhere – that is to say, it is preserved and recited in order to transmit and reproduce from generation to generation a certain religious emotional experience, and is thus regarded as a channel of religious revelation.

The first great section is that of the Vedas ('Veda' means knowledge, and is practically the same as the Greek word *oida*). The *Rig-Veda* or Royal Veda is in ten books, and contains 1028 hymns, most of them ranging in date between 1500 and 1000 B.C. The other Vedic books were compiled later. The *Sama-Veda* consists of hymns used during sacrifice. The *Yajur-Veda* is liturgical. The *Atharva-Veda* consists of charms and incantations. Two features strike us in this section. *First*, that already Indians are beginning to theorize about the gods. The hymns are not by any means all naïve folk-songs, but in many cases display an elaborate literary technique which must have involved a long period of transition from the natural to the artificial. The result is that in the tenth book, especially in hymn 129, we see this technique coupled with profound thought. The achieved end, however, is not monotheism, as in the case of the Hebrew prophets, but monistic pantheism. *Second*, the existence of a class of human beings who experience ecstasy. The latter is at first induced by a drug, generally some alcoholic drink, but for this after a time is substituted an hypnotic technique which raises the votary above the spatio-temporal order. The final consequence of this ecstasy, coupled with the effects of a hot climate, is to induce an attitude which Schweitzer has called 'world and life negation'.

The way is now clear to the second great section of sacred literature – that of the Upanishads. The word 'upanishad' probably began by meaning 'sitting close to'. But it came to mean later, 'what you got by sitting close to a teacher', secret or esoteric teaching, or teaching perhaps about the *close connexions* between the various phenomena around one, made to disciples by some holy man, in the form of a lecture or instruction, a holy man such as for example, Yajñavalkya, whose habits and technique are those of an ascetic mystic. When we say 'lecture', however, we must beware of being taken literally. There is nothing precise or clear about the Upanishads. They are not essays, but rather jumbles of lecture notes, miscellaneous quotations, aphorisms, short hymns and formulae for memorizing. Not one of them – not even the Isa, which is the shortest – is coherent, or free from interpolations. They can be used uncritically only by persons believing in verbal inspiration. Yet commentaries galore have been written upon their texts, just as commentaries on the Bible were composed by the Christian fathers. What is the net result? Not so unprofitable as might appear. The Upanishads number some 250, not all of equal importance: perhaps there are about fifteen principal ones. Taken as a whole, however, they seem to indicate a consistent development away from naïve polytheism in the direction of a monistic pantheism with a strong philosophical background. Metaphysical thinkers of today often discover that the subtle-minded Indians of this period have arrived at epistemological principles long before them. Although passages in the Upanishads are patient of a theistic interpretation, they are mostly explicated in the sense of Advaita, or non-duality. The three principal commentators were Bādarāyana (date uncertain), Sankara, *c.* A.D. 800, and Rāmānuja, *c.* A.D. 1017. Sankara, commenting on Bādarāyana, inculcates non-duality, Rāmānuja almost the exact opposite (modified duality, or Vishitadvaita, i.e. what in the west is called theism). Madhva, A.D. 1199, teaches complete duality.

In spite of the fact that these ancient documents which we have been describing are of such a miscellaneous character, they present nevertheless a kind of general viewpoint which may be called 'Upanishadic', and a kind of development which reveals logical processes of thought. There is no single well-articulated system, for there are inconsistencies and even contradictions; but, in spite of these, the Upanishads show as a general basis the first attempts at the conception of a unitary world-ground, at first water, then space, and then non-being, or in other words the conception of a developing monism; and not merely attempts at explanation in terms of science and philosophy, but also in terms of religion, since a way of living is revealed by which the individual may be enabled to exist in tune with the infinite.

The ground of all existence is stated to be Brahma. But why this word? In the *Rig-Veda* 'brahma' seems to mean 'a sacred formula or sentence'. We might almost define it as 'the verbal image of the Sacred or Holy'. From this it is but a step to the equation, Brahma=the Sacred, the most High God. At any rate, in the Maitri Upanishad we read: 'Verily in the beginning this word was Brahma.' When, however, we come to further definition, it is found easier to say what the Sacred is not, than to say what the Sacred is. So we read: Bramha is ether, Brahma is life, Brahma is joy, Brahma is the void, and so on, until it is plain that Brahma embraces all phenomena, and yet is beyond definition, as much to be called Non-Being as Being.

Side by side with the doctrine of the ground of existence develops the doctrine of the Atman. The Sanskrit word 'Atman' is closely related to some other Indo-Germanic words (e.g. German 'atmen' – to breathe, and Greek 'atmos' – breath). It denotes the invisible part of the individual, the spirit or self. But gradually the idea develops that there is but *one* Atman or Self, differentiated, it is true, into separate selves or egos, yet essentially One and the Same.

The next stage comes at the identification of Brahma with the One Atman or Great Self. Yet when this identification is reached there is, strange to say, no ultimate satisfaction to the seeker, because when he reflects upon a manifold world of daily experience he realizes (1) that since his own little self is but a misperception of what is really the Great Self, the experiences of the little self are equally misperceptions, and so the manifold world is illusory and unreal, (2) that since the Great Self surpasses definition, it is therefore rationally unknowable. But if the world is unreal, and Deity unknowable, ordinary institutional religion, with its sacrifices and celestial bargaining, becomes a mere fraud. The enlightened person, therefore, finds release in meditation upon the Great Self (even though rationally unknowable), and in conquest of the little self, with its vanities, by the practice of *tāpās* or asceticism.

Three quotations from the *Brihadāranyaka Upanishad* will illustrate this conclusion:

> *Brih.* 4.4.13. 'He who has found and has awakened the Self . . . The world is his; indeed he is the world itself.'
> *Brih.* 1.4.6. 'This that people say: worship this god, worship that god – one god after another – this is his creation indeed. And he himself is all the gods.'
> *Brih.* 1.4.15 'Verily, even if one performs a great and holy work, but without knowing that the whole world is Brahma or the Self, and that I am Brahma or the Self, that work of his merely perishes in the end. One should worship the Self alone as his true world. The work of him who worships the Self alone as his true world does not perish.'

Polytheism thus gives place to monism. The gods, goddesses and godlings are not abolished or declared in Hebrew fashion to be 'no-gods'. They are merely subordinated to the Great Self, and, though superhuman, are not more ultimate or more noncreaturely than the angels of the Hebrew or Christian Scripture.

In such a world, what is the highest blessedness? Some consider it to be dreamless sleep (*sushupti*), but others, at a later stage, declare it to be a higher condition still, in which the self becomes identified with the Great Self. This is *turīya*, in which one is 'not inwardly cognitive, not outwardly cognitive, not both-wise cognitive, not a cognition-mass, not cognitive, not non-cognitive, unseen, with which there can be no dealing, having no distinctive mark, non-thinkable, that which cannot be designated, the essence of the assurance of which is the state of being one with the Self' (*Mandukya*, 7).

The effect of such a doctrine upon conduct must be obvious. It includes a complete detachment from the affairs of this life. There is no such thing as social service. Even were the latter to be undertaken, it would have to be engaged in with complete absence of interest in the world, and it is doubtful whether it should be engaged in at all. The effect on popular ethics is also to blur all moral distinctions, since ordinary ideas of right and wrong, good and evil, do not obtain for him who has metaphysical knowledge. He is indeed, like Brahma, 'beyond good and evil'.

There are, however, some limits to the operation of this scheme. It is obviously most complete when a person dies, and next to that, when a person is sleeping without dreaming. Can it operate in life when one is awake? The answer is, Yes, if one employs a certain hypnotic technique (*yoga*) and induces a kind of waking trance.

What is the relation of all this to the belief in Karma (literally 'action'), according to which one's good or bad actions procure rebirth at death into the body of a higher or lower being? The relation is this. The Upanishad technique whereby one sees oneself as the Absolute Self is a means of release from *samsāra*, the chain of births, deaths and rebirths. Thus the *Prasna Up.* says (1.10), 'They who seek the Atman by austerity, chastity, faith and knowledge . . . they do not return', and again Brih. 6.2.15. and Chand. 4.15.5–6, 'Those who know this (i.e. the technique of the way to Brahma) go to the

Brahma-worlds. Of these there is no return'. And again (Svet. 1.11), 'By knowing what is therein, Brahma-knowers become merged in Brahma, intent thereon, liberated from the womb' (i.e. from rebirth).

With this brief account of Upanishadic literature and its doctrines we have not, however, exhausted the tendencies of the Upanishadic age to shift away from naïve religion. If there were pluralists as well as monists among the Ionian Greeks, so there were also among the Indians, and their system was known as the *Sāmkhya*, which is a word meaning 'enumeration', or 'analysis into parts without remainder'. In its main outlines it was probably established already about 550 B.C. Its essential doctrine is that from all eternity immaterial individual selves exist in countless numbers. *Prakrti*, or matter, also exists eternally; and in some way that cannot be further substantiated or understood, selves are destined to enter into connexion with *prakrti* in order that through this experience they may become conscious of their absolute and complete independence of it. In such a system there is no room for any Supreme Deity, unless as a kind of president of the college of selves. Some readers will no doubt be inevitably reminded of the system worked out by J. E. McTaggart, the Cambridge philosopher of the early twentieth century. There is no evidence that he was in any way directly indebted to the *Sāmkhya* for his ideas; but the Germans, Hegel, Fichte and Schopenhauer knew something of Indian thought, and McTaggart in his earlier years was certainly influenced by reading them.

The main concern of Indians swayed by these systems of thought was to discover how by *tāpās*, or the technique of asceticism, they might achieve such a control of the body as to render the spirit free from its interference. This technique became known as *yoga*, the process of becoming yoked with the Absolute (Indo-European root, *jog-* or *jug-*), and the adept in it is a *yogi*. *Yoga* has remained an Indian art to this day, and finds many in the West who admire and try to practise it, if only for its hygienic effects.

Together with this go the ideas of *karma*, or retributive justice, and of *samsāra*, or the chain of reincarnations. The hymns of the *Rig-Veda* know nothing of rebirth or transmigration of souls, but in the *Brihadāranyaka Upanishad* the latter is first explicitly mentioned, and thenceforward it becomes common intellectual coin among Indians, and penetrates westward as far as south Italy, where it was taught by Pythagoras in about 580 B.C., and as far eastward as Japan, whither it went as part of Buddhist doctrine. It is a tenable theory, to which certain fairly obvious objections occur; but it was held by Indians not because they liked it, but because it seemed to them probably true, a melancholy fact of the cosmic process, from which they sought to find release as best they might. Various types of technique were set forth for overcoming it altogether, either as a weary round of suffering from which freedom was desired, or as a ladder of graded existences in which the individual might, by doing the right thing, be promoted to the next birth, according to the inexorable justice of *karma*, to a higher and pleasanter kind of life, wicked persons being correspondingly punished by degradation to a lower form of organic existence.

There is something of a clash between the doctrine of *samsāra* and the pure Brahmanic mysticism which affirms the real identity of all finite selves with the One Atman or Superself. Upanishadic thought is, indeed, as a system lacking in unity and completeness. But it is typical of the Indian mind that it is always prone to hold opposites as co-existent, and to contain within the hospitable mansion of Hinduism ideas and practices which seem to us mutually exclusive.

In this, as Keyserling saw, it resembles modern Catholicism, which Heiler has declared to combine seven quite different types of religion within one institutional framework.

Out of this philosophical period emerge at least three very important quasi-religious movements, which will be here enumerated, but of which more must be said elsewhere:

        a. Jainism,

        b. Buddhism,

        c. Bhakti.

a and *b* are obvious deductions in thought and practice from the abandonment of naïve polytheism. Jainism is a kind of religion based upon the acceptance of the Sāmkhya system, but venerating a limited group of noble selves, who have achieved perfection and bliss. Buddhism is equally a kind of religion, based upon the rejection of any Supreme Being except a compound of Bradley's Absolute and the Holy Spirit of Christianity; *c* is an obvious reaction against the practical atheism of the *Sāmkhya*. It accepts the latter as the natural science and philosophy of the age, but it adds the idea of an oversoul or universal Lord, Isvara, who is so to speak *Prakrti* or Nature personified, as well as the Emitter of souls and their Preserver. Once this is accepted, life becomes not a matter of atheistic *yoga*, but of *yoga* whose object is to achieve communion with Isvara, who is said to desire the soul to have a personal relationship with Him. *Bhakti* is the emotional practice and maintenance of that personal relationship, and the impulse to indulge in it is immensely strengthened by the events of the next period.

Period six is a sort of religious reaction against the logical outcome of the monistic or pluralistic liquidation of polytheism. As a phase it is of the greatest importance and of the most perplexing origin. The main outcome in Period 5, as we have seen, is not so much pluralism as a philosophic monism which has received the name of Advaita or non-duality, and which developed as the result of a series of commentaries upon the materials of the Upanishadic literature. Of these the most famous is that of Sankara, who has already been referred to;

and his so-called *māyāvāda Vedānta*, i.e. his interpretation of the Upanishads as involving a denial of the reality of the world, has glaciated the major part of India, and conditions the ordinary thought of Hindus to this very day. It is an uncompromising pantheism, and is usually illustrated by the possibly apocryphal story of the Hindu holy man who, in 1857, when bayoneted by a British soldier, said calmly: 'And thou also art He.' It is also represented by the proverbial cliché, *tat tvam asi*, 'thou art That'. All moral and individual distinctions are in this way obliterated. The criminal and the saint are equally manifestations of the universally immanent Reality, and to believe that one is a separate individual, A, B or X is to dwell in a state of illusion, or at least a state in which one misperceives facts. And then, in certain quarters, though frankly both in past and present as a sort of 'minority movement', there comes a swing of the pendulum. It has sometimes been attributed to the influx of a new series of invaders from the north-west, though it hardly seems likely that they themselves brought in the idea of Incarnations at that point. What probably happened was that the invaders disturbed and interrupted the tranquil and normal evolution of human thought and flung men back upon a more catastrophic and less unbroken and continuous conception of Reality, just as European history from 1914 to 1940 has disturbed European religious thought from resting on the categories of smooth evolutionary progress, and has led it to demand rescue and redemption from a desperate and dangerous situation. Certain it is that in the text of the *Bhagavadgita* as it stands there is contradiction. On the one hand we read (VI. 30): 'When one sees Me everywhere and sees everything in Me, I am never lost to him and he is never lost to Me'; but on the other hand we read (IX. 4): 'All beings abide in Me but I abide in them'; (IX. 8) 'Resting on My nature again and again I emit this whole host of beings without their choice, through the power of My nature,' and especially (IV. 7): 'Whenever there is a decay of righteousness and a rising of unrighteousness, then I emit Myself. In order to save the good, and to destroy evil-doers, to establish righteousness I am born from age to age.' 'Whenever.' The word involves the idea of a discontinuity. Whence came this idea, which does not seem to occur in Upanishadic thought? The probability is that it belongs to a cycle of ideas which had been in India for a very long time, but which the exigencies of the age lifted into prominence. The idea of a series of discontinuous incarnations (not necessarily in *human* form) can be traced back to the literature of the Nordics of Iran, and is to be found in the Bahram Yasht, which forms part of the Zoroastrian corpus. In this a deity (not quite the highest god), called Verethragna, is described as successively incarnate in a series of manifestations, culminating in a man, and not necessarily occurring at regular intervals. The probability is that the doctrine here set forth was conveyed into the Ganges valley by one of the waves of Nordic invaders. It is true that when it emerges from obscurity at a later period, the name of the deity with which it is associated is Vishnu, and not Verethragna, but the similarity between the incarnations of the latter and the *avatars* of Vishnu is striking enough not to be accidental. There is some likelihood that the Bahram Yasht was not composed originally in Persia, but in central Asia, since Sir J. Coyajee has shown that it displays traces of Chinese influence and mythology, and in it the 'camel' incarnation takes the place of the 'lion' *avatar* in India, suggesting that it originated in an area where the camel was more familiar than the lion. Thus the idea of discontinuous incarnations may go back much farther than was formerly supposed.* In those

* It has lately been pointed out that in China itself, Wen-Chiang, a Taoist deity, originally a star-god, then afterwards a god of literature and scholarship, is believed to have visited the earth at *irregular* intervals, and to have become *incarnated* in the persons of various gifted men.

earlier stages it is, as might be expected, less and less like the Christian idea, but if the radiated figure of the Tak-i-Bostan be a representation of the human incarnation of Verethragna, as has lately been suggested, then new possibilities are opened up.

Vishnu is a beneficent god, of obscure origin. He is perhaps in the beginning a nature Deity, but is known as 'the Preserver' or 'Saviour', and to this extent resembles the 'Sotēr' or 'Tritos Sotēr', or 'Deliverer' of the Greeks (though there is of course no direct connexion between them). He has a number of incarnations, or *avatars*, most of them sub-human, fish, tortoise, boar, man-lion, and so on. The number is usually 10, but in one list there are 24. But it must be noted that it is Vishnu who, in his incarnation as Krishna the charioteer, is the divine-human spokesman of the *Bhagavadgita*, and it is Vishnu who is incarnate in the good king, Rama. (A Brahmin hymn composed for a festival at Mathura describes King George V as Raghubansmani, or Ramchandra, an incarnation of Vishnu, and there are certainly many Hindus who think of Gandhiji as the incarnation of this god for their own generation and its needs.)

Now this idea of an intervening incarnation is not really consistent with Advaita pantheism, and it introduces into Hindu religion an element which still coexists side by side with Advaita, and yet is out of harmony with its claims. The word used for incarnation is *avatar*, which means 'descent'. Obviously you cannot descend into a place where you are already, so the word necessarily involves the same spatial idea as that found in the Christian Nicene creed, 'Who for us men and for our salvation, came down from heaven', or in the exclamation of the Lycaonian pagans in Acts xiv. 11, 'The gods are come down to us in the likeness of men.' Those Indians who adhere to the Advaita conception say, of course, that there is no real incarnation in the *avatar*, more or less than in anything else, but that as an accommodation to human weakness and limitations, the One Reality is graciously pleased to engage in a sort of will-o'-the-wisp appearance – a beneficent illusion. (Sri Krishna Prem in his book *The Yoga of the Bhagavadgita* gives a still more elaborate explanation.) But it is doubtful whether the devout believer in the *avatar* is really satisfied with that. 'Ram' is probably as real to him as Jesus is to the Christian (though, of course, as we shall have to emphasize later, the Christian incarnation is not one of a series, but is conceived as being once-for-all, and unique, and so stands by itself). Since many text-books repeat the statement that the *avatar* is entirely phantom or 'docetic', the author has made it his business to ask a learned Brahmin whether this is really correct, and his reply is: 'I have always been brought up to believe that God "assumed" the form of Rama and Krishna,' and he quotes a commentary on the Gita as saying '*Krishnas tu bhagavan svayam*', or 'Krishna is actually God', or 'God in person'. In any case Mahatma Gandhi was hardly a phantom, at any rate not more than any other human being. So there we must leave the question.

Whatever its origin, this idea of a discontinuous incarnation does develop about 200 B.C. in India, and expresses itself in literature, and it is not at all the same as the idea which is found in Babylonia and Egypt, in which each king by virtue of his position is invested with divine honours. It also expresses itself in the extraordinary tendency to deify and worship beings of an unusual character, such as John Nicholson, Captain Pole, Colonel Dixon, Colonel Wallace, Dr Clough, a Baptist missionary, as well as a number of Indian saints, all of a recent date. In India there are two great Sanskrit epic poems, the *Ramayana* and the *Mahabharata*. Space precludes a lengthy description of their growth and structure, but as finally developed they are both built round the idea that the high god Vishnu has become incarnate for the benefit of humanity, in the case of the Ramayana in the person of Rama or Ram, the hero king, in the case of the *Mahabharata* in the person of Krishna, a charioteer. The latter poem contains one whole canto devoted to the *avatar* of Krishna, who addresses his master, Prince Arjuna, in a long series of discourses. It is this canto which has become separated and enlarged to form the *Bhagavadgita*, or song of the Lord. Professor Rudolf Otto has lately indicated the manner in which it may have been edited and added to until finally it reached the shape it bears today (containing snippets of almost every type of Indian thought). As such it is read widely by devout Hindus, and Gandhi declared his indebtedness to it more than any other literature except the New Testament. The conception of Krishna in this poem is both pure and lofty, but there is another cycle of Indian literature called the Puranas, which also deals with Krishna as the incarnation of Vishnu, and in this the moral level is much lower, and he is depicted as a lascivious daemon who has amours with milkmaids. The probability is that we have here the fusion of two separate deities under the same name. The Krishna of the Puranas is probably the naïve conception of the hero of a pastoral community, while the Krishna of the Gita, though bearing the same name, is a religious teacher or prophet, Vasudeva. Since both the Rama and the Krishna poems belong to a period of about two centuries before Christ, the idea of a discontinuous incarnation which they contain cannot be due to Christian influence. On the contrary, the idea may well have originated somewhere in the territory between Europe and India, and have taken different forms according as it moved eastward or westward. This theory may be startling to Christians, to whom it may come as a novelty, but it must be borne in mind that the doctrine of incarnation in orthodox Christian theology is not an expression of a myth in theological form, but an attempt to codify and express a real historical experience, namely the impact of the genuine historical personality and career of Jesus of Nazareth upon the world of men and women, and it need suprise no one if the attempt should have involved the use of some of the thought and language forms which are common to East and West. Moreover, to declare Jesus the unique incarnation of the Supreme God still leaves one the task of reconciling His appearance with those of other great prophets and teachers of past and present ages. This was done by the author of the Fourth Gospel, in his prologue, by the use of the idea of the Word or Logos of God, and such usage was continued by the early Christian writers to explain the work of the prophets and philosophers. But if Socrates, why not Rama or Gandhiji? The Indian, even if a Christian who places Jesus central in his thought, cannot exclude the idea that the Word of God may have enlightened some of his own great heroes and sages.

With reference to discontinuous incarnations, it is to be noted that Verethragna or Vrthrajan (sometimes, in Sanskrit, Vrttahan, as an adjective applied to Indra)=the victorious one, and the term is applied to the Sōshans, or Zoroastrian Saviour, who is expected to appear one day (estimated at A.D. 2398) as 'Lord of the Last Judgement'. In a Latin commentary on St Matthew, the Magi are represented as looking for the Sōshans or Vrthrajan. Thus the Jewish-Christian Messiah and Verethragna have actually been equated!

Two other matters must be mentioned in connexion with this period. First, the influence of incarnational ideas upon Buddhism. The detailed account of this must be left till later, and it will suffice to say here that the influence was real and profound. Second, the introduction of Nestorian Christianity into India. There is a tradition preserved in Travancore which claims the Apostle Thomas as the founder of a Christian church on the Malabar coast, and dates his arrival as the year 52. It is difficult to know how much of this to believe, since the story is embellished with extravagant miracles, but it refers to an Indian king, Gondophares, and the latter is an historical character, and actually did reign in North India in the latter part of the first century A.D. Whatever the truth about St Thomas, there certainly was a Christian community in south-west India by the fourth century A.D., and its affiliations, like those of other similar communities, were with the East Syrian church, the parent city of which was Edessa, and later with Persia. There is a Malabar tradition of a merchant called Thomas Cannaneo or Thomas of Jerusalem, who in the year 345 caused help to be sent to this Indian church, and it is possible that it is this Thomas who is the basis from which the legend given above has developed. At any rate, up to the time of the arrival of the Jesuits in 1599 the Malabar Christians recognized the church in Persia (which had sprung from the teachings of those who regarded themselves as the followers of the bishop Nestorius) as their spiritual guide. The fortunes of this community do not greatly concern us here, and it is now linked up either with Rome or with Anglican Christians in south India, but it is of importance in one special respect, as illustrating the possibility of communication between East and West even during the dark ages. We learn from the *Anglo-Saxon Chronicle* that King Alfred the Great, in fulfilment of a vow made when the Danes were defeated in an attempt to capture London, sent gifts to India in 883 to aid the Malabar Christians, transmitting them by Sighelm, Bishop of Sherborne, who travelled via Rome, and brought back from his long journey jewels and spices. In 1330 Pope John XXII sent a Dominican friar to be the bishop of these Indian Christians, and in 1757 the French scholar, Anquetil du Perron, visited Malabar and reported that on a rough estimate there were 50,000 of them in full communion with Rome, and 150,000 Syrians, divided into two groups.

Period Seven might perhaps seem properly to belong to the story of Islam and its expansion, but it must be summarized briefly here. As early as A.D. 664 an Arab force made its way into Afghanistan and took Kabul, making proselytes. Indeed, the city of Mazar-el Sherif, falsely reputed to be the site of the tomb of the caliph Ali, the Prophet's nephew, is styled the Mecca of the East, and is still a place of pilgrimage. Towards 717 the conquest of Sind was carried out, and thence the Arabs advanced and took Multan. By 1030 the western districts of the Punjab were subdued, and in 1206 Kutb-ud-Din proclaimed himself sovereign at Delhi over the whole of northern India. During the next 120 years there was a further extension towards the south. In the fifteenth century Moslem power in India broke up into a number of independent states, but these were united into a great empire by the Moghul Akbar and his successors. Akbar was tolerant of Hinduism, and tried to establish an eclectic religion, including elements drawn from all the faiths recognized in his realm. He was a descendant of Timur and Genghiz Khan, and a man of genius, but died a disappointed and baffled individual, perhaps a devout sceptic who sought truth, but never arrived at it. In the main, Islam in India (though at its lower levels corrupted by animism) has remained pure and rigid, somewhat like Ulster Protestantism in relation to Southern Irish Catholicism. It has produced one notable reforming movement, that of Mirza Gholad Ahmad, which is known as the Ahmadīya sect, and has a mosque at Woking in Surrey. It claims to be able to find much in Islam which is harmonious with Christianity, and seeks to eliminate those features of the former which are disliked by Christians and which are open to criticism. But it must be confessed that the Ahmadīya movement is not accepted as a legitimate development by the conservative Moslems, especially outside India, and its future is uncertain. The peculiar position of Islam in India is that prior to the British occupation it was the religion of the Moslem conquerors and rulers, and therefore the State religion, and its adherents cannot easily forget this, and are naturally sensitive about it. This sensitiveness led them in

1857 to join with Hindus in the Mutiny. They are also, like the Indian Christians, linked up with co-believers outside India, and therefore less inclined to take a purely nationalistic view of politics. The Wahabi reform movement from Arabia, which is rigidly conservative, has attracted a good many adherents recently in Bengal and wherever Islam is orthodox it tends to clash periodically with its Hindu neighbours, whom it calls *būt-parast*, or idolaters. Hence the riots of which we hear in the West. Since, as we have seen, the Indian Moslems number some 76 millions, they are a far from negligible quantity, and cannot possibly be ignored by any fairminded statesman in planning a scheme of dominion government. The Moslem buildings of north India are familiar for their austere and beautiful architecture (witness the Taj Mahal), so expressive of the pure but hard monotheism of their founders. Many say that they present a pleasing constrast to the sometimes gross and often dirty shrines of Hinduism.

But by far the most interesting product of the Moslem invasion has been the hybridization in religion which has flowered from the contact between Hinduism and Islam. During the fifteenth century of our era a Moslem weaver called Kabir (exact date uncertain) attached himself to a Hindu teacher called Ramanand and his disciples. He was a gifted mystic, standing midway between Hinduism and Islam, and the lyric utterances which he and his friends composed are full of beauty. He declares himself to be the child of Ram and Allah. 'O God, whether Allah or Ram,' he says, 'I live by Thy Name.' His teachings are known as the Kabirpanth, and there are about a million persons who hold themselves to be his direct followers. In the fifteenth century a Hindu of Lahore called Nanak (1469–1538) came under Moslem influence and was greatly attracted by the doctrines of this Kabirpanth. After many years of wandering to and fro in India, Nanak ended by founding a new religion and also a new political group – that of the Sikhs, whose customs are so distinctive that they tend to think of themselves as a separate race. Their numbers are approximately a little over 4 millions, and in the sixteenth century they achieved a stable organization under a series of leaders, the fourth of whom, Ram Das, erected the famous golden temple at Amritsar, while his son Arjun was the first hereditary guru of the sect, and the compiler of the Sikh sacred book, the Granth, which includes prayers and aphorisms not only by Nanak and his successors, but also by Kabir and his associates. It is rich and full of mystical beauty, and is treated with the same kind of reverence as that shown by Moslems for the Koran. For a time the Sikhs seemed to be in danger of becoming submerged in Hinduism, but in the last twenty years there has been a definite revival. Yet there is some doubt as to how far this sect is living on its past. It is said that the Granth is today as unintelligible to the average Sikh as a passage of Chaucer would be to an average British working-man. This is a pity, for there is much in the Granth which is of great nobility, and worthy to be compared with some of the finest passages in the Psalms. Nanak's call to become a teacher, as it came to his conscience, reminds us of a celebrated passage in the Pauline epistles: 'There is no Hindu, and there is no Moslem.'

Period eight, the rise of Bhakti, as we have said, overlaps periods 6 and 7. Intellectually it is the natural consequence of the theistic trend in Indian thought, but emotionally it belongs to a zone of human aspiration which extended round the whole planet during the Middle Ages of Europe. Dialectically it is the consequence of the philosophical and rationalist tendencies of the fifth period. Bhakti is fervent personal religion, and there is a quite extraordinary resemblance between the hymns of St Bernard and those of the Bhakti saints, so marked, indeed, that it is hard to believe that they are independent creations. Bhakti is first mentioned by name in the *Svetasvatāra*

Upanishad, and the attitude implied in it is not absent even from some of the Vedic hymns: but it does not become prominent till much later, and it is usually felt that its earliest real exposition is in the *Bhagavadgita*, where the main theme is the personal relationship to a god who is nothing if not quasi-personal. It could not attain to prestige until it had some philosophical background to enable it to contend with the prevailing doctrine of Advaita, but this it received in the eleventh century A.D. from Rāmānuja, whose doctrine of Vishistadvaita or modified duality gave room for a personal god, and was indeed the foundation of Indian theism. Those who wish to know more about this leader should read the valuable works of Professor Estlin Carpenter on *Theism in Mediaeval India* and of Mr Bharatan Kumarappa on *The Conception of Deity in Indian Religion, with special reference to Rāmānuja*. Rudolf Otto's treatise on *India's Religion of Grace* and his edition of the *Gita* also throw important light upon this matter. The first group of Bhakti votaries is that of the Alvars, who are Tamil saints of the Vaishnava or Vishnu cult, and flourished in the seventh and eighth centuries. Their intense religious experience is to be studied in a collection of 4000 verses attributed to them, which are used in Vaishnava worship to this day. They are notable not for any precise philosophical thought, but for their revelation of a depth of fervour produced by the idea of Deity as incarnating Himself out of love for His creatures, and desiring in return their whole-hearted devotion. One of these saints, astounding as it may seem to those who know only later Hinduism, was a woman, and others were either of low caste or even actually outcaste. One of the most famous, Nammalvar, a Sudra, declares in a lyric, 'My tongue sings to me divine songs. My body dances as if it is possessed by a deity, worships the Lord and turns back to him. . . . He does not take a few deserving only. He does not leave off the undeserving. He is

not vexed with wrong-doers nor does He love the good only.
He is unseconded nectar to those who join and love Him.' It is
this almost evangelical fervour to which Rāmānuja gave an intellectual basis, commenting upon the text of the Gita as a
Christian might comment upon the Gospels, and defining the
nature of Deity, His relation to the Universe, and the relationship existing between Him and finite selves. Deity is the
Creator, and stands in a causal relationship to the world which
He emits, sustains and re-absorbs. Finite selves are not an illusion, and, though they may find their true life and blessedness
in personal fellowship with Deity, they do not achieve their
individuality to such an extent as to annul the supremacy of
Brahma and to make Him no more than He is in the Sāmkhya system. Their true nature consists in that they have for
their inner self that Highest Self, while they constitute the
body of that Self, and are modes (prakara)of It. Deity has for
highest attribute that of love. The universe and all its contents
are real and completely dependent on Him. Selves, though
distinct from Him, can have no existence apart from Him.
Souls are true individuals whom He loves, and who share the
perfections of His nature, but owing to their own deeds are
imperfect. In his grace He seeks to lead them to a life of perfection and complete devotion to Himself, and when they
have once attained to it He will never allow them to be separated from Him again. It is safe to say that most Christians
have not the slightest idea that such a doctrine was taught in
India long before modern Christian missions entered it. It
needs to be noted, however, that almost if not quite all the
bhaktas are worshippers of idols, though they often express
contempt for the crude practices of the multitude. Thus
Namdev says, 'No guru can show me God: wherever I go
there are stone gods painted red. How can a stone god speak?'
No Hebrew prophet could be more plain-spoken. One is led
to suspect the covert influence of Islam.

Bhakti was carried to the north of India by an adherent of the sect founded by Rāmānuja, called Ramanand. He took up his abode at Benares about 1430, and the movement which he initiated produced that of Kabir, who was almost his contemporary, and also that of Tulsi Das, about a hundred years later. Tulsi Das is of special interest, because he rewrote the great epic of the *Ramayana* in such a way as to emphasize the Divine element incarnate in Rama. Tulsi said: 'The worship of the impersonal laid no hold upon my heart', and the object of his devotion is not merely Rama 'after the flesh', but Rama ascended and glorified, and even during his incarnate life never really human, in fact much more like the Jesus of the apocryphal gospels, an abnormally supernatural being. At the end of the thirteenth century Bhakti appeared in the Maratha country of western India, with the work of Jñanesvar, who wrote a poetical commentary on the Gita, but the real flowering period for the northern area was in the sixteenth and seventeenth centuries, when we find the great names of Tukārām, and of Chaitanya the Bengali, who carried Bhakti to northeast India. Tukārām's favourite expression of deity was that of the village god, Vithoba, but Chaitanya was a devotee of Krishna. Another important devotee was Dadu, a contemporary of the Great Mogul Akbar, and again we see the effect of hybridization between Hinduism and Islam. Finally we have to note the extension of Bhakti even to the rather ruthless nature god, Siva, who usually typifies the destructive energy and wild zest of tropical nature. Under the care of Mannikka-Vachar, a Tamil poet of about the year 900, he is transformed into Siva the Saviour, and the Saiva Siddhanta represents perhaps the high-water-mark of non-Christian personal religion in South India. Even towards a gross female personification of sex experience, Bhakti is also directed by the Saktas, with their fourteenth-century scripture, Devi Bhagavata.

It is said that the results accruing from Bhakti in the Marathi
and Bengali territories are not in any degree to be compared
with those achieved by Kabir, Nanak and Tulsi Das. The
cause alleged is that the *avatar* of Rama is incomparably nobler
and purer than that of Krishna. But it is possible that the influence of Islam may also have had something to do with it.
In any case, when once the leading personalities of these evangelical reformers were withdrawn, the bondage of caste and
the degradation connected with temple-worship of a gross
character threatened to return.

It is not surprising, therefore, that when the British became
acquainted with India in the eighteenth century, they formed
a most unfavourable opinion of its religion. The Krishna of
the *Gita* was almost forgotten and obscured. The Krishna of
the Puranas was worshipped, and, in Bengal especially, the
gross Tantric rites connected with the worship of Kali, the
ruthless Nature-goddess, were spreading rapidly. Yet it is
noticeable that even the early Baptist missionaries, Carey and
Marshman, were able to appreciate and to see the significance
of the Rama-cult, and they began to try to render the *Ramayana* accessible to English readers in 1806. Dr Kraemer makes
the point that when former Bhakti-worshippers of Indian
manifestations of God become Christians they do not feel that
their former devotion has in any way served as a schoolmaster
to lead them to Christ. If this is really the case, it requires
investigation, since one would have expected a Rama-wor-
shipper to regard his cultus in rather a different light.

Controversy still rages as to whether south Indian Bhakti
has received any influence from the Malabar church. It is certainly remarkable that the two movements of the Alvars and
Rāmānuja both arose in the one area of India where there had
been a Christian church for some centuries, but so far the
evidence of contact and influence does not seem forthcoming.
It seems more scientific to regard Bhakti as the local form of a

zone of religious life which had its own expression in Christian Europe, and which arose naturally as the reaction from philosophy, just as Methodism and Pietism arose in Europe in the eighteenth century as reactions against rather arid philosophical systems. Indeed, Methodism is a good analogy, on account of its large collection of hymns. The religious lyric is characteristic of this type of religion all the world over. 'Jesu, lover of my soul' is sheer Bhakti, only we have to take account of the curiously grim unlovableness of so many of the Eastern deities who are approached in this manner. (The Indian would say that the Christian object of devotion sends people to hell-fire!) Psychologists will doubtless have much to tell us in explanation of the feature that love is so often offered by the devotee without any idea of its recipient being likely to return it, and, again, of the strong sex-element in these erotic religious poems. Dr Mukerjee is at pains to justify even the extremer forms of eroticism in Hinduism as necessary concessions to an element which is present in all human life.

Period nine – that of *European influence* – is marked by three obvious features.

First, the steady permeation of Indian society by Christian missionaries and Christian missionary educational institutions, a permeation that, in spite of weaknesses and defects, has achieved much, the beneficence of which many Indians themselves are ready to recognize.

Second, the growth of a series of reformers, who have sought to rekindle the fire in Hinduism itself. Of these in particular should be mentioned Dayanand Sarasvati (1824–1883), who in 1875 founded the association called the Arya Samaj, for the revival of Vedic religion; Ramakrishna (1834–1886); and Swami Vivekananda (1862–1902), his disciple, both of whom may be described as Hindu modernists.

Third, the development of a number of prophets and leaders, who, while remaining Hindus, have tried to draw into

Hinduism as much Christianity as they can. Of these may be mentioned Ram Mohan Roy (1772–1833), who founded a reformed Hindu sect called the Brahmo Samaj, and Keshab Chandra Sen (1838–1884). Probably Mahatma Gandhi, though largely a politician, should be included under this heading. Tagore and Radhakrishnan have also had their own idea of what Hinduism should be, and it may safely be said that it is not what conservative Indians would approve.

And now, having given a brief survey of historical development, we may ask the question: 'What is Hinduism as it exists today?' The answer is not quite easy, because the only really satisfactory definition sounds circular: 'Hinduism is the religion of Hindustan.' Yet this is perfectly just. Despite efforts to represent it as in essence a universal faith, Hinduism is in its outlook as much restricted as Judaism. True, it has certain fundamental ideas which might be easily transplanted; but as an institutional system it is, as much as Nazism, a matter of 'race and blood', and is properly confined to those who belong to some specific caste, so that the only way of admission is to be incorporated as a member of a fresh caste. Once inside this rigid hierarchy one can believe or disbelieve as much or as little as one likes. Room is made for the grossest idolatry and superstition, and equally for non-theistic philosophy and for pious theism. Gandhiji has said: 'I do not disbelieve in idol-worship, though an idol does not excite any feeling of veneration in me. But I think that idol-worship is part of human nature. I do not consider it a sin', and again: 'I know the vice that is going on today in all the great Hindu shrines, but I love them in spite of their unspeakable failings.' Yet Gandhiji says that he personally finds intense solace in the Upanishads and the Gita, almost as he does in the New Testament. We shall obtain a juster view of this, as of all the great religions of the world, if we learn to think of it not as an institution but as an event. Hinduism at a particular time may be one thing, and something else at another. It is not fair to judge of it at what may be a bad period in its history. What would Christians think if Hindus were to judge Christianity by what it was in Italy under the Borgias, or Moslems if they were to be judged by the type of animistic Islam so prevalent in Morocco?

Perhaps the most deeply rooted idea in Indian thought (if we take the majority of Indians) is the lack of ultimate significance in the events of human life. The Indian, it is said, for the most part thinks of this world as a circular and unending journey, an ocean without a shore, a shadow-play without even a plot. The whole world of phenomena is simply the more or less purposeless and sportive energy (*lila*) of the Absolute Being, Who is beyond definition. Hence the ideal life is that of 'non-active Activity', the attainment by a well-defined technique of an exalted state of absorption in which one negates every movement of life, and becomes one with the changeless Absolute, beyond good and evil. Thus the world-renouncing ascetic is the type universally admired, and his renunciation is in no sense altruistic or philanthropic, but is purely self-regarding, since it is every man's business and licence to look after his eternal welfare; and to be concerned with delivering oneself from the generally accepted chain of rebirth, and from the cycle of biological existence, is not considered to be a blemish upon one's character. Gandhiji was nobly inconsistent when he made unselfish service of his fellow-men part of the discipline to which he subjected himself in order to free his soul from the bonds of the flesh, since self-forgetful service of others is a Christian, not a Hindu idea. It is true that the Ramakrishna and Arya Samaj movements engage in philanthropy, social reform and education; but their activities are not logically deducible from Hindu principles, especially the theory of *Karma*.

The above ideal of 'world and life negation' (to quote

Schweitzer again) is capable of being transplanted. Whether ultimately a correct one or not, it might easily attract a world which had given up hope about itself. But the peculiar form of it in which it appears associated with Brahminism is exclusively nationalist, and could not easily exist outside India.

There are four stages in the Hindu ideal life. The first is that of the student, in which the youth is bound by strict rules of obedience to his teacher. The second is that of the householder and married person. The third is a period of retreat, which need not, however, involve abandonment of the married state, since husband and wife may go out into solitude together. The fourth is that of complete hermit life. A well-accredited member of the British Civil Service in India once wrote: 'Asceticism makes an extraordinary appeal to practically all classes of Hindus. They feel that whatever their own manner of life, self-denial is better than self-indulgence, the suppression of passion and desires better than their gratification. To their minds temporal wealth, power, success and material well-being are, from the ideal point of view, inferior to the spiritual merit attained by one who has subdued the flesh to the spirit. Other-worldliness is a higher calling than the management of affairs.'

The observer will be tempted to reflect as to what is likely to occur if there should be an infiltration of ideas from Russia. Not a few of the younger generation of Indians have already been captured by the doctrines of Marx. The sweeping effects of the reforms initiated by the Soviet in that part of Asia which it controls are to be seen in places like Bokhara, Samarkand and Tashkent. As long as Gandhi's influence persists after his death, Hinduism may remain dominant. But should Nehru and others even more radical replace the Mahatma in the affections of his fellow-countrymen, there might be as radical a change in India as there has already been in Turkestan and China.

Something may usefully be said about the ministry in Hinduism, and its grades or types. As an institution, Hinduism partakes of the formlessness and unorganized character of all Eastern religions: but it has its sacred men. There are perhaps four clear types. First comes the *purohit*, or Brahmin priest. All priests of the higher castes are Brahmins, though not all Brahmins are priests. These *purohits* are the guardians of traditional Hindu ritual and social order. They rarely act as spiritual guides, and their temptation is to become lazy and ignorant and to prey upon the gullibility of the simple. There are few to speak a good word for them. Next there are the *gurus*. The *guru* is essentially the teacher and spiritual adviser. The better sort of *gurus* enlist almost passionate reverence, and exercise a ministry not very far removed from that of some Christian clergy in their dealings with individuals. The third type is the *sunnyāsi* or *sādhu*. The *sunnyāsi* is hardly a minister, but a wandering ascetic, who, however, commands much respect, and may even teach. Fourthly, there is the *bhagāt* or emotional devotee who, unlike the *sunnyāsi*, remains within the social structure of Hinduism, and is greatly revered by simple villagers as an exorcist.

The future of the great Indian temples is already in question. Mr Natarajan, the editor of the *Bombay Social Reformer*, declares that in many cases they are less and less resorted to by the public, who in any event do not partake in congregational worship in them, and that in the future they may be preserved as works of art rather than as centres of religion. (What of European cathedrals?)

Meanwhile, since the vast mass of the inhabitants of India still live the life of villagers, the most prevalent type of religion, where Moslem or Christian influences have not already swept it away, is the popular Hinduism of the worship of village godlings, male or female, together with the propitiation of malevolent spirits, and the worship of the greater nature deities, such as Siva and Kali (Mahadevi), consists mainly in the two activities of what have been aptly described as 'spirit-scaring and spirit-squaring'. This is pathetic, and the danger is not negligible that in a sudden revolution all this might collapse without anything adequate taking its place. Yet in fairness it is necessary to consider seriously what Professor J. B. Pratt has added, by way of comment, to his vivid description of the lingam-cultus in a village temple somewhere in India. Here is the entire passage:

'The drums are beating violently as he approaches, and wild music of strange sorts is issuing from the equally strange building before him. He is admitted (after he has taken off his shoes), and beholds a sight as extraordinary as is the noise that accompanies it. On the walls of the room are hideous images carved in stone and daubed in red paint, one representing a monkey, one a creature with a fat human belly and an elephant's head, each with an offering of yellow marigolds before it; while in the most prominent place is a stone pillar, rounded off on the top, wet with the pouring of much Ganges water, bedaubed with spots of paint, and surrounded with green leaves, uncooked rice, a few coins and more yellow marigolds. There are two priests in the corner beating tom-toms, and by the pillar stands a third, daubing it with paint, pouring water over it, placing leaves upon it, and all the while mumbling words – many of them repetitions of mere names – to which no one seems to listen. The noise becomes louder, and the old priest seizes a lighted lamp and brandishes it about in front of the much-bedaubed pillar, while the audience follow his motions with obvious excitement; and at the close of the hocus-pocus he distributes to them some of the rice which has been collected at the foot of the sacred object. The performance has been utterly unintelligible to our visitor, but the most astonishing thing about it all is the attitude and aspect of the worshippers. For worshippers they indubitably are. Some of them have been standing, some kneeling, some are prostrate on their faces. Each one has made an offering before the bedrenched pillar or at the feet of the grotesque figures on the walls, and though some seem indifferent, many give unmistakable signs of reverence, and a few show in their faces, as they start homewards, that they have found in that preposterous transaction the same sort of inner treasure which our Protestant churchgoer has occasionally carried home with him on Sunday from his American meeting-house.'

If I may give here my own recollections, I think inevitably, as I read the above words, of a little village church in France where once in the month of June I attended an early mass. The theological doctrine behind it may have differed profoundly from that implied in the lingam-cultus of the ruthless nature-divinity, Siva (life's zest personified – the very embodiment of what psychologists call 'libido'). But so far as the outward ceremonies went, I saw the use of holy water, the stiff attitude of the sacerdotal ambassador of Deity, the ceremonial lights carried and waved about, the flowers in front of the statues, themselves garish with paint. I noted the muttered prayers, to which no one seemed to give much attention. I heard the nasal sing-song of a village choir led by a woman. There was a climax of prostration; and at the end a little boy walked round with a basket of *pain béni*, of which we all partook. And as we came out one saw the faces of the congregation, and some of them recalled to me the ancient passage in Exodus, that the face of Moses shone with a supernatural glow, as he came down from the mount of God.

JAINISM

Jainism is connected with the oldest form of Sāmkhya doctrine. Its origin is obscure, but there seems reason for believing that its reputed founder, Vardhamana, was a historical character, born about 569 B.C. Legend has been busy, as ever, framing marvellous stories of his birth, childhood and initiation. He was the usual type of Hindu ascetic, and superficially it is perhaps difficult to see why the Jain community (now numbering about $1\frac{1}{4}$ million) should have troubled to remain a separate sect in India. Perhaps it owes its survival to the same psychological causes as Quakerism in the West, i.e. that a certain percentage of human beings find satisfaction in belonging to such a community. One expert says that Jainism represents the theological mean between Hinduism and Buddhism. It would need a good bit of detailed study of the documents to verify this, but certain facts stand out. First, that Vardhamana's and Gotama's periods of activity overlapped by about thirty-five years. Second, that Gotama may very well have visited Vesali and have experimented in *tāpās* with Jain disciples. Third, that both Vardhamana and Gotama were in agreement on one fundamental point, i.e. that birth and caste were of little importance, compared with the destruction of the consequences of *karma*, so that both Jains and Buddhists are alike in being reforming sects of the sixth century B.C. springing up in the lap of Upanishadic Hinduism. Jainism is less clerical in its organization, and it has always protested against limiting membership of the inner circle of ascetics to persons born of the Brahmin caste. It is also less speculative and less enterprising than Buddhism, and is remarkable chiefly for its extreme advocacy of *ahimsa*, or non-violence towards living beings, which issues in peculiar practices such as straining one's drinks to avoid swallowing organisms, filtering one's breath by a respirator for the same reason, and wearing no clothes to avoid crushing vermin in their folds. Jains have the highest standard of literacy among all Indian communities (495 males and 50 females per thousand), and their level of morality is exceptionally good. A criminal Jain is scarcely ever heard of.

The most important feature in Jain belief is the doctrine of souls. True to its Samkhya origin, Jainism (whether or not taught in this respect by Mahavira) regards the Absolute as a corporate personality of perfected souls, no one of which is supreme. This pure unfettered spirituality is called 'Jiva', and except where influence from outside has intruded, the Jains do not regard it as involving the complete comprehension of all souls in one super-soul. Jiva, in fact, if the equivalent of a deity, is a collective deity, and it is exemplified in the small body of *Tirthankaras* or heroic and enlightened individuals who have already achieved blessedness, and are the objects of Jain veneration.

There is much detail in Jain belief which seems trivial, and built on a frail intellectual foundation. Jains mostly reject the idea of a single supreme Deity, though they accept the existence of a plurality of deities who are subject to the law of transmigration as much as humans. But the main dogma of their faith is both plausible and capable of defence, i.e. that Reality is made up of an aggregate number of selves and that these have to achieve their release from the consequences of *karma* by a process of asceticism.

A sermon was preached before the Maharajah of Benares by the Jain Saint, Vijaya Dharma Suri (who died a few years ago), in which the latter asserted that it is an error to call the Jains atheists, since they believe in Paramatman, the Great Self. If Vijaya Dharma Suri is representative of his sect, my conclusions in this chapter will have to be modified, and we are presented with an extremely interesting and rarefied example of a 'High God', to whom no worship is offered.

No system in any degree similar to Jainism has evolved anywhere else in the world, except perhaps the worship of the heroes of the Positivist calendar invented by Auguste Comte, and the most original scheme set forth by J. E. McTaggart at the end of *The Nature of Existence*. It is obvious, however, that such an aspect of religious piety or thought is always possible, and that a few uncommon souls have been helped by it. In some way, it resembles early Epicureanism. Jains are at present busy endeavouring to expound their tenets in the face of the new world of an independent India. One of them, trained in Europe, has actually been Professor of Physics at a leading Indian university, and their printing presses are issuing new text-books of Jain theology, if that is the right name for it.

BUDDHISM

Siddhartha Gotama (born about 560 B.C.) was the son of a nobleman whose ancestors, the Sakyas, had perhaps held kingly rank. Kapilavastu, his native home, was a city in north-east India, the site of which is now unknown. Probably it lay somewhere in the south-eastern corner of what is today the kingdom of Nepal. There are those in consequence who think that Gotama may have been of Mongolian stock. This, of course, is not established, though it may well be that there was a Mongolian strain in his pedigree. It must be remembered that no portrait of him exists. There was no primitive Buddhist iconolatry. The earliest statues date from some centuries after his death, and are due to Greek influence. The only tradition as to his personal appearance credits him with having rather large lobes to his ears!

We are bound to note certain resemblances between the later stories of his infancy, youth and ministry, and those of the Christian gospels. There was an angelic annunciation (by *devas*) to his father. His mother was a virgin for thirty-two months. *Devas* sang at his birth. Asita, the Buddhist Simeon, predicted his future greatness. He fasted forty-nine days, and was tempted by Mara, the spirit of evil, to turn the Himalayas into gold. He performed thirty-two healing miracles, was transfigured, had an original band or Sangha of twelve followers, fed 500 persons with one small cake, had a disciple who walked on the water and sank, and when he was taken to a temple for a ceremony, conformed, but said it was unnecessary. There are also parallels in the sayings and discourses, numerous, if not very close.

(i) 'Within them there is ravening;
The outside thou makest clean.

(ii) 'Whosoever would wait upon me, let him wait upon the sick.'

(iii) 'Destroying life, killing, cutting, binding, stealing etc., this is defilement, but not the eating of flesh.'

Devadatta (the Buddhist Judas) conspires to kill Gotama, and hires thirty bowmen for the purpose. But when they see him, they fall to the ground. He makes a triumphal entry into his native city; and on the day of his death there is an earthquake.

The origin of these resemblances has not yet been conclusively ascertained, and as given by Edmunds and Anesaki a good many of them seem somewhat strained.

It is established that there was no written tradition for a very long time after Gotama's decease. India was then a bookless world. Such literary products as the Vedas must have existed orally. It is not that there was no writing, but that writing down records of any kind, literary or legal, was not yet common. The whole question of the transmission of the sacred literature of India is a very unsettled one, and it may well be that in the Upanishads and the Epics, as we have them, there will come to be detected evidence of much editing, and that in the form now before us they are much later in date than when they were originally composed or collected. The Pali Buddhist canon was perhaps reduced to writing between 88 and 76 B.C. We do not know whether interpolations got into the text as the result (at a much later date) of Nestorian Christian influence. What must be honestly reckoned with is the probable existence of a large number of appropriate folk-stories about holy persons, which influenced alike the traditions about Jesus and Gotama, and led them to assume certain forms.*

It is reasonably certain that Gotama grew up during the age which saw the growth of the Upanishads and the Sāmkhya, an age of sceptical reflection and enquiring ferment, an age also which was experimenting in *tãpãs*, and forming the technique of *yoga*. Doubtless he travelled, and visited notable teachers, and it is evident that he was soon impatient of normal family life, and after his marriage and the birth of his son, set out again at the age of twenty-nine in search of something that would bring his uneasiness to an end. Up to the age of thirty-five he found himself still on the wrong track, and nearly exhausting himself with excessive bludgeonings of the body. He was a Hindu, with a Hindu's heritage of ideas, belief in reincarnation, doubts as to the significance of human history and weariness at having to live year in and year out in a tropical climate with an entire absence of scientific hygiene. Under the circumstances it is hardly surprising that a penetrating intellect was rewarded with sudden illumination. The crowning moment came to him when, meditating under a peepul tree near the village of Uruvela, to the south of Patna, he reached the stage from which he is hereafter known as 'the Buddha', or 'the enlightened one'. After a few days he decided that he must tell to others what had come to him; so he went to Benares, and in a grove near the city he preached his first discourse, and gained five male followers. After this he continued for the space of forty-five years, travelling, teaching, and founding groups of disciples. At length he died at the age of eighty, at Kusinara in the district of Gorakhpore, about the year 485 B.C.

Such is the bare skeleton of his career. But it leaves us with

* Note an article by the late Dr J. Estlin Carpenter on this question, in *Studies in the History of Religions*, New York, 1912, a Festschrift presented to Crawford Howell Toy.

many questions unanswered. First, what was the actual original message of this oriental John Wesley? – And how did it grow into what it afterwards became?

For, indeed, the special problem of Buddhism is not so much its extent as its varieties. Christians are familiar with the distinction between Catholics and Protestants, yet these two have no more points on which they agree than the two main divisions of Buddhists, the followers respectively of the Hinayana and the Mahayana. Again, it is to some a problem as to how Catholicism can have developed out of the religious ideas contained in the Synoptic Gospels. But it is equally a problem how the Mahayana can have developed out of the texts which are held to embody the ideas of early Buddhism, if those texts be taken as they stand. We have, therefore, both in the case of Christianity and in that of Buddhism, to consider carefully the transition from the original announcements of the respective founders to the institutional forms which grew up to express and preserve within them the spirit of those announcements. Further, we have in both cases to consider the impact upon the original announcements of the view which Schweitzer has called 'world-and-life negation', carried to an extreme.

No one can even begin to understand the teachings of the Buddha who does not first master the world-outlook of the age of the Upanishads, as we have previously sketched it. The allusions in early Buddhist texts are simply enigmatic unless one is familiar with the Upanishadic phraseology and technique. Once, however, this is grasped, it is possible to see in what way Gotama simplified and developed his inherited philosophical theology.

The probability is that Gotama's own teaching underwent two sorts of development, and that in both cases it was transfigured, while the old teacher himself became almost out of date to his younger successors (a phenomenon with which we are familiar in the case of other great leaders). It is certainly the case that at the end of his life he was travelling alone, save for the companionship of Ananda, his faithful attendant, and was complaining 'How hard it is to find them who will learn!'

In an early Buddhist tradition, Gotama is asked by some men whether he can tell them the whereabouts of a female thief. He is sitting by the wayside, and answers: 'What think you, gentlemen? Which is better for you, that you should be seeking after a woman, or that you should be seeking after the Self?' They reply: 'The latter', and then he bids them sit down and be taught. We do not know the lesson on this occasion, but since 'seeking after the Self' is a phrase from the Maitri Upanishad, we can only infer that Gotama's method was to improve upon the Upanishadic technique, and to carry it farther in the direction which he had come to believe was the right one. Mrs Rhys Davids has collected a number of early fragments, all of which convey the same idea.

(i) He who has the Self as Master, let him walk with heed.

(ii) The Self is the protector of the self; who else could the protector be?

(iii) Here is a man who has made-to-grow his actions, morals, mind, wisdom, who is not a less, who is a Great Self, who dwells in the ideal.

(iv) Live as those who have the Self as a lamp.

Primitive Buddhism, as distinct from institutional Buddhism, has even traces of a post-mortem tribunal by an adjudicator or controller who is called Dhamma-Raja, the Lord of the Way. This has faded out in later Buddhist doctrine of the Hinayana.

It appears then that Gotama began with the Upanishadic background, but that he altered the scheme of it in certain important respects.

First, he was essentially practical, and sought to provide mankind with a way of living rather than of speculation. He saw life as beset by grief, impermanence and illusion, and with an almost modern insistence upon the law of cause and effect, he inculcated a method of removing passion, a technique of detachment, and a correct epistemology, which he called 'the noble eightfold path'.

Second, he was convinced that the extremes and extravagances of *tāpās* or asceticism were a grave mistake. He had tried them, and they had led him along the wrong track. For him, sane moderation was the middle path to be followed. Simple but reasonable food was to be eaten, and meditation (called *dhyana*) was to take place not when one was weakened by fasting, but after the midday meal.

Third, he saw man as a pilgrim, or wayfarer, whose task should be to fare towards a richer and fuller interior life. Recognizing the Great Self, or *Atman*, as a fact beyond dispute, he desired to apply the knowledge of that fact practically, by encouraging mankind to act habitually under the guidance of that Self, letting It serve them as a torch or lamp, so that their behaviour would be dictated by their 'better selves'. (The Self thus takes the place of the Hebrew Torah, which is 'a lantern unto my feet and a light unto my path'.)

Fourth, following directly from the last point, Gotama saw man's life as much more ethically conditioned than it is in Upanishadic doctrine. There is no talk about being 'beyond good and evil'. The follower of the noble eightfold path is as much bound by moral principles as any Christian disciple. Violence, theft, sex-offences, lying and indulgence in alcohol are all forbidden; and we read more than once of the good Buddhist as: 'Having laid aside onslaught on creatures, averse from that, he lives as having laid aside the rod and the sword, lives ashamed to hurt, endued with kindness, friendly and compassionate to all breathing living things. Having put away

taking-the-not-given, averse from that, he lives taking and
expecting only the given, with a self become pure . . . Having
put away lying speech, averse from that, he lives a truth-
speaker, a truth-linker, man of facts, who gives reasons, not a
deceiver of men'.

Fifth, in his strong emphasis upon the Self, Gotama naturally makes but very little of the individual ego. Here we come
up against a real difficulty. Monastic Buddhism, with its tendency to negativity rather than to growth in richness, exaggerated this depreciation of the ego, and attributed to Gotama
speeches and aphorisms about the *atta* or soul which were perhaps not uttered by him, but which may well be the product
of later generations commenting upon his teaching. It is
probably true that he did analyse the *atta* and show that it was
not what popular belief represented it to be, and that the Great
Self was the main factor, the string upon which a series of
sense-impressions was strung. But the violent *anatta* doctrine
of the Hinayana is as much an extreme development of Gotama's original teaching as the impersonal monism of Sankara
is an extreme development of the Upanishadic doctrine on
which he commented.

To what extent did he himself discard the notion of the
individual ego? That is what we should like to know; and if
we knew it we should be nearer to an understanding of the
way in which the primitive Buddhist teaching developed into
the Hinayana. But perhaps the question, as Gotama would say,
is not properly put; because the Upanishadic teachers themselves at least depreciated, even if they did not discard, the
notion of an individual ego. The One Great Atman is mis-
perceived when we dwell upon the permanence of our own
selves. What is called *anatta* or 'non-soul' doctrine in Buddhism is closely related in spirit to the *advaita*, or 'non-duality', doctrine of Hinduism. Actually Gotama is misrepresented
when he is said to have taught *both* atheism and the non-exist-

ence of the individual soul. So far as doctrine goes, he tended to give non-committal answers, since he shrank from encouraging the dreamy and interminable theological and philosophical discussions which even in his day were prevalent among Indians, just as they are today. He sought to be practical, and to make others practical. But it is quite clear that he in the main accepted the Upanishadic background of the Unknowable Absolute; and the Great Self, profound and fathomless, he believed to be the depths of every empirical ego. To live and teach how to live a chaste and temperate and kindly life of moderation by the aid of this Inner Light was his basic aim.

What is for him the ultimate goal? The obvious answer, and the one which springs to the lips is 'Nirvana'. But what exactly is Nirvana? A monk in Ceylon described it to Professor Pratt as 'bliss unspeakable'. But you cannot speak of bliss which is not experienced, and therefore such a description implies that the ego *can* know when Nirvana has been reached. Still, the proper course is to arrive at the root meaning of the word. Nirvana means literally 'waning out', and the natural question is 'what is it which wanes?' The answer given by Mrs Rhys Davids is important. She says: 'When first used as a religious term, it meant the waning or the making to wane of vicious disease, lust, hate, dullness.' Life as Gotama saw it was full of '*dukkha*' or suffering. Nirvana was the waning out of this suffering. It was not primarily the waning out of the little self, though this is the natural deduction. It was rather the enrichment of personality by emptying it of all ignoble selfishness, so that the little self became identified with the Great Self. What we have to remember is that to the mystic the final goal is what is called the unitive life, in which, to use the words of Meister Eckhart (Tractate xiii), 'God absorbs the soul, leaving no trace'. It is true that he somewhat modifies this startling statement in his forty-first sermon, where he says: 'In dying to her own nature and her being and her life the soul is born in her divinity. That is her becoming. She becomes so wholly one that there is no distinction except that He stays God and she stays soul.' There may be, of course, some distinction between the Christian and the non-Christian mystic (almost certainly there is), but it seems certain also that the ultimate goal implied in Nirvana is not so much extinction as another form of the Hindu Upanishadic exalted state of consciousness, *turīya* – an identification of the little self with the Great Self, in which the former is virtually swallowed up. Even the Indian may in his own idiom mean no more than does St Catherine of Genoa, an orthodox saint, when she declares: 'My *me* is God, nor do I know my selfhood save in Him.' Gotama would not commit himself to an admission of absorption. He would only say that the *Arahant* or perfected Buddhist was in a state which could not be described either as existence or as non- existence. Nirvana is therefore neither existence nor non-existence, as we use those words. It is a third state, and we can misunderstand the teaching of Gotama about the blessedness of Nirvana only if we do not recognize that Indian thinkers in his day did believe in such a state. Thus Maitreyi, the wife of the seer Yajñavalkya, asked her husband to tell her about immortality, whereupon he replied (Brihad. IV. v): 'The Self is to be described by No, No (*neti, neti*). He is incomprehensible, for He cannot be comprehended . . . How, O beloved, should he know the knower? Thus far goes immortality.' Maitreyi then says: 'Here, sir, thou hast landed me in utter bewilderment.' Immortality to Yajñavalkya is in fact describable only in such words as Plotinus uses: 'It is unspeakable, for if you say anything of it you make it a particular thing.' This is hardly distinguishable from Gotama's account of Nirvana.

So far his gospel is fairly easily deducible from the lore of the Upanishads. But we have ignored one of its most important features – its complete abandonment of caste, with all that is thereby implied. As Judaism is to Christianity, so is Hinduism to Buddhism. Buddhism could be a universal way. Hinduism has ever remained a restricted nationalist religion. Much has been made of the emphasis by the Buddha upon the statement 'existence is suffering', but, although he did emphasize it, it was not his own, but the world-negating

▨ Mahayana countries ▨ Hinayana countries

4. SKETCH MAP TO SHOW GENERAL DISTRIBUTION OF BUDDHISTS

'Plural belonging' makes the map misleading unless it is remembered that Confucianism overlaps Buddhism in China, Shinto overlaps it in Japan. In some areas like Cambodia, the two sorts of Buddhism are mixed, owing to the influx of Chinese and Annamese, who belong to Mahayana, whereas the Cambodians are mostly Hinayana.

conclusion of other Upanishadic thinkers. To say that existence is bound up with *dukkha* (sorrow), *anicca* (evanescence) and *anatta* (unreality) is not original. What is original is the *remedy* which Gotama proposes, and this is practical (not speculative), ethical, and free from extremes. Otherwise we might justly say that Buddhism is the international missionary form of Hinduism, with the Absolute for Deity.

Having then satisfied ourselves as to the nature of the original doctrine of Gotama, we can go on to investigate the causes which led it to develop as it did. For it must be frankly admitted that neither Mahayana or Hinayana satisfactorily expresses the original doctrine. Both are developments, and we are bound to consider whether they are as such justifiable. It is all very well to analyse the content of the original message, but most people are more interested in what it has become since and what it is today. How was it, to begin with, that Gotama's message, which seems to have begun as a message for laity, and even approved preaching to harlots, turned into so predominantly monastic an affair?

This question of monasticism will recur when we get to Christianity, so we may as well make a beginning with it here. We have already referred (page 55) to the rise of solitaries. Did they first begin in India on a wide scale? We should very much like to know. As Mrs Rhys Davids puts it, we cannot see them at the very outset of Indian culture. Solidarity is a great need for the invader, but when once the invasion is over, then the lovers of solitude can afford to indulge. But were there any in pre-Nordic India? We cannot yet tell. Mohenjodaro has yielded up a figurine of a male figure in a *yoga* attitude, and how much this implies cannot be determined. Once, and once only, in an early Upanishad is the word *shrā-mana* or recluse to be found, but its counterpart, *sāmana* in Pali, is common in the Buddhist Suttas, and we know that in the later Upanishads the idea of the recluse is firmly estab-

1. Australian aboriginals performing the initiation of a boy

2. Stonehenge from the air. Perhaps the best-known example of a circular open-air sanctuary of a type widely distributed in the world, the exact use of which, however, is unknown

3. Saivite sadhu (devotee of the god Siva)

4. A Krishna festival at the (new) Birla temple in Delhi. The latter was built by a wealthy friend of Mr Gandhi, with a view to drawing into a central sanctuary most of the various Indian religious groups

5. A group of
Shinto priests

6. The admission of a girl to the Parsee
(Zoroastrian) faith, performed by Mobeds
(Parsee priests)

7. Procession of a Buddhist relic to a shrine at Sanchi. The bearer
is U Nu, late Prime Minister of Burma. Mr Nehru is to be seen in
the crowd

8. Entrance to the Temple of Heaven at Peking

9. Statue of Confucius from a Chinese temple dedicated to his honour

10. Yemenite Jews keeping Seder (Passover)

11. The Kaaba at Mecca during the Haj

12. The statue of Christ over the altar in St Saviour's Church, Eltham, SE London. Virtually a modern representation, drawn from the well-known Negro spiritual 'He's Got the Whole World in His Hands'

lished. Whatever the history of the institution, it certainly belongs to Buddhism as much as to Hinduism in India, and with Buddhism it travels outside India. It is suggested that this tendency towards retreat from the world led to a warping and negativity in Buddhist doctrine.

The early centuries are very obscure, but somewhere about 270–240 B.C., in the reign of the famous king, Asoka, there was a council of Buddhists held at Patna, the rather vague records of which throw a little light on what has been happening. Asoka himself is an interesting figure. He cannot exactly be compared to the Emperor Constantine, but it is certain that he was influenced by contact with the Greek world, and he gave his patronage to the teachings of the Buddha (whom, of course, he had never known), and, from being a military leader, became a pacifist, and set up a number of rock inscriptions extolling the teaching of his newly-found faith. But Asoka had no intention of becoming a monk. He was a layman, and a layman he remained. Moreover, his apprehension of Gotama's teaching, as we see it in the pillar edicts, is less like Hinayana and more like what we have thought to have been the original announcement. But at the council of Patna there appears to have been a sharp division of opinion, and the majority at the council excommunicated the minority and expelled them from the Buddhist movement. This majority, called Vibhajjavadins, seem to have held that it was proper to analyse the ego out of existence, whereas the excommunicated, called the Sarvastivadins, held that the *Purusha*, or the Man in the man, was to grow from more to more, and so personality was to be enriched and deepened. The orthodox, if we may so call the expellers, developed ultimately into the southern Buddhists, the expelled nonconformists into the northern ones. Although there is monasticism in both, the northern or Mahayana (great system) has a more liberal outlook on life and naturally has a greater message for the laity. It calls the southern believers Hinayana (little system) in contempt, and they themselves do not use the title. These latter are probably not so far away from their fellow-Buddhists when it comes to profound philosophy, but in popular teaching the northern have two most important features in which they depart widely from their southern neighbours: (i) the conception of a Buddha-spirit, Dharmakaya or Vairoçana, which can be incarnate in a series of Buddhas or Bodhisattvas, saints who, out of love and compassion for their fellow men, refrain from attaining to Nirvana, in order to spread the saving knowledge of the way among those around them. (ii) The thought of the human soul as a continuant which may pass through a number of heavens or hells and attain a final condition of individual beatitude. The classic document of this developed Buddhism is called the Lotus sutra, and it has achieved great fame in the Far East. All the twelve main Buddhist denominations of Japan acknowledge it, and a seventh-century Chinese sage claimed to have read it 20,000 times. About a century ago a Sanskrit version of it was discovered in Nepal, and this has led many to regard it as an early writing, but its author is unknown, and its actual date uncertain, and it does not appear in any canonical list of Buddhist scriptures till the latter part of the third century A.D. The gist of the document is that a glorified and transcendent Gotama preaches for the last time to a concourse of disciples gathered upon a famous mountain peak. He is transfigured before them, and miraculous signs attend the occasion. But the chief feature of his discourse is the doctrine of the Cosmic Buddha 'in whom all things consist' – greatly resembling the Johannine Logos, or the Cosmic Christ of the Epistle to the Ephesians. 'Repeatedly I am born,' says Gotama, 'in the land of the living.' In each Bodhisattva the Buddha-Spirit is thus incarnate, and the ideal of 'Buddhification' is indeed held out to all mankind, even to the lowest and most degraded. Nirvana in this scheme is a heaven with 'social joys', depicted in a manner which reminds us of the famous picture by Tintoretto in the Louvre, representing the Beatific Vision.

Whether Buddhism without the Mahayana would have been as successful in its missionary efforts as it appears to have been, it is hard to say. Hinayana is still 'the little vehicle', because it does not and cannot appeal to the masses of any population. It is a creed for a minority. It is true that it is the Buddhism of Burma and Ceylon. But anyone who knows these countries is well aware that the real popular faith of their peoples is not Hinayana but a thinly veiled animism.

The very learned Japanese Buddhist, Suzuki, who is known and appreciated in British Universities, is disinclined to allow very much for the popular side of the Mahayana. Individuals, he says, are not isolated existences, as imagined by most people with Christian antecedents, but each acquires meaning only when thought of in oneness with the Dharmakaya. This may alternatively be called the spiritual expansion of the ego, or its ideal annihilation. Yet, as Dr Inge, in his famous essay on immortality, has said, it is not a question whether the boundaries of the ego are expanded, but whether its central nucleus remains or even exists. (Indeed, it is certain phrases in this essay which have led some critics to call him a Buddhist!) Suzuki suggests that to suppose such a nucleus is to cherish an illusion, and that the idea is offensive to Buddhists, who credit Gotama with having analysed the ego into five *skandhas*: material body, sensation, deeds, consciousness, conception. These, he says, are not combined by the work of an independent entity, which according to its own will combines them. When a certain number of units of hydrogen and oxygen are brought together, they attract each other on their own account, and the result is water. There is no need to posit an ego of water which willed to unite the two elements and to make itself out of them. Even so is it with the existence of a sentient being, and there is no need to hypostatize a fabulous being, a sort of ego-monster, behind the combination of the five *skandhas*. This is good philosophical Buddhism, and the excellent professor goes on to analyse each separate *skandha* into its component elements. But what we have here is no more the whole of the Mahayana than the quasi-pantheistic utterances of such Christians as Meister Eckhart, Schleiermacher, Kirsopp Lake or Alexander Nairne are the whole of the Catholic Christian doctrine about the soul. And we must ever beware of confusing mysticism and poetry with mathematics and prose. On the other hand, the philosophical Mahayana is said to go much farther than the Hinayana, in that it denies any soul-substance in non-sentient beings. It is, in fact, definitely against what is called pan-psychism, and says that any suggestion of the latter is also illusion, and that the reality is the Dharmakaya. It is quite clear that the latter belief effectually frees Buddhism from the charge of atheism. The Dharmakaya is not impersonal, but is capable of willing and reflecting, and is both intelligence and love (*bōdhi* and *kāruna*). Dharmakaya is in fact Deity, and is working in every sentient being, for sentient beings are nothing but a self-manifestation of the Dharmakaya. These problems were not materially different from those which confronted Christian and Moslem theologians in the thirteenth century A.D., and they are in fact basic to all thought which recognizes the categories of Self-Existence, Unity and Plurality.

The Mahayana philosophical theologians endeavoured to find some reason for the ignorance of the individual regarding his identity with the One True Self. This ignorance was recognized at a later date by Hegel, who defines religious knowledge as the knowledge acquired by finite mind of its nature as Absolute Mind, and the religious state as that in which the problems and contradictions of the world are solved. For Hegel, as for the Mahayanists, the question is 'Why should man be ignorant of his basic identity with the Absolute? If there is One Self, why do men imagine that there are many selves?' The Mahayanist answer is curious. The Absolute, it says, is ignorant of Its own nature. In order, therefore, to realize Itself, It has differentiated Itself into an infinite number of finite selves. It has cast shadows that It may see Its own shape. Man's quest for salvation is, in fact, the Self seeking to know Itself through this differentiation. It is the Self striving to get back via plurality to Its own Unity. It fails to achieve this through the external world of the creaturely, and so turns back on Itself. (This is, then, the meaning and significance of 'world and life negation.') The moment when this happens is the moment of Enlightenment – the self-realization of what is involved in the Buddha-Nature. All this, however incompatible with Hebraic Christianity, is quite familiar ground to students of the quasi-Christian medieval mystic, Meister Eckhart and his spiritual ancestor, pseudo-Dionysius, and it is typical Asiatic religious thought. The nearest point to it in Christian theology is when Eckhart says that God could not realize Himself without making His potentiality actual as Creator, namely by creating that which could respond to His love by loving Him in return, and that God, as Love, could not be satisfied without loving self-expression. But this, whether true or false, is not really the same as the Asiatic doctrine. Resuming the main point: the Mahayanist thinker seeks to obtain Enlightenment by mentally recapitulating the steps of this self-realizatory process for himself.

Space precludes much account of the Hinayana. Apart from concessions to animism, it exists mainly as a technique for absorption in the Absolute. It has no doctrine of Bodhisattvas, and among the learned monks is a sort of Asiatic Platonism, with no belief in the Buddha as a continuant, and much emphasis upon acquiring merit by good works. Major Raven-Hart's description of a Burmese monastery today conveys the impression of a community closely resembling that of the early Benedictines.

A very important issue is raised by the alleged effect of Buddhism upon human conduct. Buddhism plainly discourages the war-like spirit. In Tibet, as in China, the soldier is regarded with disfavour, and in Tibet blood-sports are prohibited, so that European visitors find it illegal even to kill game for food. It is natural to ask, 'What is to be the result if a country rich in an overplus of natural resources remains staunchly Buddhist? Will it not become the prey of militarist governments from outside?' No attempt has yet been made to maintain a State of any size upon Quaker principles. 'Would the result,' it is asked, 'be similar? Or would the absence of any attempt at fighting, coupled with readiness to discuss the needs and problems of others in an amicable spirit, end by bringing out the best that is in human nature?' Some will answer emphatically 'No. The Buddhist and Quaker States will simply be raped, on the plea of being made protectorates for their own good. Recent events have shown that this will inevitably be their fate.' There is certainly no guarantee that a military State will respect freedom of thought, speculation and discussion in its protectorates. It may well muzzle their men of science and letters and their religious leaders, and so petrify the springs of creativity in those countries. Places like Tibet can survive in a state of independence only as long as they are remote and inaccessible, or surrounded by neighbours who feel it in their interest to leave them alone or to guard them from interference.

The question is often asked: 'Can either Buddhists or Christians be soldiers if they are sincere?' It must be obvious that if all the world were to adopt their creed, the amount of killing would be reduced to a minimum. On the other hand, if a distinction be drawn between laity and fully professed members, then killing is prohibited only to the latter. Japan is largely Buddhist, as we shall see, but her laity are allowed to be strongly militarist,* and one sort of Buddhism, Zen, actually fosters a type of self-controlled character which is serviceable in war. Hence Zen is approved by the *Samurai* or military class. Something of the same judgement might be passed upon Christianity, where combatant service has not been regarded as becoming for the clergy, or for monks, but where the laity have been allowed to bear arms and to serve in *justa bella*, while certain Puritan types of Christianity have fostered the military virtues, just as certain Catholic orders (the Knights Templar, the Knights of St John of Jerusalem and the Knights of Rhodes) in the Middle Ages, combined the monastic with the military life and discipline.

The answer to the original question, then, would seem to be that in the full Buddhist or Christian life killing is excluded, but that if it be conceded that two levels of conduct are allowed, then the persons living at a lower level may be granted the concession of doing a number of things which would not be correct for those living the supernatural or full Buddha life.

It is sad to find that in Gotama's old age his own clan were massacred by a neighbouring king in the regular Prussian style. Gotama's principles were not able to tame this contemporary ruler or reduce him to good behaviour, and of course the Buddhists themselves were quite unable to protect the kinsmen of their founder.

Another problem is presented by the fact that neither Buddhism nor its parent Hinduism has any actual place for what in the West is called social service. The effect of seeing a pauper's funeral worked quite differently in the respective cases of Gotama and Anthony Ashley Cooper. The former saw in it a reason for leaving the world. The latter saw in it a challenge to transform the social order. The effect of seeing a harlot was to make Jesus say, 'Her sins, which are many, are

* This is also true of Thailand.

forgiven, because she loved much'; its effect on a Buddhist was to make him pride himself upon his superiority to passion. I do not express an opinion as to which of the two teachers was more correct in his attitude; but it is plain that the theory of life is fundamentally different in each case. When social service is adopted, as it has been by Gandhi, and also by some Buddhists in Japan, it is adopted at the expense of doctrine, which has to be modified in order to make room for it. The consistent Hindu and the consistent Buddhist, though ready to stress the virtues of goodwill and kindliness, would probably say that Western Christians over-estimate the importance of social service, and would equally argue that in a world which is so rapidly changing, and at best so full of illusion, to work for a planned society is a waste of time. They might even draw attention to the eschatological teaching of the New Testament and its reactions upon Christian practice, and point out that even some of the greatest Christian thinkers like St Thomas Aquinas and Luther have not thought of the Christian's duty as consisting in more than ambulance work. In any case, they would say, you Christians admit that you have only a leasehold tenure of the earth, and therefore it seems rather futile to take so much trouble about creating an earthly paradise. Buddhists would insist rightly upon the ethical ideal of their founder, but would say that a planned and reformed society is an idle dream, since all the world is *anicca*, i.e. evanescence. Western Christians might make the retort that in a sense they, too, believed that to look for permanence on earth was to look for an impossibility, and that their advocacy of social service was not of the same order as that of the Bolshevik, since their vision was not limited by the boundaries of an earthly paradise. They would say that they worked for a better social order because they believed in the infinite worth of the individual soul, whose destiny is to them not limited by the span of earthly life. And so the argument would go on.

It is also doubtful whether these Indian systems are really friendly to the progress of empirical science, since if the external character of so-called 'events' is without significance, the main motive for their study and investigation is withdrawn. But then the study of the terrestrial world was equally discouraged by the medieval Christian schoolmen, who thought it neither profitable nor really possible, and wished to restrict scholars to theology, astronomy and logic.

What happened in the first years after the departure of Gotama from the scene of his labours is not easy to know. We seem to see a body of rather happy and informal people, not necessarily living in the well-established monasteries of later years, but spending about half the year in going about, and the other half, the rainy season, in huts. Their primary mission is, so to speak, to 'the lost sheep of the house of Israel'. They do not think of going to other lands, only of spreading their new word throughout India itself. The change comes, as we have been led to think, after the council of Patna, and Mrs Rhys Davids aptly compares the situation to that in France after the revocation of the Edict of Nantes, when the Christian nonconformists of France left their home-country not of set purpose, but because they had no option. If this is so, then we must see in the first missionary efforts of Buddhists which were of an external character an accidental discovery that the new movement had a message for the larger world, rather than an express understanding to carry out the 'marching orders' of the founder.

We have it, at any rate, that for some reason or other there was expansion of Buddhism about the third century B.C., and that this expansion went eastward, and tended in the main to take the form which we know as Mahayana. But here again it is not quite correct to divide Buddhism into Northern and Southern. It is true that the analytical school established itself in Ceylon, Siam and Burma, and the progressive or Mahayana in Nepal, Tibet, China, Korea and Japan. But in the last three countries there are types of Buddhism which are, strictly speaking, neither Northern nor Southern, but which form a separate Eastern school, sometimes called the Sukhāvati or Paradise group (see the section dealing with Amida-cult in Japan).

Here for the time being we must leave the story of the spread of Gotama's gospel, and it will be taken up again in the course of the next chapter.

In 1920 it was estimated that there were 138 million Buddhists in existence, as compared with 564 million Christians, but it is difficult to obtain more recent figures. Buddhism is not expanding much today, but in places it is showing considerable power of rejuvenation. A computation which includes nominal Buddhists in all Asiatic countries gives the total as near 750 millions. The renewal of Asian solidarity as evinced at Bandung, coupled with the menace of Marxism, is drawing Theravada and Mahayana Buddhists into closer cooperation, and a body of scholars is at present engaged in producing a revision of the Buddhist sacred canon of scriptures.

CHAPTER VIII

China and Japan

MONGOLIAN man divides into three groups: northern, southern and oceanic. Of these, the northern comprises the various types of Turk, and a number of peoples such as the Finns, Lapps, Bulgars and Magyars: of all of whom It must be said that they have been greatly modified by intermarriage with northern and western Europeans, of Nordic and Alpine stock. To this same northern group belong the various peoples of East Siberia, and the Manchus of China. There is a strong element of northern Mongol in the Japanese and Koreans, as well as in many Russians (in the latter case owing to the western incursions of Mongols in the early Middle Ages). The southern Mongols include the Chinese proper, the Burmese and Siamese, the peoples of French Indo-China and the various tribes of Tibet and the Himalayas. The oceanic Mongols include most of the peoples of the East Indies except the Australoid jungle and other tribes, the Malays and proto-Malays, and, strange to say, the inhabitants of Madagascar.

We know very little about the origin of the civilization of China, but it appears (though not the most ancient) to be the oldest continuous culture in the world. Some think that it came from south-west Asia, and point to resemblances between Akkadian and Chinese words and astronomical systems. These, however, need not imply actual colonization, but only trading intercourse, either by caravan routes (which are of great antiquity) or by sea-borne traffic from a port called Eridu at the head of the Persian Gulf, which was a centre of commerce some four or five thousand years ago.

The Chinese, although long centuries have unified them into a fairly homogeneous nation, contain a number of different types. Until recently only Neolithic deposits had been found, but since the beginning of the twentieth century rich Palaeolithic deposits have come to light, especially in the loess area, and it now seems clear that early man was as least as active in China as in France. Most striking of all has been the discovery of very early human remains near Peking. A considerable Neolithic culture datable at about 2000 to 1500 B.C. has been found in the north-east and north-west, and in the north-west has been found pottery resembling early specimens unearthed in Babylonia, and dating from before 3500 B.C. This culture is regarded as the eastern expansion of a great prehistoric culture-province extending from Central Asia to Iran, Syria and Egypt, long before 4000 B.C. Physically these early inhabitants of China may have had a more European appearance, but Central Asiatic tribes, Turki, Tungus, Mongols and Manchus, invaded the country at various times and modified the early type, while there are also connexions with Siam and Burma. Dr Hu Shih, the able modern historian of China, has divided Chinese religious development into three periods:

1. The Sinitic age, extending from about 2000 B.C. to 300 B.C.
2. The age of Buddhism.
3. The Chinese Renaissance, which began with the triumph of Neo-Confucianism and has lasted to the present day.

The Sinitic period is the product of two distinct civilizations: first the Eastern or Shang, which preceded the year 1200 B.C., and which in the matter of religion is characterized chiefly by ancestor-worship and the cult of the dead, and second the Chou or Western, so called because it came in from the west with invading conquerors (we may well query whether they contained any proto-Nordic elements!). Chou religion is associated with the worship of Shang-ti or Hao-Tien, and this is not necessarily a monotheism, but at any rate centralizes upon a Supreme Sky-god.

The worship of Shang-ti, supreme ruler, goes back, however, farther than 1200 B.C., and this suggests that even in the Shang religion there was a high god. But Shang-ti is not precisely a creator, because the primitive idea was of a more or less spontaneous evolution out of the Self-Existent, by the rhythms of Yin and Yang. Much later, in a prayer of the Ming period – that is to say, after Christ – the idea of creation is introduced. But it seems as though to this 'high god' idea another was added by the Chou conquest, since about 1100 B.C. occurs the word T'ien, which is found in old poetical classics, the Shu King and the Shih King, and these have much to say about Heaven as Ruler, but employ the word T'ien, though making it correspond very much to our vague term 'Providence'. But the earliest ideographic symbol for T'ien is 𡗗, which is plainly anthropomorphic, and must surely denote 'the man in the sky'. Later the symbol became more stylized, as 天, and today it is 天, which has been analysed as — =one 大=great thing. T'ien is really used in two senses, (a) sky and (b) god, and it is said that Confucius seems to have used it mostly in the second sense and but rarely in the first. Professor Giles has expressed the opinion that T'ien probably denotes 'god' in the passive, and Shang-ti 'god' in the active sense, but one would have thought that the opposite was more likely to be the truth. It may be supposed that the depersonalization of the ideogram goes along with the depersonalization of the idea, which we shall have to record.

The ancient book of Rites or Li-Ki recognizes four great sacrifices: the Kiao, the great Hsiang, the three Hsien and the one Hsien. Of these the Kiao is offered to Shang-ti. It was always offered by the Emperor in person as Son of Heaven (a title much like the Greek 'Huios Theou', or 'Son of God', applied to some Roman Emperors). The ceremony goes back at any rate to the Bronze Age, and it is believed that there were several Altars of Heaven, though the most famous was at Peking, and in its present form is still to be seen there, unless the Japanese have bombed it.* It was rebuilt as recently as 1889, and consisted of three concentric white marble circles, with a central platform. A vestry or blue-roofed chamber stood in its precincts, but otherwise all the ceremonies connected with the sacrifice took place in the open air, as at the altar of Zeus at Pergamum – though under umbrellas if necessary! The rites as performed in the nineteenth century were most elaborate and dignified, on a scale rather to be compared with that of a pontifical high mass in St Peter's at Rome or at Westminster Cathedral, with musicians, choir, incense and elaborate liturgical prayers and hymns. The sacrifice included, besides incense, offerings of silk, wine, inscribed paper and bullock's blood, and there was a spot set apart adjoining the altar for the slaughter of the victims, and also a fire for the burning of the offerings.

Chinese religion from 3000 to 1200 B.C. much resembles other Bronze-Age polytheism. If there is a high god, there is also a large array of inferior deities and spirits. There are nature and fertility festivals, and in the harmonies of dance and song and the mating of men and women the rhythms of nature are believed to be expressed and embodied. These ancient Chinese appear to have been not unlike the Greeks as we see them in the pages of Homer. They had wives and also concubines; they preferred sons before daughters; they hunted and fished; they tilled the soil; they fought; and were organized under a sort of feudal system. Their religious world was pluralistic. There were spirits of heaven and earth, spirits of departed ancestors and daemons of storm and drought. The relations

* Up to 1942 I hear that it was intact. It is now in Communist hands.

between Deity and humanity were on the level of '*do ut des*', exactly as they seem to have been among many in Athens when Plato wrote his 'Euthyphro'. We may also note that the reputed founder of the Chou dynasty, which in 1122 secured the hegemony of the feudal States, and who was believed to have lived about 2500 B.C., was also believed to have been miraculously born:

> his mother
> reverently offered up sacrifice
> That she might not be without children
Then she stepped in a footprint made by T'ien, and conceived.

. . . .

> When she had fulfilled her months,
> Her first-born came like a lamb;
> There was no rending, no tearing,
> No injury, no pain,
> In order to emphasize his divinity.

During the next period, 1200 to 300 B.C., we enter upon the transition to philosophy. Kung-fu-tzŭ, better known under the latinized form of his name as Confucius, was born in the small feudal dukedom of Lu (part of the present province of Shantung) about the year 551 B.C. He is a clearly defined character, and is said to have descendants living today. It has been usual to say that the other world-famous philosopher, Lao-tzŭ, was born a little earlier (about 604 B.C.); but more recent researches have tended to reduce him to the proportions of a very legendary figure (also, like the founder of the Chou dynasty, reputed to be virgin-born), and some doubt remains as to whether he ever existed at all. The teaching associated with his name may belong to a later period, and may have been the product of a number of thinkers; or it may be that there was a teacher who proclaimed what are called Taoist doctrines, but that we do not possess his real name. In any case, the fame of the reputed Lao-tzŭ rests more upon the work of a later disciple than upon anything that is known about the sage himself. Both the systems of Confucius and of Lao-tzŭ make use of the idea of the great Tao, which is certainly much older than their day in Chinese thought. Tao is difficult to define strictly. At first it seems to mean simply the course of Nature, but in the hands of philosphers it comes to resemble an impersonal deity, or to be the equivalent of the words in Greek which are rendered 'Reason', or again it is not unlike the Logos of Graeco Roman and Hellenistic Hebrew thought, or like the Dialectic Process of Marxism.* In other respects it resembles the Absolute of modern idealist philosophers. The main difference between the Confucian and the Taoist systems is that the former prescribes an active attitude towards the world, and the latter a passive. The doctrine attributed to Lao-tzŭ inculcates a kind of quietist mysticism, a sort of tranquil spontaneity in all one's life, in which considered action and independent thought are eschewed, since Nature is so beneficent that it is better not to interfere with her machinery. Confucius, on the other hand, was a rationalist who favoured a practical conservatism, in which the duties of one's day and station were carefully prescribed. Confucius was by no means nontheistic. Although he tended to de-anthropomorphize Deity, and used the word which is usually translated 'Heaven', instead of any personal name, he used it with obviously theistic implications. 'Heaven,' he would say, 'has entrusted me with a mission'; and he spoke of the ideal man as one who stands in awe of the ordinances of Heaven. He was a strange and rather imperious character, and, like the Buddha, he is to us best typified by such a teacher as John Wesley. That is to say, he travelled much, proclaimed a message in season and out of season, formed little groups of followers, suffered dangers and hardships, and exhibited much general organizing ability.

* Tao (pronounced 'Dow') is the official rendering of *Logos* in the Protestant Chinese version of St John's Gospel.

Like the Buddha, he was practical. But both Easterns differed from the great Western evangelist in their tendency to relegate theology to the background. Both avoided speculative issues and stressed the importance of ethics. To Confucius the whole duty of man consisted in preserving the right relationship towards each of one's fellow human beings. He seems therefore entirely practical and this-worldly, and enjoins no ordered ceremonies or sacrifices. Yet, as in the case of the Hebrew prophets, it is doubtful whether even Confucius, with his recognition of Heaven, would have scorned to perform the ceremonies which had been handed down as part of the piety of his nation. He was, as has been said, intensely conservative, and inculcated a great respect for authority; and he may therefore have taken for granted much which he does not mention. Life to him must be vigorous and positive, carried on with balance and moderation, and avoiding all extremes. This doctrine of the mean, so much resembling that of Aristotle (and also the Middle Way of Gotama), is greatly developed by the later Confucian scholar Meng-tzŭ, or Mencius, who was born about 451 B.C.

But perhaps the most important and controversial element in Confucian theory is its doctrine of man. Meng-tzŭ, expounding the teaching of Kung-fu-tzŭ, declares that every man possesses in himself the four principles of benevolence, justice, propriety and wisdom, and that man has only to obey the law within himself in order to be perfect. This optimistic valuation of man is plainly the reverse of what is to be found in the writings of St Paul. That great Christian, it will be remembered, wrote 'All have sinned and come short of the glory of God', and again, 'I find a law that when I would do good, evil is present with me', and so on. Some modern critics have praised Chinese optimism, and have contrasted it favourably with what they call the sin-obsession of Christians, and it is certain that thoughtful Chinese have deprecated the emphasis laid by some Christian missionaries upon mankind as 'children of wrath', saying that it tends to undermine (especially in the young) that self-respect which they regard as a cardinal and legitimate virtue.

This matter must, however, be regarded more justly. While it is true that Confucianism proclaims the essential goodness of man, it is certain that Confucius himself was saddened at his failure to get his rude contemporaries to realize the good within them and to teach them gentle manners. He died more or less broken-hearted; for the teaching to which he had devoted himself was so contrary to the spirit of his time, and to the struggles of the individual war-lords to obtain in turn the mastery, that, although it was intended to bring about a regeneration of social life, it had at the time almost no results. Moreover, it seems certain that even the thoughtful contemporaries of the sage felt that he had not proclaimed the whole truth, for we find a number of opposite tendencies asserting themselves in other teachers who followed. The most impressive of these is Mo-ti (470–390 B.C.), who said that the orthodox Confucian doctrine was erroneous, because agnostic and determinist. Mo-ti declared, 'We *can* know God, and we must base our conduct upon his moral character. His will is love, universal and without distinction: war is against his nature, and nothing will work except love.' Mo-ti has been almost ignored until now, but he is really the most amazing phenomenon, in his monotheism and ethical ideals like a Hebrew prophet. Even Meng-tzǔ, who did not agree with him, said, 'Mo-ti loved all men, and was ready to wear himself out in the service of human beings. In a long life of such service, he endured hardship and opposition in pursuing his ministry of reconciliation.' His great idea was 'impartial love for all', and he sought to trace all the confusion, crime and oppression of his day to one root – selfishness or lack of mutual love. His diagnosis will commend itself as correct; where opinions will differ is as to the kind of remedy to be prescribed. Again, between 332 and 295 B.C. another new leader of thought, Chwang-tzŭ, endeavoured to substitute Lao-tzŭ for Confucius as the guide to life, and succeeded in making his theory prevail for a time. Taoism has in recent centuries been so much identified with polydaemonistic religon of a debased sort that it is necessary to bear in mind that, as taught by Chwang-tzŭ, it is of the mystical type described above. A change of dynasty in the year 221 B.C. still further favoured this revival of interest in Lao-tzŭ, for in that year a very able Asiatic autocrat, Shih-huang-ti, seized the Imperial throne, and endeavoured to make a clean sweep of tradition, and to build, à la Lenin, an entirely new social order. Taoism he found not uncongenial to his plans, but the conservative tradition of Confucius he felt to be an obstacle, and he therefore ordered the destruction of all Confucian literature, and forbade the doctrines of the sage to be taught any more. But Confucius was too deeply fixed in the affections of the Chinese people for his memory to be uprooted in this way. When the autocrat died after twelve years of power, his innovations did not endure. His government broke up, and a new adventurer founded the famous Han dynasty, which lasted nearly 400 years. This new Emperor, Liu Pang, not only restored the public teaching of Confucian principles, but went much further than anyone before him, in performing for the first time on record a sacrificial offering at the tomb of Confucius. The latter is from now onwards regarded as a kind of supernatural being, instead of as an extremely human teacher. It is possible, as Mr Carl Crow has done, to reconstruct from the traditional records a very vivid picture of this human teacher, and it is plain that during his lifetime he never claimed for himself the kind of position with which he has been invested. True it is that respect for ancestors, emperors and heroes is not perhaps far removed from the veneration now bestowed upon the spirit of Confucius, but the cultus itself has much more in common with the *avatar*-ideas of India than with anything in Chinese wisdom.*

Yet there were still other dissentient voices. In the fourth century B.C. there was another teacher who founded a school of ethics. This was Hsun-tzŭ, who was a complete heretic, and taught that men are not by Nature good but evil: Nature must therefore be overcome by nurture. This, except that there is no suggestion of salvation by grace, might almost be mistaken for evangelical Christianity, but Hsun-tzŭ put his faith in education, not in conversion. His doctrines met with much opposition, and his rationalism was hostile to current Taoist principles. Thus he said that we ought to domesticate and regulate Nature instead of praising her and meditating upon her.

Mo-ti, Chwang-tzŭ and Hsun-tzŭ represent, as it seems, minority movements in Chinese thought albeit important ones. The really vast change which now impends is from outside, and comes from the west. In the sixth century A.D., Buddhism entered the country, and within a century of its arrival two other religions also arrived, that of the Manichaeans (see page 290), and that of the Nestorian Christians, both presumably travelling along the great trade route which runs horizontally east and west through the Tibetan mountain ranges. Of these three, Buddhism was by far the most important. It must be understood that it arrived in the Mahayana form. Had the Hinayana come to China it is doubtful if it would have registered so great a success. As it is, according to Dr Hu Shih, 'Buddhism came with irresistible force and broke down the fatalism of Confucianism and Taoism . . . and brought home to the Chinese the indestructibility of the soul'. This must sound strangely to any who have come to overstress the *anatta* doctrine of the Hinayana. The fact remains that the sort of Buddhism which entered China had a considerable eschatology, and rich teaching about the future life with its heavens

* See pages 137 ff.

and hells. It also had a new ethic which was not that of Confucius, but bore the same relation to it that the Christian supernaturalist ethic bore to the secular and worldly-wise ethic of the Roman Empire. There were also the same objections to it. It was accused of encouraging celibacy and of breaking up family life, by discouraging filial piety. Modification took place on both sides. To this day, Buddhism is the faith which the Chinese regard as suitable to turn to when it is a matter of dying or caring for the dead. Yet Buddhism was itself adapted to fit the Chinese, and instead of remaining a purely world-denying mysticism, it became a strong force for the moulding of the characters of men and women who were to take their place in the utilitarian and world-affirming life of the Chinese and Japanese peoples. This seems so curious that we nearly forget that it is a statement which almost exactly describes the corresponding adaptation of world-renouncing Christianity to the needs of the Western nations. The worship of the universal Buddha-spirit as the Absolute Deity, and the emphasis upon compassion, gentleness, love and purity, were matters of vast import to China, and the ideal of the *bodhisattva* is very different from that of the Chuntzŭ or princely man set up by Confucianism – as different as the ideal of the Christian saint is from that of the high-minded man of Aristotle.

With the advent of Buddhist propaganda Confucianism was for a time depressed, and those who prefer it are apt to regard the next few centuries as the sterilization of China. But this is really unjust. China owes an incalculable debt to Buddhism in respect of art and philosophy (see page 178), and in any case the Buddhists adopted a policy of conciliation, while the Chinese are by temperament given to compromise. There was thus a tendency to fusion, and Zen Buddhism (Ch'an in China) is probably due to a blending of Taoist intuitionalism with Buddhist ideals. This took place during the T'ang dynasty, about A.D. 574, and at the same period Confucianism revived under Imperial patronage. During the Sung period Confucian and Buddhist ideas were fused, but earlier, between 750 and 810, there was considerable rivalry between Confucians and Buddhists. During the T'ang period Islam also reached China through visiting traders, and the first mosque was built at Canton. (There are still Moslems in China, but they are a relatively small, self-contained community.)

The final and in some ways most important development in Chinese thought proper comes with the Neo-Confucianism of Chu Hsi, or Chu Tzŭ, who lived from 1130 to 1200, and has been called the St Thomas Aquinas of China. His is the most subtle metaphysical mind that China has produced, and from him proceeded the only complete system of philosophy that China has been able to develop. Separated from the West, he demonstrates how impossible it is for the human mind to work very differently even in spots geographically far apart, so long as it has to use the same categories. There is considerable divergence of opinion as to his religious beliefs or disbeliefs, and it is only fair to give both sides of the picture. On the one side he has been represented as a materialistic monist, who denied the existence of a personal god and the immortality of the soul, on the other as a theist, at least in the sense in which Dr Inge could be called one. What are the facts? Chu Hsi was a philosophical theologian and speculative thinker, not an evangelist or a prophet. Hence his attitude towards a good deal of popular piety was disapproving. In his anxiety to stress the spiritual character of Self-Existent Being, he tended much as other Chinese sages (or need one say 'Chinese'?), to depersonalize it. Professor Hocking goes so far as to suggest that one of the chief contributions of the East to religious thought is to make room for the avowedly non-personal element which is present in Deity. All may not agree with him, but his position is certainly capable of defence. Again, the natural temperament of many average Chinese is materialistic and utilitarian

once more, need one say 'Chinese'?). Hence the elements in
the writings of Chu Hsi which seem to tend in the direction
of a monistic atheism receive among his countrymen an emphasis which they do not find in the pages of their author. An
expert who has made a complete study of the works of Chu
Hsi declares that although individual immortality seems to be
depreciated in some passages, such as those in which he compares individual existence to waves of water, in others Chu
Hsi differs specifically from his Buddhist contemporaries in
saying that instead of sinking one's individuality in the universal, it is one's business to develop one's mind to the utmost
and to bring it into harmony with its source, and that in this
way one's individuality will not be obliterated, but intensified.
Here we have an apparent contradiction which can be
accounted for only by saying either that it is just a typical
example of the capacity of the Oriental for what Hocking
has called 'plural belonging' i.e. in this case the capacity to
hold apparently mutually exclusive beliefs simultaneously; or
that Chu Hsi changed his views as he went on, or yet again
by supposing that scholars have not yet fully mastered the
meaning of the terms as used by the author himself, and
so are liable to misinterpret the sense of passages in which they
occur. Any one of these three solutions is still possible. Then
with regard to theism; while it is plain that an estimate of
Chu Hsi's doctrine depends upon really knowing what he
meant by 'Li' and 'Ch'i', and their mutual relations, commentators differ widely in what they say; some finding an uncompromising materialism, others a species of pantheism.
Thus Maclagan says, 'The identification of Heaven with Li
makes the universe more than merely material, but it is not
unfair to say that it makes God less than personal, and this less
theistic interpretation is borne out by the subsequent history
of orthodox Confucianism'. On the other hand, Bruce tries to
avoid misleading us by sticking close to the actual statements

of the sage. Li, according to Chu Hsi, is the Supreme Ultimate, the Primordial Substance, the Guiding and Directing Principle which determines the form of everything that exists, and causes it to be. Li vivifies, constructs, composes and informs the whole. But the component principles of Li are love, righteousness, reverence and wisdom. (In what sense 'reverence' is here used is not clear.) But these principles are attributes of mind. Chu Hsi is rather puzzling when he says that Li is a property of mind rather than mind itself, but he goes on to add that Li is ethical. It is that which gives law, and without it mind would have nothing in which to inhere. Probably we are only on our way to understanding this religious philosopher. We are ourselves like Chinese trying to make sense of Aquinas, but not knowing much about medieval Latin, and still less about classical Latin. Saunders says attractively that Chu Hsi, when he talks about non-being (*wu-ki*), a potential cosmos, and the Absolute (*tai-ki*), Pure Being, is nearer to the transcendental God of St Thomas than to the Brahman of the Vedanta. As to Ch'i; a French writer renders it '*matière*', yet since Chu Hsi says that it includes every form of existence, it appears to be much more the equivalent of Sir Arthur Eddington's mind-snuff. Li is eternal, but eternally generates Ch'i. This sounds remarkably near to saying that Deity is eternal, but eternally generates the creaturely. It would all seem pretty good natural theology; yet the results are, as we have said, in effect less favourable to theism than might be supposed. Confucianism as shaped by Chu Hsi remained stable and unchanged for some 700 years, with extraordinary conservatism. It was the basis of the education of the mandarin class, and a subject for examinations; and it thus became the background of the life of every educated Chinese gentleman. But its result was to depreciate most kinds of cultus, and to produce cultured and urbane agnostics, somewhat of the type evolved by Western classical public-school education, with a Stoic background and a great insistence upon the repression of one's feelings.

Into the Chinese world of the seventeenth century came the Christian movement. It had been there twice before, once as we have already mentioned, in the sixth century, and again in the thirteenth, when some Franciscan friars penetrated to Peking and founded a church; but in neither case had the results been permanent. Now in a later age arrived the Jesuit missions, and later still the Anglican, Baptist and other Reformed Church emissaries. In the nineteenth and twentieth centuries have also come the disturbing influences of recent European and American secular thought, Darwinism, Marxism, Humanism and Nationalist Fascism. All these have produced and are producing profound changes. Many Chinese have gone to the United States Universities, and Chinese religion is in a stage of extreme transition, in which Chinese trained in the numerous Christian Universities exercise an influence which is out of all proportion to their numbers, while many other of their compatriots are quite as definitely critical of Christianity, which they regard as intellectually naïve, and unsuccessful in controlling the West. Marxism at the moment is in the ascendant, and the situation is so fluid and unstable that it is difficult to predict the future. Mr Liu Wu-Chi in his recent Pelican book has tried to appraise the position of the old Chinese culture, which it is hard to believe can remain submerged entirely and for ever. But China has never been patient of interference from foreign powers, and it may well be that this older spirit of Chinese nationalism will re-assert itself in a modified form, though if it does, that need not mean a revival of Christianity, unless it should reappear in a thoroughly Chinese form. Americanized Christianity, or even Chrsitianity with a European bias, can hardly be expected to succeed.

The Chinese, unlike the inhabitants of India, cannot fairly be described as a religious people; that is to say, their thought is neither naturally theocentric nor mystical. They are practical to a high degree, and although Self-Existent Being is acknowledged as the Background of life, their chief concern is with their own material welfare. Hence, when converted to Christianity, their main question is, 'What is going to be its direct value to me?' and they have in consequence been compared to the British, who admittedly take somewhat the same line.

Whether rightly or wrongly, a people steeped in Confucian thought will always naturally tend towards an optimistic anthropology. The sense of human inadequacy goes only with an intense perception of the transcendent holy God. Chinese wisdom, with its vague theism and its preoccupation with human relationships, is in consequence less sin-conscious than Hebrew and Christian prophetism, and also less world-negating than the thought of India.

A few typical passages from Confucian thought may be appended here.

(1) *From Appendices to the Yi-king*, a pre-Confucian document, with commentaries and additions attributed to Confucius:

(*a*) The great man is he who is in harmony, in his attributes, with heaven and earth; in his brightness, with the sun and moon; in his orderly procedure, with the four seasons; and in his relation to what is fortunate and what is calamitous, with the spirit-like operations (of Providence). He may precede Heaven, and Heaven will not act in opposition to him; he may follow Heaven, but will act only as Heaven at the time would do.

(*b*) God (Shang-ti) comes forth in a certain area to His producing work; in another He brings these processes into full and equal action; in a third they are manifested to one another; in a fourth, the greatest service is done to Him; in a fifth He rejoices; in a sixth He struggles; in a seventh He is comforted and enters into rest; and in the original area He completes the work of the year.

The above indicate the way in which Confucius refers to Deity as the constant but rather vague background to his ethics.

(2) *From a handbook of Confucian teaching*, issued by the Prime Minister of Manchukuo for use in schools (the passages are taken from the Analects of Confucius):

i. It is in accordance with the nature of things, that of all beings on earth Man is the noblest. Uprightness belongs to Man by virtue of his birth; if he loses that, he is in peril.

ii. The commander of a mighty army may be carried off into captivity, but the humblest man of his people has a will which need never be surrendered.

iii. The true scholar and the man of true virtue will never seek to save themselves at the cost of their moral integrity. In its defence they will be ready to sacrifice life itself.

iv. If truth has been revealed to you in the morning, you may die when night comes without repining.

v. Among the truly educated, there is no distinction of classes.

vi. Tzŭ-king asked if the Master could give him one word to serve as rule of life. The Master said: 'Would not "reciprocity" be such a word? What you do not wish others to do to you, do not do unto them.'

vii. The gentleman (chün-tzŭ), contemplating the world, is free from unreasonable likes and dislikes. He stands for what is right.

viii. Even when contact is made with uncivilized peoples, kindly sympathy (jên) must not be withheld. (Jên=as nearly as possible Greek Agapê, as used in 1 Cor, xiii.)

JAPAN

The Japanese, though superficially resembling their Chinese neighbours, are a very distinctive people. Comparisons which represent the Chinese as the Greeks of the Far East and the Japanese as its Romans are apt to be misleading, but it is certainly true that the Chinese resemble the Greeks in their passion for art and philosophy, and the Japanese the Romans in their power of assimilation, their lack of originality and their readiness for discipline. Just as the Greeks civilized Rome, so the Chinese have civilized the Japanese, and Buddhism has done for both much of what Christianity did for the Greek and Roman world. Buddhism has had a curious power of evoking new life, but in the end of calling out strong opposition to its great claims. Is this again the story of Christianity in Europe, and is the stimulus provided by both due to their widening and deepening of the value of the human spirit! Both certainly had such an effect: Buddhism in its emphasis on the More to be found in everyman, Christianity by its stress upon the worth to God of every individual human soul, and both by the vista of Eternal Life which they opened up.

The prehistoric inhabitants of the islands which constitute Japan are referred to as 'earth-dwellers' or 'dwarfs', and very little is as yet known about them. They were at some period displaced by the Ainu, who were an eastward movement of an ancient group of white-skinned people, survive today in the north, and are of a strongly hirsute appearance, reminding one of a certain type of Russian *mujik* or peasant. The Japanese proper are of two sorts: the aristocratic or *Daimyo* type, who are northern Mongols, similar to the Koreans and Manchurians, and the plebeian, who are southern Mongols of the stock from which the true Malay is derived.

Prior to A.D. 522 the ethnic religion of Japan was apparently much the same as Chinese polydaemonism. From that date onwards Mahayana Buddhism was introduced via Korea, and the Chinese word Shin-to (the way of the Gods) was also introduced to describe the non-Buddhist religion of the country. As in China, so in Japan, the ethnic divinities tended to become incorporated in the Buddhist scheme as Bodhisattvas. This syncretism was followed by a reaction, and between 1700 and 1841 the national religion was purged of all Buddhist and Chinese influences, and for the time being was reduced to Mikado-worship. There followed a revival of Buddhism, which has continued very nearly to the present day, but has latterly been overlaid by a renewed nationalist reaction, in which Shinto has re-asserted itself. Indeed, in 1870 the attitude of patriotic Shintoists towards Buddhism was much the same as that of patriotic and fanatical Nazis towards Christianity. Buddhism was regarded as a noxious foreign intruder, to be expelled in favour of a return to pure and undefiled national religion, and the cry '*haibutsu kishaka*' (abolish Buddhism and down with the priests) resounded everywhere. But this violence gradually abated, and twenty years later Japanese Buddhism was more alive than ever. It was, in fact, found impolitic to disturb a faith which had so deeply affected the life of the people, and the problem was solved by a legal separation of what is called 'state Shinto' from the control of the Bureau of Religions, and its transfer to the tutelage of the Japanese Home office (Erastianism with a vengeance). This has left 'sect Shinto', some (but not all) Buddhism, and Christianity free to develop as disestablished, voluntary and purely religious movements. so long as they do not interfere in politics, or raise any objection to the performance of the rites and ceremonies of state Shinto.

Several points stand out as worthy of special attention.

(1) *The Nature of Shinto.* – As it existed in 1940, it was divisible (we have already seen) into two distinct forms: (*a*) state Shinto, which closely resembles the cult of the Sovereign in the days of the Roman Empire, plus a good deal of ordinary ethnic polytheism of the domestic sort, together with a cultus of some 110,000 shrines; and (*b*) sect Shinto, which is extremely varied, and in one of its forms almost approximates to

prophetic monotheism. The fundamental idea in Shinto is that of *Kami*, which may perhaps be rendered as 'the sacred', but which is also the equivalent of the Polynesian *mana*, and of the Latin *numen*. The shrine, or *jinja*, is usually of a simple and naturalistic character and represents the stylization of natural surroundings, as distinct from the rather elaborate architectural achievements of Buddhism. One cannot help being reminded of the tabernacle of the ancient Israelites, and it is noticeable that there is a *honden*, or holy place, and *haiden*, or holy of holies. (I hope no British Israelite will take hold of this as evidence that the Japanese are some of the lost ten tribes. There is no more evidence for their being Semitic than for their being Nordic!) There is a curious 'fundamentalist' cosmogony which has actually been taught in the Government manuals for schools, and which represents the world as the product of the copulation of two divinities, Izanagi and Izanami, from whom was born Amaterasu the Sun-goddess. She in her turn is the ancestress of the Mikado. It has been found impossible to account for this female divinity on euhemeristic principles, any more than it is possible to euhemerize Jahveh, who walked in the garden of Eden in the cool of the day. Amaterasu is undeniably a solar myth, and modern educated Japanese are hard put to it to square the fundamentalism of certain powerful Government officials with their own scientific education. It is not surprising that some react in the direction of Marxism. Others try to allegorize the mythology after the manner of Plutarch, or of modern Biblical critics in dealing with the book of Genesis.

There is much controversy as to whether state Shinto is or is not a religion of an exclusive character, or whether it is not merely an organized means of promoting loyalty and patriotism. Dr Holtom's view is that it is the former, and he considers it questionable whether it would long survive the spread of an agnostic attitude towards the *kami*. It certainly seems to be in the position of an established faith, and there is a Government department – the Jingikwan – which regulates its details, just as there is another – the Jibusho – which controls Buddhism. These supervise not only the priests and nuns, but also ecclesiastical music, the Imperial tombs, State funerals and the reception of foreigners. In addition, the Emperor exercises the right of lay patronage and investiture in respect of certain ecclesiastical offices. Perhaps the nearest parallel to Mikado-worship as existing in 1940 is the reverence prescribed towards the person and statue of the Emperor under the Roman régime, and this Roman ruler-worship seems to have been introduced from the middle East.

Sect Shinto has about 17 million adherents, and is therefore by no means a negligible element in the national life. It has been classified into five groups:

i. The purely religious or conservative sects (3).

ii. The Confucian sects (2).

iii. The mountain sects (3) – the Japanese, not being naturally mountaineers, regard mountains as the abode of the *kami*.

iv. The purification sects (2) ranging from superstitious lustration to asceticism.

v. The faith-healing sects (3) especially Konko kyo.

Not being under State control, these bodies are freer in their various expressions (to this extent resembling English Nonconformity), and satisfy a number of needs. The last group is by far the most interesting, and deserves much more study than it has generally received. The first sect – Kurozumi kyo – is the creation of an individual called Munetada (born 1780), who came to believe that by earnest contemplation of sacred things he would gain so complete an understanding of the relations between the *kami* and man that the divine life would entirely take hold of him and he would be transformed into a living *kami*. His underlying conception of the world has been described as a solar pantheism, but in his teachings about the Great Spirit of the Universe and in his doctrine of the brotherhood of man he comes very near to Stoicism. The second sect – Konko kyo – is even more interesting. Its founder, Kawate Bunjiro, was born in 1814 at Kibi, 100 kilometres westward of Kobe, in an agricultural area near the inland sea, and, as far as can be discovered, remote from Christian influences of any kind.* He began by being a worshipper of a daemon called Konjin, and during this period of his life married and had several children. Always pious in a polydaemonistic way, he displayed at the same time strong ethical tendencies. In 1855 occurred the turning-point in his career, when, during a severe illness, he apparently began to have doubts about Kinjin. Three years later we find him claiming to have a special revelation from the other world – god-possession – which declared that Deity was one, good, and always the companion of those who trust in him. Some of this he seems to have derived from the teaching of Munetada, but he believed his message to have been sent to him by God direct. The problem is thus pushed farther back for solution, and we are compelled to ask whence Munetada derived the impulse to teach as he did. At the beginning of the nineteenth century contact with European evangelical Christianity had hardly begun in the Far East, nor indeed had Japan at that period begun to copy the West in the way that she did at a later date. Unless, therefore, it can be shown that Munetada owed some of his ideas to the Catholicism of the disciples of Xavier the Jesuit – which has never been established – we are bound to conclude that the monotheism of these two Japanese is an independent product, as independent as that of Zarathustra, for example. In point of fact, however, Munetada's doctrine differed considerably from that

*No Christian influence was possible in Japan from the massacre of 1637 until after 1858, and work by Western missions did not begin in earnest till 1873.

of Bunjiro. Munetada conceived the Ultimate Deity as Maternal and Feminine, and his theology was pantheistic. Bunjiro's god is cast more in the Hebrew type, and is transcendent, but homely. Here are a few extracts from the sacred literature of the sect, which consists of four collections of brief but pithy logia, transmitted orally at first, for Bunjiro left nothing in writing. There are about a hundred paragraphs in all, gathered together after his death by various devoted disciples. Here are a few of them:

God is the Great Parent of your real self. Faith is just like filial obedience to your parents.

With God there is neither day nor night, neither far nor near. Pray to Him straightforwardly and with a heart of faith.

God has no voice, and His form is unseen. If you start to doubt, then doubt has no end. Free yourself from fearful doubt.

Do not worry but believe in God.

The believer should have a faith which makes him a friend of God. He should not have a faith which makes him afraid of God. Come near to God.

Bunjiro did not immediately form a separate sect, but in 1867 became a Shinto priest, though apparently not a very orthodox or disciplined one. He specially repudiated the prevailing Shinto use of charms and amulets, and laid great stress upon the possibility of direct communion with God. But his most remarkable feature was his possession of a kind of dual consciousness. A simple and humble farmer, he allowed himself during his 'god-possession' or 'god-consciousness' to be called by the name of the 'Living God', or 'the great god Konko', though he never permitted anyone to address worship to him direct. Here, indeed, we do seem to reach a point of dependence upon Munetada's teaching, for it will be remembered that the latter claimed to have discovered the technique for establishing a union between himself and the *kami* which would virtually transform him into one of the latter. Bunjiro died in 1883, at the age of 70.

The third sect in this group is the Tenri kyo. If in Kurozumi kyo and Konko kyo faith-healing occurs as part of the result of communion with God, in Tenri kyo it is the central feature. Indeed, the sect has been called the Christian Science movement of Japan. The founder was a woman, Maekawa Miki, who was born in 1798, and was mated at the age of twelve to a young farmer of twenty-three. Her family were keen Jodo Buddhists, and she married on the understanding that she should be allowed by her Shintoist husband to continue her Buddhist devotions daily. Twenty-eight years after her marriage, when she had already borne six children, she experienced a crisis of a revelational character. She continued in trance for three days, and at the end a healing of herself, her son and her husband is recorded. She now became a veritable saint, possessed by God and intensely unworldly, since she dismayed her husband by selling all the family property and devoting the proceeds to the relief of poverty and suffering. She underwent considerable severity of treatment at the hands of the police, who at first regarded her as either a witch or a mad woman. She was also accused of propagating a new cult without a Government licence (much as the early Christians were), and of disturbing the public peace. Eventually she won toleration, and on her death in 1887 she left behind her a considerable body of followers. A year after her death the Government gave them legal recognition, and in 1908 Tenri kyo gained complete legal and institutional independence, since when it has expanded to a membership of over 4 millions. There is a sacred book comprising a number of religious lyrical utterances, the first two of which were composed in the years 1867 and 1875, corresponding to two publications by Mrs Eddy in 1866 and 1875. These coincidences are, to say the least, remarkable, but, as with Bunjiro and Munetada, it is impossible to establish any direct indebtedness, or even indirect borrowing. One can only surmise that when ideas are in the air they may pass, by some extension of E.S.P.,* to people who are not in actual contact with their originators.

Space has been given to an account of these sects not because of their size, but because most text-books, though furnishing a correct account of ordinary Shinto and Buddhism, ignore the very peculiar phenomena which they present. It is natural to point out that they are all late eighteenth- or early nineteenth-century foundations, and that Western influence *must* have come in somewhere; but, since the latter cannot be established, it is impossible to avoid the conclusion that in Konko kyo we have an example of an independent approximation to prophetic monotheism, which may throw some light on the causes which led to the early developments of Christian theology. It is of course unlikely that the sect founded by Bunjiro could ever have grown to the size and influence of the Christian Church, and no serious comparison is intended between the characters and careers of Bunjiro and Jesus of Nazareth. But the point is, of course, that there *is* an analogy between the two leaders in respect of their alleged dual consciousness; and this should be taken into account in estimating the phenomena of prophetic inspiration, for it now seems probable that a dual consciousness such as led to the formulation of the theological doctrine of the two natures in the one Christ is to be encountered among a number of ecstatics, and that whatever uniqueness is held to have resided in Christ must be sought, by those who accord Him a unique position, less in the fact than in the quality of His dual consciousness.

(2) *The Nature of Japanese Buddhism.* – This has a number of well-defined sects, which not only are of intrinsic interest, but also reproduce in a curious fashion the contrasting doctrines and problems of institutional Christianity, and so furnish a most interesting psychological study.

During the earlier period (eighth century A.D.) the older

* See p. 30.

sects were introduced from China, among them the Kegon and Ritsu, and the relations of Shinto and Buddhism were exceedingly free, and even casual. Anthropomorphic images do not figure in Shinto, though symbolic emblems occur. But as in China, so in Japan, it is Buddhism which introduces statuary and temples of an elaborated plan. Yet here again we must call a halt. Is it really Buddhism which does this? We have seen that in its earlier stages there was no Buddhist iconography. It was the influence of Hellenism on India which caused the development of Buddhist art. We are therefore justified in saying that indirectly it was Hellenism which caused the outburst of artistic activity in Buddhist China and Buddhist Japan. Local forms developed, no doubt, but the inspiration came from the east of Europe. And since this influence is to be seen also in that estimate of man which is of necessity associated with incarnation doctrines, we must revise what has been said of the effect of Buddhism upon China, and say that it was not Buddhism in its pristine form which was able to inspire, but Buddhism as interpreted in the Mahayana, and therefore less after the pattern of the Upanishads, and more after that of the India of the Ramayana.

Towards the beginning of the ninth century A.D. came the introduction into Japan of the two great sects of Tendai and Shingon. Both are still strong today in numbers and influence, and they were established there by two famous leaders, Saicho and Kukai, better known as Dengyo Daishi and Kobo Daishi. Tendai (Tien Tai in China) was a Chinese attempt to found a kind of comprehensive Buddhist church by recognizing all known forms of Buddhism, with the doctrine of the Lotus-sutra as its crown. Shingon, on the other hand, is a transplantation of a late form of Indian Buddhism, which is also found in Tibet as Lamaism. It is extremely complicated, and has an esoteric as well as a popular doctrine, but its main idea is that the *whole* universe is the self-expression of the Buddha-nature, called in this case Vairoçana; and thus in its symbolism the austerer and more terrifying aspects of cosmic energy are depicted, which is not generally the case in Japanese Buddhist art, where figures of benevolent saints abound – Bodhisattvas, who, although buddhified Nature-deities, are of a uniformly philanthropic character. Tendai is centred upon the doctrine that all human beings possess in capacity the Buddha-nature, such as was to be seen in full measure in Sakya-muni or Gotama, and that therefore the purpose of life should be to realize and to develop this nature (just as St Paul talks about 'Christ being formed' in his converts). The Tendai, Shingon and Kegon sects practise a rite of initiation called Kwanjo which is ceremonially true to type, and consists in sprinkling with water, being blindfolded and subsequently seeing a sacred image. But Kwanjo, as it is called, is not performed on children, nor is it an admission ceremony in the strict sense of the term, but rather an exceptional privilege reserved for those desiring to approach higher mysteries (rather like higher grades in Freemasonry). According to the philosophical theology of the Tendai, the Buddha-nature is present equally and wholly in a grain of sand or on the point of a hair. It in fact corresponds almost exactly to the idea of the immanent Logos (without, of course, its complement in the transcendent Father, or of Brahma in Indian thought). The main idea of Shingon being cosmotheism, it concerns itself chiefly with the development of spiritual life from blind instincts to complete enlightenment by realization of one's self as the Great Self or Supreme Buddha, Vairoçana. Quite plainly, Tendai and Shingon believe in 'works' as a means to salvation, and prescribe a certain ceremonial technique for the attainment of the highest bliss.

Very different are the tenets of the later sects. Amida or Amitabha is to begin with a benevolent deity, possibly of Iranian origin, who gradually comes to be regarded as a Bodhisattva, though he is hardly an historical character. The cult of Amida appears to have begun in India about the first century A.D., whither it probably came from Iranian districts. It cannot, therefore, be due to Christian influence, as has sometimes been conjectured, though Christian soteriology may conceivably have owed something to a similar Iranian doctrine penetrating westward. Amida is entirely unknown in the earliest Buddhist texts, and though the latter inculcate, as we have seen, a doctrine of being 'those-who-have-the-Self-for-a-lamp', they imply a doctrine of works, since the quest of the Self is an activity rather than a passive reception of influence. But Amitabha or Amitayus, Measureless Light or Life, is conceived as a Bodhisattva whose immense merits avail for the salvation of others, and Amidism consists solely in resting upon the merits of Amitabha, not in any action that we may perform. To this extent, therefore, Amidism closely resembles the Pauline doctrine of the Epistle to the Romans, and its interpretation by Martin Luther, since it emphasizes salvation by faith alone, 'sola fide', without any trust in one's personal merits.* But this does not involve any connexion whatever with Christianity. The same contrast is to be found in Indian Bhakti theology, where there is a distinction between the 'cat' and the 'monkey' schools of salvation-theory, the former holding that Deity saves mankind as a cat picks up a passive kitten with her teeth, the latter maintaining that there must be co-operation between mankind and Deity, just as a young monkey holds on to the mother who carries her offspring about. (This idea of co-operation, familiar in Christian theology as synergism, or 'working together with God', is also found in Islam, where Mohammed is represented as having said: 'Tie thy camel to a palm-tree, but also commend it to the care of Allah.') The truth is that we are here dealing with a fundamental oscillation in the human outlook upon the

---

* *jiriki* = (lit.) one's own strength, i.e. works.
  tariki = (lit.) strength of another, i.e. grace.

nature and activity of the Self-Existent Being, and this psychological phenomenon is one which can arise anywhere independently when religious thought has reached a certain stage, no matter what that Being be called.

The cult of Amida was introduced from India into China before A.D. 300, and spread after two or three centuries to Japan. At first it influenced only the existing sects, which prescribed *meditation* upon Amida – not simply invocation. But invocation and the repetition of the name of Amida are of the essence of this cultus, and it is this aspect which in the twelfth century A.D. is proclaimed by the real exponent of Amidism in Japan, Honen, and by his successor, Shinran. Honen, who has been called 'the Japanese Luther', was born in 1133, and founded the Jodo sect; and Shinran, who was his devoted and favourite disciple, continued his work into the early thirteenth century, and founded the Shinshu or Shin sect, which is really the Jodo-Shinshu sect, i.e. the true or genuine Jodo community. Honen prescribed 'many callings upon' the name of Amida, but not in the sense of 'works' – rather as an exhibition of trust and utter dependence. Jodo means 'pure land', and the doctrine is that Amida was a person who became a Buddha, but for the love of humanity renounced Nirvana in order to save mankind by teaching and example, and that by faith anyone can become a Buddha and go to the pure land or Paradise where Amida reigns. This sounds like Evangelical Christianity, and the technique is surprisingly similar. But Amida is not a real historical figure, and he performs no atonement by the sacrifice of himself; and, further, the mechanical recital of his name would have been repudiated by the historical Jesus, who condemned 'much speaking' and 'vain repetitions'. Indeed, the recital of the name of Amida is more in line with the recital of the Catholic rosary: so the analogy must not be pressed.

At the same time it is not unreasonable to regard these later

Japanese sects as 'Protestant' in comparison with the Tendai and Shingon. Shinran prescribed marriage of clergy, whereas the earlier Buddhist ecclesiastics are on principle celibate.

Such doctrines were bound to arouse a reaction; and it came in the latter part of the thirteenth century with the rise of a remarkable man, Nichiren by name, who fiercely attacked the Jodo and Shinshu sects, saying that they were not real Buddhists at all, and calling people back again to the doctrine of the Lotus-sutra, and to the system of the Tendai as Nichiren believed it to have been taught at first. Nichiren was thus a counter-reformer. But he was not quite a parallel to the European type, since, although Buddhism in general has been independent of political attachments, Nichiren maintained not that what he taught was true, but that it was the business of the Government to enforce its acceptance; he was thus somewhat Erastian in his leanings. Nichiren's Buddhism is more than any other form of the whole movement based upon a sacred book, for it exalts the Lotus-sutra with real fundamentalist enthusiam.

The last and most curious Buddhist sect to be mentioned is Zen. Here again we have a system which has been introduced from China, where it was founded, according to the usual tradition, by an obscure and half-legendary teacher called Bodhidharma. There are those who claim that he never existed at all, and that the name is simply a made-up one. But if this is so, then we have to account for the rise of a new method of approach to essential Mahayana Buddhism which shows marks of original genius. Is it possible for it to have been the product of a school of teachers, or does it not seem to demand a founder? Zen in Japanese is the same as Ch'an in Chinese or Dhyana in Pali, and means a technique of meditation. To understand Zen we must go back once again to the doctrine of the Buddha-nature which is said to be in all things. This is the Great Self, and in China it became identified with the Tao. In Ch'an Buddhism, in fact, Buddhism entered into close relationship with the essential principles of Taoism. Now the Mahayana, though on the one side richly institutional, was on the other side strongly intellectual. It developed (as we have seen) a philosophy of the relation of the Great Self to the many, and sought solution of the problems of life through the mind. But the teachers of Zen protested against this. They declared that no real solution was attainable along these intellectual lines, and sought to direct men to a better path, the way of intuition, wherein by 'satori' or a sudden jolt, or by meditation on a paradox or 'koan', they would be enabled to see without any complicated intellectual processes their actual relationship to the Buddha-nature. The peculiar and rather eccentric technique of Zen is all subordinated to this principle, and it all ministers to this end; and it is just because he has not grasped this, that Sir Charles Eliot avows a lack of sympathy with Zen.

Further points in it which are of great importance are the emphasis upon the doctrines of 'wu-wei' or inaction, and of the union of attack and defence, of subjectivity and objectivity, of passivity and action. Wu-wei has been compared to the action of slender branches of trees when covered with snow which weighs them down. Instead of resisting the weight of the snow actively, which might easily lead to the fracture of the branches, the latter bend spontaneously under the weight of the snow, and then it slips off the end and falls to the ground, so that the branches right themselves. Even so the man who seeks to attain enlightenment should not resist intellectual difficulties, but should let them destroy themselves by their own weight. This has sometimes been regarded by commentators as the counterpart of Christ's command 'Resist not evil', which, although in its original form probably an *obiter dictum* meaning 'Do not take up arms against the Roman government', was in the hands of his disciples converted into a general maxim. On this point it may be said that the original injunction is no doubt based upon a principle similar to that of *wu-wei*. But this principle is nowhere so explicitly stated in early Christian literature as it is in Zen Buddhism, where it leads finally to the picturesque development of it into the sport of 'Judo'. Here the fundamental principle is to let one's opponent overthrow himself by his own force or weight, and one's manoeuvres are concentrated upon yielding or slipping to one side so that the force or weight opposed to one ministers to its own defeat. The union of attack and defence, which is also a part of the technique of 'Judo', is also applicable to the realization of enlightenment. The disciple must never separate himself from life and regard it in a detached way. He must regard himself as a part of life, and he can attain to realization of the Buddha-nature only by ceasing to think about it objectively and by living as part of it. This has by some been compared to the Marxist principle of the union of theory and practice, which it certainly closely resembles.

A few examples will best illustrate the working of Zen principles. Two questions and answers are often quoted as made by Zen pupils and replied to by their masters: 'What is the Tao? Usual life is the Tao,' and 'What is the Buddha? Three pounds of flax'. The meaning of the above is not far to seek. The disciple is told that he need not go into retreat and investigate intellectual mysteries, in order to discover the Buddha-nature. On the contrary, he will find it in ordinary life. Again, the Great Self within one's self is to be discovered not by the curious technique of some forms of Dhyana, but in doing one's ordinary menial task such as spinning or weaving. It is rather like the injunction of Jesus – Not 'lo here or lo there', for behold the kingdom of God 'is within you', or 'in your midst'. The Sacred, the Supernatural and the true way of living in harmony with the latter are to be found, not in something artificial or peculiar, but in ordinary life. One Zen expert, feeling cold, lit his fire with a wooden statuette of Gotama. When someone expostulated with him, he said

'There are no holy images'. In other words, there is no line to be drawn between the secular and the sacred. It is rather like saying 'Going to church? But all the world is church'. Of course the teachers of Zen constantly went much farther than this in seeking to jolt their disciples into sudden insight. Sometimes it took the form of a box on the ear, or a blow with a stick; sometimes there are glimpses which remind us of St Francis making Friar Masseo turn round and round till he was giddy, or of the two holy friars who played see-saw. Or again, absurd paradoxes are set out for consideration, such for example as the goose and the bottle:

'A long time ago, a man kept a goose in a bottle. It grew larger and larger until it could not get out of the bottle any more. The man did not want to break the bottle, nor did he wish to hurt the goose. How would you get it out?'

This Koan, or paradoxical riddle, as it is called, is usually a choice between two equally impossible alternatives. It is an image of the great Koan which is presented by life itself, an *impasse* which cannot, so the Zen teachers say, be ended intellectually. Man, for example, is confronted with the antithesis, 'freedom or determinism'. The solution comes in the flash of insight which is called '*satori*'. It is perhaps incommunicable – certainly on intellectual lines. You can only see it, or not see it.

The success of Zen in Japan has been rather curious. It is the one form of Buddhism which has appealed to the military caste, and to athletes. But the main thing about it is its tonic effect upon those whose countenances are 'sickled o'er with the pale cast of thought', or who are hide-bound by convention.

There are those, indeed, who say that Christianity is at present radically in need of a Zen movement in order to be set free for further progress, and that the essence of Zen is to be found in many of the Gospel sayings, as well as in the doctrine of the prophet Jeremiah and in the lives of the saints. But this is a highly controversial topic, which cannot be fully argued here, and it is referred to at this point only for the sake of honesty and completeness.

(3) *The Impact of European ideas, Christian and non-Christian, upon this Japanese complex of religious activity.* – It is important to avoid exaggerating the size of the Christian community in Japan, for it is still only a small percentage of the population: but its influence is entirely out of proportion to its size. Besides the Roman community, which dates back to the early Jesuit missionaries, there are an Eastern Orthodox, one founded by a Russian missionary, Bishop Nicolai, an Anglican, and various Protestant communities. American missionaries of all kinds have been influential; and Japanese Christians have received training both in Europe and the United States. Newspaper evangelism has been employed in recent times with notable results; but naturally the risk has always existed of Christians in Japan (as elsewhere) becoming less truly typical of their own national traditions, and so obnoxious to a nationalist Government. It is therefore worth noting that in the past few years a genuinely Japanese movement has sprung up, led by Toyohiko Kagawa. This, which is known as the 'Kingdom of God movement', has no exact parellel in any other part of Christendom. It is animated largely by the desire to promote better social conditions, especially among the depressed industrial workers, but also in agricultural districts, and it has aimed at planning a kind of co-operative society which shall serve as a counterblast to non-Christian communism. It is too early to judge whether its success, which has been considerable, is likely to prove more than ephemeral, but of the remarkable personality of its founder there can be no doubt. The war with China disturbed all such work (and Kagawa was for a time placed under military arrest), but it has been noted that, in spite of hostilities, Chinese and Japanese Christians tried to maintain their contact with each other. What effect the Second World War has had upon Buddhism

can hardly be judged. For many years there has been an attempt, especially noticeable among Shin Buddhists, to investigate the causes of Christian success, and to copy Christian institutions. In 1920 a Buddhist monk was found studying the methods in use at the church of St Martin's-in-the-Fields, London, and adaptations have been made of Christian hymns, though only in a superficial manner, the underlying doctrine remaining essentially Buddhist. We may note that the latest action on the part of an independent Japanese Government was to prohibit the occupation of all higher posts in the Japanese Church by foreigners. This is obviously an extreme nationalist move, and will greatly embarrass the Christian communities, but it will do so only in proportion as they have so far failed to train Japanese leaders. Where this has happened, the effect may well be to make the Church more truly Japanese. by casting it back on its own local resources.

The Japanese were described before 1940 as the strongest people in Asia, and, although they may have caused anxiety by their crude exhibition of power politics (no cruder than what is to be seen in Europe), there is hope that this phase in both continents may ere long spend itself, and that their undoubted gifts of organization and discipline may be employed in a better cause than that of destruction, and that, whether they become increasingly Buddhist or increasingly Christian, they may grow to emphasize and appreciate other virtues than those of the man-at-arms. At the time when the first edition of this book appeared, the head of the Department of Education at Tokyo was said to be an enthusiastic Zen Buddhist, who also practised Shinto!

It is too early to estimate fully the effect on State Shinto of the Mikado's public renunciation of his divine ancestry, made in December, 1945. Buddhism may be the gainer, or Christianity; or there may be a swing towards Marxism, as in China.

The most recent phenomenon is the somewhat rapid development of new syncretistic religions in Japan.

CHAPTER IX

Hebrew and Christian Religion

HEBREW religion has been described by Dr Leo Baeck in clear terms: 'In its briefest form it is the idea and challenge of the One. This challenging idea is first the One thing, the One thing that alone is needful, that which has been commanded, the Good, the Right. Secondly and mainly it means the One Being who has proclaimed this One Thing and demands it from men, the One God, beside whom there is none else. And finally it means the unity and totality of man. It means that through this One Thing, and therefore with his whole heart and soul, man is to serve the One God and Him only. All that the prophets from Moses downwards have taught, all the way in which the religion has tried to express itself anew, are, however different the ways in which it has been expressed, just this: that there is only *one* reality – the One God, His commandment and the doing of it . . . In each man, therefore, there is a unity, or to speak more accurately, a totality, that corresponds to the unity of God. This is an essential element in the doctrine of what is called ethical monotheism. From man is demanded conduct that is exclusively and absolutely related to God. To the One and only valid Thing man can give himself only if he yield up to it all that he is and all that he has; only thus can he serve the One God and acknowledge Him as the only one. All half-measures, all that savours of neutrality towards the Good, all bargaining or making terms with it, are thus excluded, as well as all lethargy and all mere pose, all that antiquity regarded as the ideal of the wise man. This demand for definite decision, this sternness. this "Thou shalt, thou shalt not", is the core of Hebrew religion. Here the Good is not, as it was for Plato, a mere idea to which men can rise by contemplation of it; nor is it, as Aristotle taught, the golden mean or *via media* between two extremes. It is the imperative, the categorical. It demands the man wholly and absolutely. It demands that his will be set toward the One and Only and against the Many and the Manifold, and this it claims to the end, even to martyrdom.'

All this is profoundly true, and it creates an immense gap between Hebrew religion and every other system. This conception of Deity was the inheritance of Christianity, and, whatever its truth, it is the background of Christian theology and the foundation of all Christian conduct and character.

It is, however, of vital importance to distinguish between the religion of Hebrews in general, and the religion of the Hebrew prophets. The Hebrews themselves were Semites, and practised a polydaemonistic cultus not very far removed from that of the nations round them, with the super-addition of a great god, in their case Yahu or Yahoh, who might or might not have a female consort. (Sometimes the name is El, and in the Ras Shamra tablets El has a consort.) When isolated from the influence of the prophetic movement, Hebrews were prone to sink back to the level of other peoples, as they did periodically in Palestine itself, and as they appear to have done at Elephantine. Much that is recorded of their religious institutions in the literature of the Old Testament displays affinities with the general zone of Bronze-Age religion. The recently discovered Ras Shamra tablets show that early Syrian polytheism lies behind much which is to be found in the Bible, both in beliefs about the gods and in the matter of festivals and ceremonies. The relation of these to the monotheism of the prophets is similar to that between Arabian polytheism at Mecca and the stark transcendent monotheism of Mohammed in his most uncompromising moods, i.e. violently antithetical.

Super-normal states such as those enjoyed by clairvoyants and prophets may be the result of a natural gift of emotional and ecstatic insight. But in earlier times they have been confused with sub-normal or abnormal states of a pathological character, approximating to hysteria or epilepsy; and sometimes the discovery of the effect of certain herbal drugs or of alcohol has led to the employment of artificial means to induce abnormality. For example, the earliest attempts at a Yogic technique known to us seem to have been associated with the use of the alcoholic drink Soma; and in Hellas it was discovered several years ago that the Pythia, or spokeswoman of the god Apollo at Delphi, sat upon a tripod over an omphalos with a central tube, through which smoke was apparently blown up around the tripod from a subterranean chamber. This smoke was probably produced by the fumes of burnt barley, laurel-leaves and (especially) hemp-seed, the latter having the effect of hashish, and producing frenzy. Music of a cacophonous sort was also resorted to by some types of ecstatic. But all these artificial aids to prophecy are scorned by the higher grade of Hebrew prophet (or *nâbi'*), who depends solely upon his natural (or supernatural?) gifts. Our word 'prophet' is unfortunately used to translate a number of different terms. *Prophētēs* in classical Greek means the official at a temple who on feast-days expounded the mythus of the God. Later the word is used of ecstatics, and in the Septuagint is the equivalent of a number of Hebrew words, each with a different significance. The *ro'eh* and *chozeh* were diviners, seers or clairvoyants. The *nâbi'* might be these as well, but he was chiefly a speaker, called by God, whose heart 'bubbled over with goodly words'.

The immediate problem therefore is: 'How did the great prophets as a series come to develop when and where they did?' For the fact is indisputable that from the vague and shadowy figure of Moses onwards there is a tension among the Hebrews between a series of isolated figures who seek to divert the nation from the paths of ethnic into those of prophetic religion, and it is equally indisputable that in the end these isolated figures triumph, and fasten, first upon the Jew, and subsequently upon the Gentile, a religious ideal which is not a mere reformation of an older faith, but a revolution breaking away from it.

Several answers have been proposed, not perhaps incompatible with one another. The standard answer is that God intervened and spoke through Moses and the prophets, and ultimately through Christ, and that in this chain of religious leaders there occurred 'a down-rush from the Super-conscious'. The evolutionist believes that the transition was not so markedly abrupt as it might seem, and that although it came 'in the fulness of time', when mankind was ready for a unitary conception of Deity, and ethnic polytheism had exhausted itself, it did not do so discontinuously, as the orthodox believe. The anthropologist thinks that the sudden appearance of prophetic monotheism may have been due to political leading on to religious imperialism, or to hybridization between proto-Nordic peoples (chiefly Mitanni) coming from the north-east and colonizing and marrying in Mesopotamia, Syria and Egypt. This he thinks may account for the sudden appearance in Egypt of the reforming king, Ikhnaten, whose mother was a Mitannic princess. It is also thought by some that perhaps the Davidic dynasty in Palestine may have been partly Mitannic as well as Hebrew, and traces of non-Semitic blood are thought to be detectable in such peoples as the Amorites. Perhaps all three answers are correct, though a fourth is also possible: that, given certain conditions, prophetic monotheism may develop anywhere quite naturally, though it may not everywhere possess the same dynamic force of expansion.

Much has been made of the fact that the name Moses is in form Egyptian, and it has therefore been suggested by Freud, following Sellin, that Moses himself was an Egyptian religious reformer and follower of Ikhnaten, who transferred his energies to the conversion and liberation of some subject Semites, and was then killed by them in the wilderness at or near Kadesh. The evidence for this reconstruction of early Bible history is very meagre, and it is quite impossible to build upon it any such elaborate theory as Freud has done. Still, Moses remains a very great figure, albeit a shadowy one, and it is certainly the case that the eighth-century prophets themselves (such as Amos and Hosea) thought of the Hebrews not as arriving at a new doctrine at that period, but as deserting and rebelling against a more spiritual worship to which at the time of the Exodus they had been summoned, and which might even have had its roots in the earlier secession of Abraham from Ur and its polytheistic society. Such a belief is too deep-rooted not to have had *some* foundation in historical fact.

Once again it is important to stress the general principle that any religion is to be judged not by its possibly humble origins, but by what it grows into. It is indisputably certain that by the time a remnant of the Hebrews had decided to return from Babylon, and, by permission of their Persian overlord, to rebuild and inhabit the capital of the southern Hebrew Kingdom, that remnant had achieved an insight into the Divine nature, which, as expressed in the words of its prophet, is unlike any other pre-Christian insight in quality (see Isaiah xl. 12 to end). This is not mysticism, such as occurs in the literature of India. Hebrew prophetism is profoundly ethical and dynamic. The prophet is certain that he is called by God to declare to men one absolute message that comes from the living God. He is only incidentally concerned with prediction. Some of his spiritual ancestors may have been soothsayers and clairvoyants, but *his* concern is with the Word of God to man. If this involves the interpretation of the future as well as of the present, that is incidental. It is the commandment of God that he must preach. 'The Lord said unto me, Say not, I am a child, for to whomsoever I shall send thee thou shalt go, and whatsoever I shall command thee, thou shalt speak' (Jeremiah i. 7).

The so-called prophetic books occupy about one-half of the Hebrew Bible or Old Testament, and fall into two divisions: (a) moralized histories, (b) homiletic utterances and proclamations, comprising fifteen books, if we exclude Daniel. Each book is a collection of passages, some of them interpolations later than the main bulk, grouped and edited under a single name. The main features in the outlook of these greater prophets may be quite easily recognized, and are to be found not only in the actual utterances of the seers themselves, but also in the moralized histories which precede them, and in a number of the Psalms.

History, according to the compilers of these books, is the unfolding of the purpose of Deity, who works in it and through it, and shows definite purposive intention in His dealings with all nations and individuals, and not merely with the Hebrews. The latter are His instrument for making known His nature and purpose, and therefore the name by which He is known to them is His name for the whole world. He is omnipresent, and transcends the entire universe. Hence to localize Him by the use of images and temples is an accommodation to human weakness, perhaps inevitable, yet to be deprecated, and outgrown as quickly as possible. He is of infinite holiness and majesty, and the perfection of moral goodness. Hence He has no pleasure in ritual sacrifices and no need of them. In so far as these represent an emotional attitude towards Deity they are not wholly worthless, but as attempts at quantitative bargaining they are both worthless and pernicious. A life of habitually right conduct, affectionately devoted to the observance of the divinely appointed moral law, and the practice of a neighbourly spirit of good-will towards one's fellow-men are the only sacrifice God needs.

This scheme omits, as will be plain, any declaration about the problem of the suffering of the righteous, and also about the difficulty that *habitually right conduct is not achieved merely by learning or being taught*. It is sometimes asserted also that the prophets have nothing to say about the more tender aspects of the Divine character, and proclaim only Holiness, Sovereignty and Law. This at least is incorrect; for Hosea and also Malachi declare the Divine Love, and the forgiveness and healing of the penitent. The book of Job, though cast in the form of a drama, and not strictly speaking a prophetical work, makes some effort to envisage the problem of the benevolence of a Deity who allows the righteous to suffer. But it leaves the matter unsolved, since in the end Job reposes only in blind trust and in contemplation of the unsearchable wisdom of Deity. It needs faith in the Christian doctrine of the cosmic significance of the Cross to satisfy men's doubts on this tremendous problem, and without that faith even the Cross itself remains part of that problem. The two alternatives are to say with the poet Cowper:

> He who wore the thorn-crowned head and bleeding brow
> Rules universal nature,

or to say with D. H. Lawrence: 'Jesus trusted in God, and God let him down.' But this is anticipating. To the Hebrew prophets human suffering and human rescue from destruction are still mysteries unprobed.

And further. As pre-Christian, this doctrine of God remains nationalist. In Jonah, in parts of Isaiah and in Malachi is to be found the idea that it is the duty of Hebrews to convert Gentiles, or that God cares for non-Jews. But even then it is the chosen people who are to dominate others. By the time of the Crucifixion (A.D. 29) there must have been a considerable number of admissions to the Jewish Church, both from the Semitic and non-Semitic populations of the Mediterranean world. The Maccabean princes had employed coercion to

Judaise the inhabitants of Galilee and Idumaea. It was a case of 'Conform or clear out'. But elsewhere conversion to Judaism was voluntary, and the propaganda of the Diaspora Jews, in spite of opposition, met with amazing success. Synagogues were open to foreigners, and both Philo and Josephus describe the character of proselytes. Exactly what status the *sebomenoi* or God-fearers enjoyed (as referred to in Acts xiii. 16) must remain uncertain. It is, however, perfectly plain from Tacitus (*Hist.* v. 5) that the proselyte to Judaism became virtually identical with a Jew. He learned 'to despise the gods, to cast off the fatherland, and to hold parents, children, and brothers in contempt'. He adopted, in fact, the *radical displacement* of one religion by another. As Th. Reinach observes, we cannot account for the enormous growth of the Jewish population in Egypt, Cyprus and Cyrene, without assuming a large admixture of Gentile proselytes, who were circumcized, and kept the food-law. It is vital to remember all this, if we are properly to understand the way in which Christianity began its spread, for it is only after the impact of Jesus Christ upon the Jewish world that real use is made of the Jewish diaspora (or dispersion) and its proselytes to create a *new universal or common world religion*.

The Christian Church began as a sect of Jews, claiming to be the true logical and spiritual development of Judaism. It adopted the Old Testament as its basic Scriptures, and while discarding, after the first Council of Jerusalem, the rite of circumcision and the eating of *kosher* food, it used in other respects the same methods in making proselytes as were used by the Jews themselves.

Baptism, of a sort, was a Jewish custom before the time of Christ, and was not invented by Him or His apostles, but merely adopted as the initiation rite of the new fellowship, while the rite of communion, still central as a social religious ordinance for most Christians, is now seen to have developed out of a Jewish religious meal held on the eve of the Sabbath, though Jesus and His followers gave to it a new and piercing significance, and non-Jewish traditions and customs assimilated it to sacrificial feasts of a type common all the world over.

The reader of the Old Testament will therefore do well to keep a sense of proportion in reading, and avoid attaching too much importance to ritual ideas and regulations, since these are actually of secondary interest, and constitute only the points in which Hebrew religion resembled other religious systems, rather than those in which it differed from them and showed its specific genius. All religions tend, unless relentlessly pruned, to conserve mutually imcompatible ideas and practices (e.g. the Lepchas of the Himalayas have two perfectly distinct and irreconcilable religions, Lamaism and the Mun religion, which they practise on separate occasions). Mankind is reluctant to jettison any element which seems capable of recalling valuable religious experience. Hence ritual sacrifices persist right up to the fall of Jerusalem, side by side with ethical and moral precepts as well as doctrines about God which are inconsistent with their retention. The same combination of incompatibles is to be found in Christianity, and this is due partly to its inheritance of the Old Testament as a sacred book, partly to over-rapid expansion leading to the incorporation of imperfectly converted heathen, who sought to retain as much of their sub-Christian beliefs and practices as possible.

Many writers allege that the transition to Hebraeo-Christian monotheism from any other form of god-belief is not achieveable by way of an evolution, but only by way of a breach. Faith in the God of Jews and Christians is to them not even the result of a reform, but only of a revolution (or as others would say, a discontinuity). The difference between the many gods and the One God is according to them not a difference in number, but a difference in nature. It is due not to a numerical unity, but to the actual content of that unity. The One God is not greater than the many gods, like Zeus – He is far above all gods. He is not a fusion of all their attributes – the kind of *one* god in whom perhaps Plato and Plutarch believed; but an entirely different sort of Being, not a superman, but entirely non-anthropomorphic, and incapable of being fairly likened to anything else. Such allegations may be balanced perhaps by pointing out that the fine monotheism of Zarathustra himself may have approximated to this belief, and that, as we have seen, it may actually have influenced Hebrew thought during the Persian period; and again that the Absolute Deity, Brahma, is equally non-anthropomorphic. But there is this difference between the highest stage of Hebrew religious belief and the belief in Brahma, that the latter represents Deity as really non-moral, the apotheosis of cosmic nature, beyond good and evil, the former as 'the Holy One, the Cause and Guarantee of the One Good Thing, The Good, The Righteous, to whom man can draw near only through the One Thing, only by doing justice, loving mercy and walking humbly with God'.*

The problem that naturally interests us is the validity of this claim to a discontinuity. Is the alleged sharp separation between prophetic monotheism and the other kinds of religion real, or is it only apparent? No author would be honest if he were to ignore the claim in silence, and equally no author would be truly scientific if he allowed himself to express a biased judgement upon a matter which is perhaps incapable of complete and absolute proof in either direction. All that can be said here (and it is saying a good deal) is that (1) conversion in the Christian direction *does* certainly appear to be of a discontinuous or revolutionary character, (2) the effect of accepting prophetic monotheism, as far as the positive fruits of character are concerned, is marked and, one might be justified in saying, unique.

There is, however, another point to be considered. The fact

* Leo Baeck, *op. cit.*

that the great religions have in the main grown up in areas be-tween which, at the time when they matured, intercommuni-cation was not easy, has resulted in each one becoming in-volved in the complex of a separate cultural life. Consequently to pass from one religious group to another has come to mean to sever one's connexion with the entire adjustment to life and the entire way of living into which one has been born, and into which, therefore, one fits by tradition, because it is the way in which all one's relations and fellow-citizens choose to live. Religion in such circumstances is much more than a belief or theory superimposed upon a neutral system of social life. It is actually a social system, and to abandon it is to ostracize oneself from all other members of one's cultural group.

This shows the strength and weakness of Latin Catholicism. It is essentially the religion of the Mediterranean world of dark-whites, and of their kinsfolk and dispersion. Hence the conspicuous ease with which it can assimilate to itself peoples in other parts of the world who belong to similar racial and cultural groups, forming part of a zone of religion and culture extending round a large part of the planet. A good example is the Portuguese colony at Goa, where Mediterranean Cathol-icism has easily adapted itself to the needs of the Dravidians of south India, because both Portuguese and Dravidians are ethnologically somewhat akin. Quite as striking is the way in which anyone of southern Irish antecedents is almost certain to be either a Catholic or an anti-clerical. Whether in Aus-tralia or the United States, true Irish conform to this principle. So consistent are they that, when Bishop Gore was found stating, as soon as he became acquainted with the system of Anglo-Catholicism, that he felt sure it was the only sort of Christianity for him, it was no surprise to find that he came of good Irish stock. And the southern Irish are of course mainly of Celtiberian antecedents.

On the other hand, Anglo-Saxon Protestant missions do not

succeed to the same extent except among the sub-Dravidian or Australoid outcastes and jungle-tribes, where the cultural complex is easier to break down. Even then the radical displacement policy of such sects as the Baptists has had the effect of destroying many of the more beautiful features of communal life, instead of modifying them to Christian use. Hence the Puritan Christian communities stand out as isolated blocks, with much less culture than the Moslems, whose institutions, though they tend to impose an Arabic culture and to make it international, are at any rate closer to the ordinary habits of the Oriental than those of Englishmen. The perception of this has in recent years led to fresh efforts at adaptation on the Christian side. The *sangha* and the *ashram* have been introduced into Christian circles in India, and European architecture and music have given way to native forms of church-building and hymnody.

It may be urged, then, that part of the apparent discontinuity betwen Hebraeo-Christian and other religion is due to the necessity for a cultural break, and that where this can be avoided the transition from the one to the other need not be so difficult. This thesis is arguable, though not entirely convincing. There is no necessary connexion between concessions to ethnic religion and assimilations of ethnic culture. Protestants have not always refused to allow the latter (one knows of examples in Ceylon and Egypt), but Protestantism would never agree to go as far as Catholicism has done in actually absorbing pieces of ethnic religion into its system.

Future centuries may see the breaking down, for weal or woe, of many cultural barriers, and the disappearance of many of the lesser types of local institutional system. The spirit of nationalism is said to militate against such a growth of uniformity, but, however proof nationalism on a large scale may be against the levelling influences of an international movement, on a small scale it is vulnerable to threats from totalitarian socialism, and it is a question how much local variety, if any, the latter will tolerate, whether in religion or in matters of a more external character. It is a further question whether any totalitarian socialism could be compatible with prophetic monotheism. It would seem unlikely that it could. Hence the conversion of the majority of the citizens of such a State to either Christianity or Islam would indeed involve nothing short of a revolution. There could be no easy transition, no concordat. It is a serious reflection that while the rights of man, according to Mr Wells, include complete freedom of worship and religious belief (or as some might say, the right to be a person, even at the risk of being wrong), the form of government now developing in at least three countries in the world denies such freedom to the individual, and it is significant that one of these States, Turkey, is rejecting Islam just as Russia and her satellites are rejecting Christianity, and that Russia, with complete consistency, is rejecting all religion alike, Christianity, Islam and Buddhism, in favour of a new system, which, though it sets science in opposition to all religion, puts in place of the latter a doctrine of the Self-Existent Being as Dialectic Process; and this, though at least in essence as much a religion as Hinayana Buddhism, and no more deterministic than the extremest Calvinism, seems to deny any real freedom to the individual, and is thus the dialectic antithesis of non-Calvinistic Christianity.

But to go back to the doctrine of the prophets. True monotheism is not simply the affirmation that God is one, but, as Oman has said, that the world is all God's by reconciliation to His meaning in it and His purpose beyond it. 'The prophets.' he continues, 'were very far from regarding all religion as good. A religion which sought God's blessing, while disregarding His mind, they did not think to be unreal or even lacking in zeal, but so far were they from thinking that it should be approved, or even tolerated, that they denounced it as, more than the worst politics, man's most dangerous enemy and God's most hated abomination.'

The story of the Hebrew people as it is given in the Old Testament is so well known that it does not seem worth while to repeat it here in detail. Briefly it may be summed up in a few lines: the emergence of a Bronze-Age people into prominence as a small but wealthy kingdom which soon split into two sections, and was successively swallowed up by Assyria and by the second Babylonian empire. It was during the period of the dual monarchy that the great prophets first appeared one after another, and their line extends almost to the time of the conquest of the Middle East by Alexander. Prior to the exile the prophets had no majority in the nation. They were pulling against public opinion, and although some of them, like Isaiah, may have occupied positions of high honour in the State, others, like Amos, were of the country yeoman or squire type, and some, like Ezekiel and Jeremiah, were of the priestly caste, but out of sympathy with their contemporaries. We do not know how much of their message was a growth kindred to what, as we have seen, was rising up in Egypt and Iran, but the more we study it, the more does it seem clear that the Hebrew prophetic interpretation of life and history is of a unique quality. Yet the best in Hebrew religion is not necessarily that which comes latest. The exile cut off the Hebrews for a time from the sacrificial system of their temple, and this, although linked with a code of moral law, had been in many respects very much like that of other temples in the Middle East, of which the ruins have been excavated and studied in recent times. The result, as is well known, was that, under the influence of prophetic tradition, the exiles developed a non-sacrificial type of worship, and almost wholly discarded the practice of temple rites in favour of what has been called a 'word-of-God service', which is as much distinct from their former cultus as the practices of a Buddhist hall of meditation are from those of a Hindu temple. This 'word-of-God' service those of them who chose to return home brought back to Palestine, and thus laid the foundations of domestic worship, as distinct from worship in a building set apart for the purpose, and of 'meeting-house worship', as distinct from rites centring upon an altar. From Judaism such types of cultus passed into Christianity, and developed there into family prayers and the services of reading and preaching with which Christians all over the world are familiar. The influence of the same religious exercises is to be seen in the devotions of Islam, which, as we shall see, began by being very friendly towards the Jews. The reading and preaching of the Law and the Prophets makes both Judaism and Islam, as Kraemer has said, religions in which 'The Word became Book', not like Christianity, in whose doctrine 'the Word became Flesh'.

What is for us significant, however, is that the concentration upon the book led to the growth of a class of scribes or commentators, by whom nothing new could be tolerated, but only an interpretation of the old. Hence, with a code of religious regulations in their hands, they could never be creative, but only casuistical. Jewish church life in the first century A.D. was thus both earnest and moral, but almost entirely lacking in generosity of outlook. Its teachers, the greater Rabbis, surprise us sometimes in their utterances by passages of rare beauty, almost equal to those in the Gospels; but in the main they are disappointing. Judaism is spiritually a spent force. Though it may be said that it gives birth to the Christian movements, it is also true that as soon as it has done so, it for the most part rejects its offspring. 'He came unto his own, and his own received him not.'

The fortunes of Hebrew religion after the rise of Christianity are seldom studied as much as they should be, by either Christians or non-Christians. They are in fact neglected in much the same way that the study of post-Tridentine

Roman Catholicism is by Protestants. It will, therefore, be right to devote a little attention to them before we leave this section.

Most people know in a general way that after the conquest of Babylonia by the Persian king Cyrus in or about 540 B.C. he allowed such Jews as wished to return to Jerusalem and to rebuild the walls of their city and set up their temple again. What is not so generally known is that relatively few of the Babylonian Jews availed themselves of this permission, so that not only were the northern 'ten tribes' dispersed after 722, but a considerable number of those who were the descendants of the exiled Judaeans of Nebuchadrezzar's day were also absorbed into the Babylonian population, or at least remained behind in Mesopotamia. The Palestinian Jews of the post-exilic period were therefore indeed a small remnant of the whole nation,* and besides those in Babylonia there were others in Egypt, and these latter learned to speak the *koinē* Greek of Alexander's empire, translated their sacred books into the same language and lived a separate life from those in their home country. Thus there grew up two distinct sections of the Jewish people, those who lived in Palestine and those who lived outside it, and these latter became more and more assimilated to the particular country where they happened to live, so that whereas in the first century A.D. there were Greek-speaking and Latin-speaking Jews, and also Babylonian Jews, by the Middle Ages there were Spanish and German and Polish Jews, just as today there are British and American Jews. Members of the dispersion have in the past been

* I regret having to omit the story of the Maccabaean revolt against Antiochus IV (the 'Nebuchadrezzar' of the book of Daniel) and of the life of Jews in the period after the Alexandrian conquests, but for this readers may be referred to Dr Charles's *Between the Old and New Testaments*, and to Prof. Gwatkin's essay in Peake's *Bible Commentary*, pages 607–611.

encouraged to live not more than ninety days' journey from Jerusalem, and with this went the obligation up to the year A.D. 70 to pay a tax of half a shekel annually towards the up-keep of the Jerusalem temple, and to visit it for the Passover every year if possible. But these ties came to an end after the destruction of the temple by Titus, and many have tended to lose interest in the fortunes of the Jews' religion after this point.

It must, indeed, be admitted that the enthusiasm for pros-elytizing passed over into the ranks of the Christians, and that the Jews themselves became introverted and more like the citizens of a besieged city, especially when, after the rise of the Christian Church to a position of dominance in Europe, they were treated with something of the severity with which in the second century they had treated the Christians in (for ex-ample) Smyrna, Ephesus and Lyons. But two blacks do not make a white, and the persecution of the Jews is one of the re-proaches of the Christian Church, and a sin for which many Christians today are showing a genuine if tardy repentance. Religious animosity was in the Middle Ages mingled with anti-Semitic nationalism, and Jews had to wear a distinctive hat and badge, and live segregated in ghettos. In the supposed interests of English life Edward I in 1290 expelled 15,000 Jews from his realm. The French kings in 1394 also expelled thou-sands similarly from theirs, and the Spanish government, ap-parently with the slogan, 'Spain for the 100% Spaniard', in 1492 massacred vast numbers of Jews or drove them out from the Iberian peninsula. It is indeed estimated that 200,000 to 400,000 left that country. The modern German attack is there-fore no new thing, but only a particular instance of a general tendency which is reflected in the pages of the rather unhis-torical book of Esther. In the Middle Ages the Jews were toler-ated in parts of Germany only on condition that they and all their belongings became virtually the chattels of the Holy Roman Emperor, to be used as and when it suited him. Life grew so unbearable for these German Jews that they in many cases migrated into Poland, where they became numerous, and returned to the Reich in appreciable numbers both before and after the setting up of the Weimar republic. In the seventeenth and eighteenth centuries such Jews as remained in Germany were roughly treated, and it is not as well known as it should be that Karl Marx and his family received baptism not from conviction but to save them from cruelty, and Marx's bitterness against Christians is largely to be traced to his early experiences.

From these sad events it is a relief to pass to some of the brighter features of later Jewish history, which serve to show that it was not entirely barren. Although in a sense a certain narrowing and petrification descends upon the faith of the Hebrew people after it had fructified in the immense product of the Christian movement, yet it would be unjust to ignore certain features of Jewish life, and certain illustrious names, whose bearers wielded an influence far outside the limits of their nation.

What kind of religion is it which during the Middle Ages and even earlier gradually takes shape as characteristic of Jews? and what kind of character is it which they admire? The answer is that the Jewish religion becomes a patient and legalistic piety, and the hero of it is the suffering righteous man, perhaps typified by the figure of Tobit (familiar to those who have see the play by James Bridie, even if they have not read the Apocrypha). The careful and even meticulous observance of the Torah or law is accompanied by daily and weekly devotions, and by the keeping of certain great fasts and festivals. These, after centuries, are invested with a holiness and mellowed dignity such as belongs to some ancient gothic church, and are treasured as part of the spiritual tradition of the nation, which gives to those who observe them faithfully the air of a spiritual aristocracy. Observant Jews have something of the conservative exclusiveness and dignified culture which also belong to members of old practising Roman Catholic families, and their liturgy embodies much which plainly developed in earlier centuries into parts of the Christian liturgy, and also hymns and prayers which, although much later in date than the apostolic age (or perhaps for that very reason), breathe a high standard of theistic devotion. Indeed, except for occasional lapses into nationalism, many of the prayers might be used by any theist who did not own specifically the Divinity of Christ. There is no sacrificial element, now that the temple services are ended, as it would seem, for ever; but the principal acts of worship are (1) the daily morning service, which includes the two hymns Yigdal and Adon Olam (both medieval, and the former based upon what is called the creed of Maimonides), (2) the services for the Sabbath, including the reading of the law, and six devotions, two, Kiddush and Maarib, for the eve of the Sabbath and four for the day itself, (3) services for the seven Festivals and finally (4) the service for the day of Atonement. Space forbids a full exposition of all these, but perhaps the most interesting features of them are (a) the general resemblance in structure between the daily morning service and the morning and evening prayer of the Anglican Church, and (b) the resemblance of Kiddush to the Eucharist. Of course in the daily service the actual prayers are different, but the sequence of the devotions is very similar. First comes the Introduction or Preparation, then the Praise, then the reciting of the Shema and the Shemoneh 'Esreh, then the Tachanunim or series of petitions for grace, then the Reading of the Law (on Mondays and Thursdays), and finally the concluding section, which comprises the singing of another hymn and a psalm, the recital of the ten Commandments and Thirteen Principles of Faith, and the reading of two stories (i) Abraham's sacrifice, (ii) the gift of the manna to the Israelites and a prayer for sustenance. We have here, as will be seen, a non-sacrificial service with a fairly quick change from one devotional type of exercise to another. The inauguration of the Sabbath seems to have been a domestic service long before the beginning of the Christian era, and continued so for many centuries, and indeed is still a home service; and the synagogue service of inauguration is not older than the end of the sixteenth century A.D. This domestic ceremony begins with the lighting of two candles by the woman of the house, to symbolize the joy at the approach of the festival which is the woman's privilege to proclaim. Then comes the 'Kiddush' or sanctification of the day, said by the head of the household. This is not simply a prayer, but a prayer uttered over bread and wine, at the ordinary meal. There is evidence that this little service might be said at Passover time a day early, so as not to clash with the Seder or Passover service proper. It is thought likely, therefore, that Jesus and His disciples celebrated it in this way, and that the subsequent confusion of what happened with Seder itself is due in the first instance to the obvious fact that in the house of Mark's mother, where they met, there was no Seder that year, owing to the anguish and disorder caused by the arrest of Jesus. The Eucharist is thus not something which happened only once, but the last of many celebrations of Kiddush in which Jesus and the Chaburah or brotherhood of His disciples took part, and on the occasion He took opportunity to say something which not only gave it a new significance, but apparently made it a regular and continuous custom for the new community which sprang out of His Passion and Resurrection.

The principal Jewish festivals are Passover or Pesach, Pentecost or Shevuoth and Tabernacles or Succoth, but there are other minor ones such as Purim. On the eve of these the service is similar to that for the eve of a Sabbath, but shorter. The other services are as on the Sabbath except for certain additional acts of praise proper to the special occasion.

Fast days are of two sorts: special ones appointed in com-memoration of some important occasion or of some tragic event such as the destruction of the Temple in A.D. 70, and general ones such as the penitential season of ten days at the beginning of the New Year, which culminates with the Day of Atonement.

All these various devotions have left their mark upon Christian forms and methods of worship, and more is perhaps owed to them than to Gentile liturgical forms, though litanies and manual acts in Christian public worship show signs of modelling upon pagan temple practice. Just as in Christian and in Moslem tradition (as we shall see later), so in Judaism the repetition of certain well-worn devotional formulas is prescribed in order to mould character. The two chief ones in this case are the Shema, 'Hear O Israel, the Lord our God, the Lord is One', and the Eighteen Benedictions or Shemoneh 'Esreh, a long series of blessings which has undergone revision and additions during the centuries, but which may in embryo go back to about 175 years or more before Christ. It will be observed that the Catholic practice of having a fixed liturgical framework, with variable matter adjusted according to the season, is already in operation in Judaism.

To sum up; the orthodox Jew, especially in Eastern Europe, has a belief in God which consists largely in an assent to the mathematical unity of the Godhead. He is not greatly conscious of sin or shortcoming, and really believes that it is possible to keep the law correctly from one's youth up. In the place of sacrifice he has erected a system of merit, and from the days of the first-century Rabbis he has practised casuistry seriously, and has probably transmitted this also to the heritage of Catholic Christians. He still thinks of his race as the Chosen People. None of these remarks would be true of the more Liberal Jews, of whom there are a great many in Anglo-Saxon countries. Some of these are almost Christians in a latitudinarian sense, and some are philosophical theists. Some are agnostics, and even anti-theistic, and among these we may reckon the many Jews who have turned Marxist.

But we must not forget that in the Middle Ages, before the great expulsions, there were Jews who might have been called Liberal, and who not only lived on friendly terms with their Christian neighbours, but also exercised no small influence upon Christian thought. Of such was Ibn Gabirol (1021-70), who in his day was one of the leading authorities in Europe upon Greek philosophy, and was indeed appreciated more by Christian than by Jewish scholars, so that the medieval schoolmen are indebted to him for much which appears in their pages. Another was Moses Maimonides (1135-1204), probably the greatest of all medieval Jews. Not only is he the author of the two famous hymns which are used in the daily morning service, but he was also a prolific writer, seeking among other things to spiritualize the secrets of the Old Testament on the lines of Alexandrian allegory, as had previously been done by the famous Jew Philo (20 B.C.). Maimonides by his vigorous treatment set aside traditional Rabbinism, and Dr Box has observed that in spite of being condemned and publicly burned, the works of Maimonides have received more and more recognition, and that is probably true that today no serious Jewish theologian would dispense with them. The influence of Maimonides extended outside the boundaries of Jewry, and is traceable in the writings of so great a Christian theologian as St Thomas Aquinas, as well as in those of Albert of Cologne, who actually incorporated whole sections of Maimonides in his works. It is further important to recognize the influence of another distinguished Jew of a much later date, Spinoza the Dutch philosopher (1622-1677), who is on the one hand still described by his old epithet of 'the god-intoxicated man', and on the other hailed by Plekhanov as the father of modern dialectical materialism.

So he may be, but the modern dialectical materialist says that Plekhanov went too far in calling Marxism a sort of Spinozism, since he holds that although the work of Spinoza in its entirety finally forced him to embrace a materialistic conception of substance, Spinoza's use of the term 'nature' denotes nature in the narrower meaning of the word, as tangible matter, opposed to thought and consciousness; and therefore Spinoza, in repudiating the equation of God and Nature, as he does in his letter to Oldenburg (the Secretary of the Royal Society in his day), is really using the word in its narrower sense, and not, as in the Theologico-Political Tract, as Nature in its entirety, The Whole, or The Super-Universe, or The Absolute. And so they say that this undoubtedly most religious Jew is a metaphysical pantheist, and can be used by communist philosophers only when stripped of his theological terminology.

Here we must leave the Hebrews, conscious that many topics have not been adequately dealt with, notably their legal casuistry in the interpretation of the Torah, the religious aspects of Zionism and the development of Jewish mysticism. The former two must remain untreated, but the latter we can best consider briefly when we come to survey mysticism as a whole.

CHRISTIANITY

In a short survey such as the present one it would be painfully easy to fail to treat with justice the great religious system which today covers so large a part of the planet. In the endeavour to avoid such injustice, let us try to consider the subject under certain clear heads.

(1) Origin and earliest developments.
(2) Phases, up to the present day.

In considering these we shall also be able to ascertain the

nature of Christian belief, since it is indisputable that it is of a rich variety, and has been subject to evolution. Christianity is in fact a huge organism, quite as much as Buddhism or Islam.

Origin and Earliest Developments

Looking back over the past 180 years, we can now see that the earlier investigators of the New Testament were mistaken in supposing that the Christian movement began with the activity of a teacher like Socrates or Confucius, owed its remarkable success to his didactic ability, and was at a later date perverted into a mystery-cult with a divine cult-hero. It is now plain from the analysis of the documents that even during his life-time there was never a point when it could be said with certainty that the Gospel was purely an announcement made *by* Jesus, and not also an announcement *about* Jesus. Both elements are always present. True, in the earlier part of the public ministry, prior to the famous conversation with Peter at Caesarea Philippi, the first is more evident than the second, and in the later half of the ministry what is called the 'Messianic self-consciousness' of Jesus does seem to develop more than in the earlier half. But nowhere in the earlier half can we say definitely that it is wholly absent.

It is also plain from the analysis of the documents that the surprising initial success of the Christian movement was due to the announcement of the career of Jesus by the apostles as a supreme Act of God. Jesus himself is undoubtedly recognized as a genuinely historical character, a genuinely historical human being. But not a single one of his followers ever dreams of talking about him as though he were just an exceptional Jewish rabbi, of the same species as Gamaliel or Johanan ben Zakk'ai, only more distinguished. Though addressed as 'rabbi', he is always reckoned as something more, just as John the Baptist is 'more than a prophet'. However the fact may be accounted for – as mistake or as insight – Jesus stands isolated, and, there was no interval of oral tradition in which for the time being he occupied a lower place. The primary impression is that from the first he is felt to stand simultaneously on both sides of the gulf separating Creator and creaturely; and this impression is prior to, and is not dependent upon, the subsequent circulation of accounts of an alleged miraculous birth, or of a series of nature-miracles. These were held credible and congruous only because of a previous impression. If the latter was due to a mistake then it was a very great mistake, since upon it has been built the entire edifice of Christianity. In a scientific treatise this is perhaps the limit of what may rightly be said. When, however, the expansion and effects of the Christian movement are taken into account, the overwhelming probability remains that in some way or other the original disciples were correct in their estimate, but that neither they nor their successors have yet been able to express that estimate in a formula wholly satisfying to a world biologically re-knit, geologically re-surveyed and astronomically intimidated. Even now the Christian movement is relatively very young, for it is not more than about sixty-six generations away from its founder, and this, compared with the age of the earth or of the human race, is a very short period. It is also evident that ideas about incarnation, and doctrines about man held elsewhere than in Christendom, throw some light upon the value which has been set upon the human Jesus.

Any attempt at a brief summary of the earthly career of Jesus of Nazareth is bound to lead to criticism from both the conservative and radical directions. Taking a middle course, it may be described as follows. So far as we can tell, he was born some six years earlier than the date which Christian tradition had chosen to fix as the first year of its era, and the year of the crucifixion was probably A.D. 29, that is to say when he was in his thirty-fifth year. If we may believe the so-called infancy sections of the canonical gospels, which from their sober and restrained dignity command attention, he was actually born at a small village outside Jerusalem called Bethlehem (literally bakehouse*), where his parents happened to be lodged during the taking of a census. There seems no reason for doubting that, although poor Jews, they were in some way connected with the royal family of their nation, and the birth may very well have taken place in the yard of a caravanserai. The stories of the magi, of the shepherds and of the massacre of the children, as well as the flight into Egypt, may easily contain a substratum of fact, although they may also have been shaped in the course of telling to fit the demands of proof-texts. The well-known north Palestinian town of Nazareth seems to have been the final home of the family, though Capernaum is also spoken of as 'his own city'. Joseph is described as a *tektôn*, which has been rendered 'carpenter and builder', not simply 'joiner'. There is no special reason for doubting the truth of the story of the visit to Jerusalem when the boy Jesus was of the age of twelve. It is too much like the reminiscence of a bright and (as we might say) intelligent lad to be summarily dismissed. After that we have to confess to an entire absence of information until he has nearly reached the age of thirty.

Something may be said for the benefit of British and American readers about the effect of comparative studies in recent years upon our study and appreciation of the Christian gospels.

It has been found increasingly fruitful to recall that the Christian movement originated on the Asian side of the Aegean, and that even though Jesus and his disciples may have been bi-lingual, it was probably in an Asian tongue and to Asians that the message first came. Many sayings and episodes in the New Testament are better understood if we realize their

---

* Though Dr S. A. Cook informs me that a god Lahamu has been suggested. Beth-lahamu=house (or temple) of L. *Cf.* Bethel=Temple of El.

background. Thus the saying in Mark ix. 17 is rendered in the (Peshitta) Syriac version 'my son hath a roof-demon'. This Syriac is of course not the original text, but a translation from the Greek, but it fairly well reproduces the kind of idiom in which the Palestinian peasants expressed themselves, and in the Middle and Far East the roof-demon has been a well-recognized bogey, who is believed to slide down over the eaves into children's sleeping quarters and to afflict them with convulsive ailments. Again, the episode at Cana in Galilee is much better understood when we realize that in the Middle East in Christ's day there were temples, mostly connected with the cult of Dionysus, where it was popularly believed that the god on a certain festival occasion caused the fount of water in the temple to flow with wine. Pausanias, in his curious 'Baedeker guide' for Greek tourists mentions temples where he says this was believed to happen, and I myself found traces of the same belief at temples both at Jerash in Jordan (the Gerasa of the Bible) and at Leptis Magna in North Africa. The intelligent reader of the Fourth Gospel would be expected to understand the allusion, and to infer, whatever we may suppose to have happened at Cana, that 'a greater than Dionysus is here'. And again: Professor Widengren of Upsala has recently drawn attention to a ceremony which took place in connexion with the ruler-worship of one of the small Syrian states. Here the king on an appointed day was ceremonially robed in a silver garment, and at dawn stood or sat on a raised dais where the rays of the rising sun could 'transfigure' him (the Greek word used is the same which is applied to Jesus in the story in the gospels in Mark ix. 2). The king then made an oration to the assembled congregation and was acclaimed with divine honours as the epiphany or incarnation of the sun-god. (Readers may recall the passage in Acts xii. 21.) Any intelligent reader of the Marcan story in the end of the first century would at once see that the evangelist intended to imply: 'Here is something far nobler than your faked and staged epiphanies of petty Levantine princelings such as Herod. This is the real thing – the King of kings coming into his own.' And once more: all the references to feet-washing in the New Testament are seen in much better perspective if we realize that they are the normal part of etiquette in matter of hospitality among Asians who habitually wear sandals or go barefoot in a hot and dusty milieu. I have myself a photograph, taken in India, of a *guru* or holy man having his feet washed by his disciples, and a Presbyterian missionary some time ago actually recorded that he had seen an Indian woman after washing the feet of a guest, stoop down and ceremonially wipe them with her long hair as an act of courtesy. Instances of this sort could easily be multiplied, and they do not need that their implications should be stressed.

The beginnings of the birth story are believed to be known. The evidence from the great scholar Origen, in his controversy with the pagan Celsus, is that the text of Mark vi. 2 was originally 'Is not this the son of the carpenter?' The two genealogies given in the synoptic gospels, though differing in details, both agree in attempting to prove the Davidic descent of Jesus, and they are therefore genealogies of Joseph, who is actually referred to in Matthew i. 20 as 'thou son of David' (cf. also Luke i. 32, ii. 4, i. 69 and iii. 31). It is thought that the story of the Virgin Birth appeared as an article of belief after the year A.D. 70, and by A.D. 150 had replaced the earlier view, with a few exceptions. The development of a malicious Jewish report that Jesus was the illegitimate son of Mary and a Roman soldier appears about the same time, and is evidently a counterblast from the Jewish side, since it is not heard of earlier, and is not mentioned in the synoptic gospels, though there may be a covert reference to it in the fourth gospel (viii. 41) which is datable about A.D. 100. The doctrine of the Virgin Birth had great apologetic value, and not only harmonized with the pre-suppositions of the pagan world,* but served as a most useful weapon against those orientals who taught that the historical Jesus was merely a ghostly 'appearance' or emanation from the Prime Mystery, and not a real man at all. But belief in the reality of the Incarnation is not dependent upon the doctrine, even if it be true that the unique birth is congruous with it, and radical views have been stated by two Anglicans, the late Professor J. M. Creed and Dr H. D. A. Major, who both hold that the record of a birth in full wedlock had been changed by about A.D. 70 into the record of a Virgin Birth, and that the evidence from the New Testament in Romans i. 3 – earlier than any synoptic gospel, Hebrews vii. 14, Revelation xxii. 16, John i. 45 and vi. 42, and various synoptic passages in which Jesus is addressed as 'Son of David', and Joseph and Mary are spoken of as 'his parents', support this belief. Against this must be set the probability that the old Roman Creed is very early in its original form, and that the Virgin Birth is affirmed in it; and it is not unfair to press the point, as the orthodox do, that so unique a person as Jesus may well have had a unique beginning to his earthly career. But the radicals go further still, and suggest that the original form of the birth story was that Jesus, like Isaac, was a 'child of Promise', and that Joseph and Mary may well have had some special spiritual experiences in connexion with the conception and birth of their first-born,† which have got attracted into the form of a story similar to those current in non-Christian

---

* Both Merlin, the legendary British magician, and Plato were reputed virgin-born by many. Plato was sometimes described as the off-spring of Apollo by a woman. Philo thus refers to Zipporah: 'When Moses took her to himself, he discovered she was pregnant, but not by mortal man.' (See Lietzmann, *Ch. Hist.*, vol. 2, p. 153, E.T.)

† The Matthaean story purports to come from Joseph, the Lucan from Mary, and it seems captious to deny the possibility of some such origin for each.

circles, though much purer and more dignified. There is therefore, according to this view, a substratum of real spiritual truth in the birth of Jesus as a discontinuous Act of God, even though it may have subsequently received a somewhat materialistic transformation. The radicals also think it possible that the original birth took place at Nazareth, which is called (Luke iv. 23) the *patris* of Jesus, and that the association with Bethlehem is due either to the connexion of Joseph with it, or to the influence of the prophecy in Micah v. 2. It is significant that in the report of the Doctrinal Commission appointed in 1922 by the Archbishop of Canterbury, which appeared after lengthy deliberations in 1938, and therefore, on account of the European crisis, was overlooked by the public, the following sentences occur:

'There are some among us who hold that full belief in the historical Incarnation is more consistent with the supposition that our Lord's birth took place under the normal conditions of human generation. In their minds the notion of a Virgin Birth tends to mar the completeness of the belief that in the Incarnation God revealed Himself at every point in and through human nature,' and: 'We also recognize that both these views, i.e. the latter and also the older traditional one, are held by members of the Church, as of the Commission, who fully accept the reality of Our Lord's Incarnation, which is the central truth of the Christian faith.'

Physically we know little about Jesus. The gospels refer to his commanding presence and to the effect of his eyes, when fixed upon people. But it is impossible to feel sure that the various reputed likenesses have any resemblance to the original. The earliest portraits of Peter and Paul are strongly characterized in the second-century catacomb paintings, where the former is represented as having a rough rounded grey beard and shaggy head, and the latter as bald, with a black pointed beard. But the earliest figures of the Good Shepherd are beardless and idealized – sometimes of the Orpheus, sometimes of the Apollo, type: no portraiture can have been intended. Later pictures may be assimilations to the Zeus or Dionysus type.* There is, however, some reason to believe that certain representations of the bearded Christ, copied by an artist from catacomb paintings since destroyed, and now in the British Museum, are not forgeries but fair reproductions of a much more primitive attempt at portraiture, and that so steady and uniform a tradition must have had some foundation. In earlier times than St John Damascene (c. 730) there were two schools of opinion, the one based upon the text in Psalm 45 ('thou art fairer than the children of men') the other on Isaiah 53 ('there is no beauty that we should desire him'). But St John Damascene says that his beard was slightly forked, but not long, his hair with a parting down the middle, his face oval, his eyes bright, his complexion olive-tinted, his attitude slightly stooping. The descriptions which represent him as a hunchback look suspiciously like malicious inventions. There is no sound textual evidence to support them. Like much else in the Slavonic Josephus, they seem to be interpolations in the text of that author which are unknown to any commentator on it earlier than the time of the first Crusade, and certainly to hostile critics of Christianity, such as Celsus in the second century, who if they had known of them would certainly have not failed to make use of them.

It is a serious misjudgement to say that Jesus grew up in isolation from the civilized world of his day.† It is incredible that

---

* Professor A. B. Cook considers that the great statue of Zeus Olympius, by Pheidias, 'stupendously noble, and dignified in its moral grandeur' – it carried no thunderbolt, and suggested the rule of righteousness rather than of violence – though destroyed in A.D. 462, must have influenced the artistic conception of Deity in general, and of the historical Jesus in particular, as Deity incarnate.

† Readers may find a development of this theme in my *Everyday Life in New Testament Times* (Batsford).

he should have known nothing of the Gentile atmosphere or the Greek colonies of Decapolis (Tentowns), no great distance from Capernaum, or that between the ages of twelve and twenty-nine he never visited Jerusalem, with its relatively complex society. It has been pointed out that important caravan routes ran near Nazareth, and that no observant person could fail to have gleaned much information therefrom regarding 'all the kingdoms of the world and the glory of them'.

The actual duration of the public ministry is doubtful. Probably it lasted rather less than two years. There was a period of activity covering some twelve months, ending about the time of the Passover with a group of events associated with the feeding of the multitude, and a second period of about nine months, spent mostly in retirement, and ending with a final journey to Jerusalem at the beginning of the month of April. Just before this journey occurs the confession of Peter at Caesarea Philippi, in which he declares that Jesus is, in some sense that is not specified, the Messiah. This is the turning point in the ministry. Jesus accepts the statement, but with qualifications. It is no sign of an unbalanced mind that he does so, for his contemporaries were expecting a conquering hero to appear, and he rejects totally the role of a military Messiah, and thereby forfeits the support of many otherwise friendly disciples. He will set up no Empire of the East. His transfiguration in fact is real. Not only is he now isolated from the greater number of observant Jews, but he has also alienated the more fiery nationalist patriots. He has chosen the larger mission, the founding of a Kingdom that is not of this world, but is nevertheless, like the Kingdom of Daniel's Man (Dan. vii), world-wide. And in the end he comes to see that this Kingdom cannot be realized unless he is willing to embody in his own person the ideal of the Suffering Servant (hitherto held to be represented by the nation of Israel) and give his life a deliverance for many. Readers must turn to the many good books written in recent years which give in greater detail both the teaching and the earthly career of Jesus;* there is no further space for them here. In any case the so-called Sermon on the Mount, the parables and the occasional sayings are familiar, and easily accessible, and careful study of them will reveal that Jesus did not merely reproduce current Judaism, but 'fulfilled' it in accordance with his own claim, displaying at the lowest estimate supreme original genius, and constructive transformation of his material. It must suffice to say that it is no longer profitable to expound the teaching as though the Teacher were a mid-Victorian Liberal. Jesus is always less a teacher than someone who acts. It is the coincidence of the teaching with the personality and the career which gives it its poignancy, and also its authority.

The story of the arrest and execution is too well known to need repetition. There was no rescue. The sentence was carried out, and the movement apparently crushed. At the end of the first Good Friday there remained perhaps one completely loyal Christian in the world, and he apparently dead. It was remembered that on the cross he had been heard reciting the 22nd Psalm, and the strange words of the colloquy between the martyr and his God were honestly reported (with all the embarrassment which they involved, unless it is remembered that like the 40th Psalm, which seems also to have been in his mind, the 22nd ends with a paean of triumph).

For the rest, I must be allowed to repeat without comment what I have written elsewhere, on the understanding that it represents what Christians say about themselves and their creed. Others may, if they will, hesitate to take the leap of faith which it requires, and in a scientific manual it is no part of the author's business to demand assent, or to disparage disagreement.

Christians observe that to believe that Jesus was a failure

* See Bibliography.

leads nowhere. The Kingdom obviously did come in. Indeed, so gross, so petty, even superstitious and wrong-headed were many of the blundering attempts to explain the significance of Jesus for the world, that to the impartial observer the one and only perfectly attested miracle (in the old-fashioned sense) must seem the fact of the vital and active existence of the Christian movement in the world today. This fact is due less to secondary circumstances of a political nature than to the attraction of Jesus for the hearts of men, and to the sense that at the supreme crisis in his career he won through and emerged victorious, and that that victory, in whatever terms it is described, was the culmination of a supreme Act of God in which Jesus purposefully chose his part, and not a mere martyrdom which was forced upon him. By what kind of 'certificate' this conviction established itself, opinions are bound to differ. The conservative view is that the living Jesus rose bodily from the tomb, which was thus rendered empty, and that his physical integument was wonderfully and suddenly transformed. Others will say that we can have no certain knowledge as to the fate of that integument, but that from it there issued (as from a slough) a new and glorified and wholly spiritual Jesus, whose Presence has never since departed from the commonwealth of his followers, but who is known and felt by them in daily and hourly intercourse. To these latter the experiences commonly called 'Resurrection appearances', the Ascension, the conversion of St Paul, the visions of the saints (such as Pascal, Marie Lataste, the Sadhu Sundar Singh, &c.) and the intimate communions of ordinary everyday Christians are all equally authentic, veridical *and mental*; and they point out that the earliest documentary evidence for the risen and living Jesus makes no reference at all to the empty tomb. Here again the Anglican doctrinal commission had a word to say which affects all English-speaking Christians at any rate:

'If a general principle is to be laid down, we may say that Christian faith is compatible with all such critical reconstructions of the events underlying the narrative (of what happened at the first Easter) as would not have the effect, if accepted, of invalidating the apostolic testimony to Jesus as the Lord who rose from the dead. To speak more positively, we are of opinion that it ought to be affirmed that Jesus was veritably alive and victorious; that he showed himself alive from the dead to his disciples; and that the fact of his rising, however explained (and it involves probably an element beyond our understanding) is to be understood as an event as real and concrete as the crucifixion (which it reversed) and an act of God, wholly unique in human history.'

Cautious as such statements are, they constitute a charter for wise and reverent but essentially liberal thought about the fundamentals of Christianity.

There are two modes of regarding Christianity as to its origin: (a) The appearance to an outsider, (b) the account it gave of itself. *To an outsider* the chief factor would have seemed the Jewish diaspora or dispersion. Any new religious movement springing up among Jews stood an excellent chance of spreading itself, since in almost every centre of Mediterranean and Gallican population there were at least small communities of observant Jews, who from time to time re-visited their mother-city, and who had contacts with other Jews. About the year A.D. 29 a new religious movement did begin. At first it was purely Palestinian, but very soon it attracted adherents from the diaspora, and spread to Antioch in Syria. This city became a base for propaganda, and, under the enthusiastic leadership of a bilingual Jew of Tarsus, the new movement travelled westward through Asia Minor, crossed, like other Oriental cults, into Europe and eventually reached Italy, Gaul and Spain. Our outsider would have noticed that after A.D. 70 it became predominantly non-Jewish, mainly, it would seem, because Jewish interests were so largely centred round a political deliverer that the notion of a purely religious Messiah failed to appeal, but also, perhaps, because the unique position claimed for the founder conflicted with the stricter Jewish monotheism, while an association with Goyim in fellowship and worship was repugnant to Jewish nationalists. Thus in the second century A.D. the Jews appear as the bitterest enemies of the Christians, and an unhappy feud began which has prevailed with sinister results on both sides to this very day.

What the outsider saw, however, as we learn from Pliny's famous letter (A.D. 110), was the quiet but rather rapid growth of a movement, with many branches, which, instead of spending its religious emotion upon some semi-mythical figure such as Dionysus, directed it upon the historical Jesus with a devotion recalling the Bhakti of India (though not Jesus as he walked in Galilee, but Jesus as he is described in Revelation 1, i.e. a glorious figure, more like an epiphany of Apollo), and pledged iself to a life of ethical probity in his service, crowning all with a simple communion meal of a type similar to Jews and Gentiles alike. Since in some senses the Roman Empire was a totalitarian State, this was disturbing to the outsider, for the Christian asked no leave of the Government to engage in his worship, and would have nothing whatever to do with the official Imperial religion, with its cultus of Caesar, of Dea Roma, and so on. He was every whit as exclusive as a Jew, but, as it seemed to the Roman official, without a Jew's excuse; and it must be borne in mind that the *good* Roman was just as serious about his own religion as the Christian.

What, then, was *the account which the movement gave of itself*? First of all it claimed to be the complete and legitimate heir of Jewish monotheism, and insisted that what had hitherto been the property of one small nation was now to be the common world-religion for all time. It thus took up the missionary propaganda of the Diaspora, and carried it further, with the greatest enthusiasm, and, as it seemed, with a much more impressive technique. Second, it claimed that, although the entire universe was the self-expression of the One Good God, the highest single piece of self-expression for dwellers on this plane was to be found in the total career of Jesus, *past, present and future*. It claimed, so to speak, 'the Christianity of Deity'. It was from the first what Kagawa has called it today, 'the Jesus-religion', and the quasi-sacrificial death and alleged resurrection appearances of Jesus were the culmination of its announcement. It treated Jesus as fully human,* incorporating in its sacred literature passages which spoke of him as 'a man that hath told you the truth', and 'a man approved of God among you', but it interpreted him in terms of Incarnation doctrine, capable of being placed in series with other incarnations, yet in quality and historicity unique, not merely a peak in human evolution, but a discontinuous once-for-all initiative of the Divine within the spatio-temporal order, and it called its announcement Good News, not so much a demand made by God, as something given by God to the human race which, if appropriated, must alter radically the tempo and quality of its life. Third, it affirmed, in common with other religions, that human life on earth is not devoid of significance, but has abiding consequences, for weal or woe, and it placed the judgement and decision upon each individual soul in the hands of the glorified Jesus, as being the image of the invisible God.

It therefore called upon all mankind without exception to become members of a new Koinonia or Fellowship, in which they might practise a new sort of life, and by which the world

---

* Even the Athanasian Creed, so-called, says that Jesus had a human soul as well as body, so that the Word of God acted *through* Him. As Dr Temple, late Archbishop of Canterbury, said in effect in his book *Christus Veritas*, 'Take away the action of the Word of God, and what we have left is *not* the body but the body-soul complex, the personality of Jesus of Nazareth the prophet'.

might be regenerated. This new life was to be inspired by what has been called 'Christ-mysticism', i.e. the communion of each individual with the One Good God through the personality of Christ. ('He that hath seen me hath seen the Father.') The above three claims it still makes today, and it claims further that its developed valuation of the historical Jesus is a *growing into* rather than a growing out of the truth – a true deduction and not a distortion.

Such a movement was bound of its very nature to be imperious and exclusive. As long as it did not stray from its Hebraic anchorage it was unlikely to make any compromise with the ethnic religions. Compromise began only after persecution ceased, and church membership became diluted by the influx of ex-pagans possessing no Hebraic background.

A proper scientific estimate of Christianity has been hindered by the convention of confining the study of it to the earlier centuries of its growth. Actually the only way in which to see it with justice is to see it as a whole right up to the present moment, with the arrow pointing forward. The reason for emphasizing this is that from about 1699 onwards (or if we include the Jesuit missions in Asia, from about 1520) an entirely new and unprecedented expansion of Christianity has taken place, and this expansion has been intensified since about the year 1800, so that today there are few areas on the planet where there are not at any rate *some* Christians, while large tracts of Africa and parts of Asia which 100 years ago were entirely non-Christian have now new, flourishing and actively expanding churches. The existence of large and influential Christian communities in the American continent must also be recognized.

Again, it is no exaggeration to say that the understanding of the essential Christian announcement is much clearer now than it was fifty years ago, and that at no time has the intellectual expression of that announcement in terms of current thought been completer than today, while the application of Christian principles to social service seems to have reached its maximum in some areas during the last 100 years, however lacking it may have been in others.

Against this must bet set the severe shrinkage due to the loss of ground by institutional Christianity in Russia and in Germany, and to a lesser degree in almost every country. The collapse must be contrasted, for the sake of fairness, with the collapse of Islam, say in Turkestan, which is very complete, and with the adaptability and resilience of even Western Christianity in new centres of population. But so rapid has been the change to the age of applied science, that all the institutions of religious life, non-Christian as much as Christian, have suffered from inability to keep pace with it.

Meanwhile it may help to a juster understanding of the whole position if we enumerate (2) *The phases through which Christianity has passed*. It began, as we have said, as a Jewish sect. There was a steadfast expectation that the humiliated and crucified Jesus would return in majesty to triumph over his enemies. This was expressed in the rather crude symbolism of Jewish apocalyptic, but there is no evidence that Jesus himself ever gave sanction to such expectations, though he certainly spoke of his return. Gradually the cruder apocalyptic belief faded, and was replaced by what is called the realization of eschatology,* the sense of the abiding Presence of the Living Jesus, and the sacramental communion with Him which frequent Eucharists afforded. That there would be a last judgement was not denied, but the interest in it receded into the background, except in times of crisis like the fall of the western Roman Empire. Many came to believe that for practical purposes Jesus had already returned or was constantly returning

---

* Professor C. H. Dodd stresses the apparent recognition of this 'realization of the time' by Jesus Himself in His own utterances as recorded in the Synoptic Gospels.

(where two or three were gathered together in his name), and stress became to be laid upon such texts as 'Lo I am with you always, even unto the end of the world', or upon the doctrine of the Real Presence in the Holy Communion. About the time of the first Jewish war in A.D. 70, or even a little earlier, the Christian movement passed into an obscure phase, from which it emerged, about the year A.D. 96, as predominantly and increasingly Gentile, an illegal religious association, enjoying local and periodic immunity, but always liable to suppression or attack at the hands of a conscientious provincial governor; and so it continued until A.D. 313. Then from the Emperor Constantine it received the fateful gifts of both toleration and privilege, and seventy years later it had become for weal or woe the dominant legal expression of religion inside the Roman Empire, while even that portion of it deemed unorthodox (because Arian) had come to exercise considerable influence among Goths and Vandals, and beyond the boundaries of the Empire there were native churches in Armenia and Georgia, and some Christians in Persia. During the period of the so-called barbarian invasions, the Church became the residuary legatee of Imperial culture, and suffered less from actual heathen than from unorthodox Teutonic invaders, since it converted the former, and gradually subjugated the latter. But from about A.D. 300 onwards the really serious feature is the growth of celibate asceticism within all parts of the Christian community. This has been attributed to several causes. The cessation of persecution encouraged efforts to compensate for its tonic effect by introducing a sterner self-discipline. Oriental life-negating influences, with special doctrines of the malignity of matter, and the consequent sinfulness of sex experience even in wedlock, no doubt contributed to the result. Passages were found in the Gospels which seemed to endorse and justify the abandonment of the married state. But most potent influence of all was the prevailing sense of the decline of society. Secular thought (taught by the Stoics) considered that the peak of excellence was passed, and that the world was perishing and running down and reaching its last end, and must arrive at zero before the next cycle could begin. Even then there would be only a dreary repetition of the past cycles. Taxation was heavy, and people ran away into the Egyptian desert to escape from it. The Graeco-Roman world was relatively nerveless and exhausted, and large families (or even children at all) seemed troublesome. But when people begin repressing their instinct to procreate they are asking for trouble; and the necessary self-tortures of the Christian ascetics and the tormenting sensual visions of the cloister and cave are the nemesis of those who are trying to lead an unnatural life. Of course many of the best monks and nuns sublimated their sex impulses by keeping themselves busy, either as agriculturalists, craftsmen, teachers or scholars and evangelists; and to these European life owes an incalculable debt. Sometimes it occurs also that a celibate is able to endure greater hardships and dangers than someone who has given hostages to fortune, and in certain cases the damming up and restraining of the sex-life have produced a nature of an altogether richer and more concentrated sort than would have been possible under other conditions. But it must be honestly admitted that the ascetic phase which set in after A.D. 300, and which endured unbroken until the time of Luther – and after that continues as an indispensable part of Catholic Christianity – is a phase which brings medieval Catholicism very close to Hinduism and Buddhism, far closer than many Christians are yet willing to recognize. Let anyone take a map of England (let alone the continent) and mark on it the sites of monastic ruins, and then date and classify the results, and obtain if he can from such books as Dr Coulton's* a record of the numbers of inmates in these houses in proportion to the population, and he will be

* Most recently those of Dom David Knowles.

startled to discover how different was the sort of Christianity from that of his own day, especially if he is what is called a 'Protestant'. It will no doubt astonish Londoners to know that documentary records show that in the Middle Ages almost every city church (and there were a great many – nearly one in every street) had attached to it its anchorite or anchoress, a solitary ascetic (probably with long hair and the characteristics of a fakir, especially in regard to self-torture), who was either vagrant or enclosed in a cell or 'ankerhold' built into the church wall. (One suspects that the eccentric figure of Solomon Eagle, the naked ascetic who went about the city during the time of the plague and fire in the reign of Charles II, was a solitary survival of these gruesome creatures.) There was no thought of a Christian planned society, only of ambulance work in a world already doomed; and the contemplative life was considered the noblest.

And then, with revolutionary force, came the phase of disruption, first in 1054 the severance of East from West, and then about 1520 the severance of Catholics from non-Catholics, whether Eastern or Western. This latter had its origin partly in the revival of the study of Greek free thinking, but also in the restoration of the study of Christian literature in the tongue in which it was first written, especially the writings of Paul, the bilingual Jew of Tarsus referred to previously. This remarkable man, whose letters to his converts began to be collected somewhere about A.D. 139, has through them exercised a unique influence upon Christian thought: Augustine the Great, Luther, Calvin and today Karl Barth being deeply indebted to him. He was indeed the first to think through the implications introduced by Christian belief. There were also forces of racial antagonism at work. The Catholic pattern of Christianity continued to persist either in unreformed Caesaropapal Russia (with more monks and nuns than ever), or in the countries subjugated by Islam, as a repressed sect, or in

Southern and parts of Central Europe, as a powerful and re-generated force, tardily but genuinely reformed. But in Britain (excluding southern Ireland), Scandinavia, Holland (till recently) and part of Germany, Christianity recreated it-self after simpler patterns upon the basis of new and different interpretations of vernacular Scripture. Yet the same circum-stances which brought about this appeal to documents and unbiased private judgement in the evaluation of Christianity also brought about a change in men's attitude to the external world and to the analysis of their own minds. They began to feel themselves free to experiment and explore, to classify and draw inferences, and even if necessary to make mistakes in the process. Copernican astronomy, the discovery of the New World, Greek free thought and the beginnings of empirical science all tended to turn men's minds away from other-worldly contemplation, and to encourage activist views of life.

Thus the next phase in the history of Christianity is a very confusing and perplexing one. The disrupted bodies were for the time fiercely intolerant of one another. They saw them-selves cloven apart over fundamentals, and sometimes the new forms of Christianity powerfully affected political ideology (as when Calvanism and Huguenotism seemed to lead straight to republican oligarchy and the overthrow of the divine right of kings). Passions swelled high, and blood sometimes flowed freely. But with the spread of rationalistic science and the approach of an age of reason rather than of emotion, the idea of mutual tolerance began to spread, and from the appearance of John Locke's *Letters on Toleration*, 1689–92, to the Roman Catholic Emancipation Act of 1829 there is, in Britain at any rate, a steady stream of development, and in the nineteenth century we see the almost complete abandonment of coercion by Christian bodies, and also the vast new missionary expan-sion previously referred to. Meanwhile the eighteenth century brought the development of literary criticism of the Christian scriptures, and especially of the Gospels, beginning in Germany and extending to other countries.

And so we enter the phase in which we live at present, one which has been labelled 'ecumenical'. Its main features are (i) efforts at federation, reunion or mutual understanding, (ii) continued expansion, (iii) renewed hostility by the world.

External danger has driven religious people, whether Christian or non-Christian, to consider whether the principles which unite them against a purely secular view of life are not perhaps greater than those which divide them. Yet the enemy is not precisely non-religion or anti-religion. At one time, no doubt, it seemed as though a line could be drawn between (let us say) theists and anti-God propagandists. Now, however, the proper distinction would seem to be between one sort of religion and another. Even then it would not be correct to divide into Christians and non-Christians, since in certain fundamental respects a Christian would find himself much more in sympathy with a Tibetan Buddhist than with a central European Fascist, though the latter might pay lip-service to the historical Jesus, wilfully misinterpreted. Or again, a Christian could not help feeling a considerable measure of agreement with a Communist of ex-Moslem Turkestan, where the collapse of the horrible government of the Emir of Bokhara has led to an emancipation of women and to a cleansing of society which are in complete harmony with the desires of progressive Christians.

Nevertheless, for our purpose, the main features of this period have been (i) the extensive growth of what has been called 'the new Christianity', with an art, a worship and even a literature of its own, and (ii) the numerous and never-ceasing efforts to look at Christianity as a common world-religion in a sense in which no other age has ever looked at it. A scientific observer must, of course, record the possibility that this specific instance of religion is no more destined to be the final world-faith than the League of Nations inaugurated in 1919 was destined to be the final form of the World-State. That is only fair. But he must certainly add that the ecumenical movement in Christianity has done more than anything which has preceded it in history (more even than Stoicism) to render familiar the idea of a common world-family of human beings, possessing in common a single spiritual creed. If Communism avows a similar ideal, it owes the origin of that ideal to its rival (or perhaps to the fact that Karl Marx was a Jew, standing on the shoulders of many generations of Jews who looked for some kind of realization of the Kingdom of God on earth). Never before, in spite of formidable opposition, have Christians thought more consistently or courageously about transforming the world, and never before have they shown so much enterprise in constructive works of loving-kindness. They are in the present decade suffering a severe setback. But it is not as great as that which they suffered in Europe during the Dark Ages, and it must be noted that the present setback is one which affects the security of much which is presupposed under the heading of natural religion and pre-Christian ethics – things which, even if Christianity were submerged, were thought at least to be safe. It now becomes evident that they are not safe, and that their fortunes are in some way or other bound up with those of the basic creed of Christianity.

To find a common formula for expressing the total activities of all types of Christian Church-community is not difficult, even in the case of the sects which renounce any connexion with the world of culture and are fundamentalist and adventist. It may be said that the objects which are aimed at are threefold:

(i) To bridge over the centuries which separate any individual soul today from the original experience of contact with the living Jesus. This embraces all devotional exercises, whether sacraments, Bible-reading, the delivery and hearing of sermons, or merely listening in silence.

(ii) To organize and unify the personality of the individual around the Living Person of Jesus, and where that process is hindered, or has been broken by rebellion or falling away, to restore and regenerate by inducing confession, and declaring the Divine forgiveness of the truly penitent.

(iii) To build up an habitual type of behaviour and to form a consistent character, in the fellowship of a community.

In nearly all cases there is also a fourth aim (absent perhaps from the smaller world-renouncing sects), which is of supreme importance.

(iv) To transform not merely individuals, but the whole structure of society, so as to express in its social, political and economic life, in its art, its recreation, and its science and philosophy, a sense of being God-centred and God-controlled, 'God' being interpreted as symbolized and expressed in and through the human character of Jesus.

Christians are bound to assume that by far the larger part of the life of their movement lies ahead of it; and they cannot wisely regard the past as for ever fixing its form.

They have a strong and firm belief in the continuance of the individual's conscious experience beyond the grave; but they are not officially tied to a detailed and precise forecast of it. Plainly 'the resurrection of the body' and 'a spiritual body' are phrases which commit the Christian to the continuance of recognizable personality in some form or other – what has been described picturesquely as 'further experiences of John Smith'. But this need not be materialistic, a mere resurrection of relics. Moreover, there is much to be said in favour of a belief in what has been called 'conditional immortality'. Abiding consequences, whether they be expressed as the antithesis between life and death or between heaven and hell, are certainly part of the Christian creed, held in common, be it noted, with other creeds. What, however, Christians can never allow is that individual souls whose virtue has been achieved at severe cost not only to themselves but to those who have loved them and trained them and agonized over their development – that these should at death merely be absorbed into the depths of a vague and featureless Infinite. They feel it is too much to ask them to believe *that*.*

If Christians are to be allowed to give their own account of themselves, the central position of the Cross in Christian belief must be explained. Suffering of some sort is a natural datum in human experience. It may either be submitted to as inscrutable (Islam), or regarded as the result of a wrong attitude to life (Buddhism), or accepted and conquered creatively as part of life's adventure (Christianity), or evaded as far as possible, after the manner of hedonists. But the last solution looks what it is – ignoble. The universe being the place we find it to be, the greater the aspiration to virtue, the greater the possibility of suffering. Thus the deliberate choice of the Cross by Jesus interprets the whole of life. No one without shirking can evade the possibility of his own Calvary, and readiness to accept that possibility is the condition of properly fulfilling one's vocation, as well as a large part of the spice of life. Thus the Christian says that the Cross, instead of being a regrettable flaw in the constitution of things, is actually the Will of God both for Himself and for all His creatures. Its cheerful acceptance is the secret of the art of life, and the only way to victorious living. Self-centredness is also a universal tendency in individual life. Even in the sub-human creation it may express

* Necromancy or spiritualism is still, in spite of its many adherents, a most debatable affair, and its alleged phenomena, where untainted with the suspicion of fraud, are often, though frankly not always, explicable as the results of E.S.P. (see p. 26).

itself as the will to survive biologically at all costs – as a para-
site or as a predatory super-animal. This will in itself is no
more evil than the 'cool self-love' of which Bishop Butler
speaks in one of his sermons. But its over-emphasis leads to a
nearer and narrower good being preferred to a higher, remoter and more ultimate good, and this exaggerated self-love
is what is called carnal freedom or more shortly 'sin' (German, '*Sünde*'), i.e. that which sunders or separates from fellowship with God.

The Christian doctrine of man is fundamental at this point.
Christians are committed officially to a very high belief in the
potential greatness of man. He is a little lower than God (Ps.
viii). He is made in the image of God (Gen. i.) The spirit of
man is the candle of the Lord (Prov. xx. 27). Yet Christians
are equally committed to the belief in man's utter need of
God. Man needs God. Man cannot be all that he ought to be,
or fulfil his grand possibilities, if he tries, as he so often does,
to be the artist of his own social and individual life – 'on his
own', so to speak – apart from the life of God. Even the fine
aspirations and endowments with which he begins are actually
what we call them, 'gifts'. We acknowledge this when we use
the ordinary hackneyed terms 'talents' and 'talented'. St
Paul's famous phrase (1 Cor. iv), 'What hast thou that thou
didst not receive?', is unanswerable. Yet man's disaster is that
he is always trying to be 'on his own'. His delegated and real
capacity for free action, though it is indispensable for the
highest grade of noble character, is nevertheless, by the very
reason that it *is* freedom, prone to misuse, and as a matter of
fact is continually being misused. Man is, like all living organisms, self-centred, but what in the sub-human creation is
less obviously harmful, in man becomes positively frightful.
Hence man needs rescue not from ignorance or from evanescence, but from sin, as previously defined.

Since we all at some time feel the urge to evade or rebel, or to make a narrower choice when faced with the issues of life, it is really true that the identification of ourselves with the Person of Jesus, who deliberately chose the Cross, does 'take away the sin of the world' by emptying us of the wrong impulse and filling us with new life. This 'new life' is what Christians mean by the rather hackneyed technical term 'grace'. And again, because Christians believe Jesus to stand on both sides of the gulf which divides the Creator from the creaturely, it is therefore fair to say, so they hold, that his choice not only reunites humanity in fellowship to God wherever human beings appropriate what he did by identifying themselves with him, but also makes reparation or *atonement* to the Divine standards of right and wrong wherever these have been violated by wrong human choices. Obviously the only adequate reparation for such violations could be made by God Himself, since humanity is found wanting. Hence humanity is in duty bound to assent to the Divine action, and to share in the reparation by repeated self-identification with it. It is this appropriation of and self-identification with the action of God in Jesus which is referred to when Protestants speak of 'justification by faith', and Catholics of 'assisting at Mass or the Eucharist', the latter being the dramatic representation of the Action of Calvary. Any who do not hold as a living reality the Hebraeo-Christian belief about the moral holiness of Deity will find this doctrine hard to follow. But it may be fairly claimed that if the *belief* is once assumed, the *doctrine* is a straightforward deduction from it.

The technique is not unlike that of Buddhism, where the disciple by habitual meditative exercises puts on Buddhahood and embraces the Buddha-life. But of course the ideal is different, for, as Iqbal Singh has pointed out, Gotama and Jesus are not really alike, but stand for two distinct modes of approaching Reality. For Jesus, Love is the last word on the nature of Reality. Gotama is concerned more, as Renan has said with 'la pensée pure'. Thus it is possible to accept or reject Gotama's doctrines on intellectual grounds, since they spring, as we have seen, from the fount of philosophical thought. But one cannot treat Jesus in this dispassionate and detached manner. One gets emotionally involved with him, and one must either love him or wrestle against him. This is the elucidation of the phenomena of men like Nietzsche and D. H. Lawrence, and it is involved in the Barthian statement that it is impossible to approach Christianity without what is called the risk of existential thinking, i.e. thinking in which one's very existence is challenged and called in question, and which cannot therefore be detached or dispassionate.

The Christian idea of prayer is so much misconceived that some attention must be paid to it.

The precise position which interests and even agitates the minds of most thoughtful people, especially in the present age, may be thus stated.

An essential feature of Christian God-belief is that it affirms what Gilbert Murray has called 'The Friend behind phenomena'. That is to say, it declares the Self-existent Being to be describable as the Wise, Loving, Holy and Supreme but Self-limited Parent. Communion and reconciliation with this Parent are considered to be the core of the life of every person who lives Christianly. But now comes the difficulty. Is it permissible to ask, or reasonable to expect, that the Wise Parent should direct or alter the course of events at our request? Most naïve religions have allowed their members to petition the gods or God for temporal blessings, and sometimes to bargain for them. Bargaining *is* perhaps excluded from Christianity, but petitionary prayer – is that allowed? Can we ask and expect that 'the Friend behind phenomena' will at our urgent plea save a country from military defeat or invasion, an army from destruction or a beloved friend or relative from death? The difficulty is an acute one: for if Jesus really taught that such prayer was right, and if it appears on ample evidence to be vain, then he is proved on a most vital spiritual issue to have been in error, and his authority is fatally diminished. No special pleading on his behalf can be of any avail. He shrinks to the dimensions of a kindly but mistaken prophet.

Let us examine the situation more closely.

First, it is quite certain that most of those persons who were included in the large-scale conversions to Christianity possessed a background of belief in naïve petitionary prayer for temporal blessings. They would therefore read into the sayings of Jesus an endorsement of their habits.

Second, the Gospel records as we have them show signs here and there of having been corrupted (at least unconsciously) in a sub-Christian direction. A good instance is the insertion of the word 'openly' in the text of Matthew vi. 6 after 'thy Father which seeth in secret shall reward thee'.

Now these two considerations make it necessary that in stating the teaching of Jesus about petitionary prayer we should confine ourselves only to the very few Logia which seem to give his teaching on this subject at first hand beyond a doubt.

(i) *The Lord's Prayer*. – Here there is a three-fold alignment with or surrender to the Divine will, followed by an apparent petition for 'daily bread' ... But the word translated 'daily', 'epiousion', though rendered probably in the Old Latin, 'quotidianum', i.e. 'daily', was *interpreted* at least as early as A.D. 235 as 'the Bread from Heaven'. (Cf. Tertullian: *De Oratione* ... '"our daily bread" is better rendered spiritually as meaning "give us day by day Christ our True Bread ... for He saith I am the Bread of Life."') In accordance with this, St Jerome, in revising the text for the Vulgate during the fourth century, put 'supersubstantialem' for 'quotidianum'. Here, then, is no request for material good, but an expressed desire that one may have the Mind of Christ in all one's daily dealings; and this is at any rate in harmony with the teaching of the Fourth Gospel, i.e. about A.D. 100, so it looks like a very primitive and stable tradition.

(ii) *The Gethsemane Prayer.* – 'Nevertheless not my will, but Thine, be done.' Comment here seems unnecessary.

(iii) *'Ask . . . in My Name'* (John xvi. 23, 24). The condition of a successful petition to the 'Friend behind phenomena' is here given. But it does not mean 'Use my name as a lever'. Such an interpretation, though common and conventional, is sub-Christian, and must be rejected. 'Ask in my name' can mean only 'Ask as *I* would ask . . . in *my* spirit, or according to *my* will'.

(iv) There is a fourth passage, in the Third Gospel, which cannot be placed on a level with these others on account of the Lucan tendency to the rewriting of sources. After speaking of fathers who do not give stones for bread or serpents for fish to children who ask for food, Jesus is represented as adding: 'If ye, then, being men of the world, know how to give good gifts to your children, how much rather shall your Heavenly Father give the Holy Spirit to them that ask Him.' Yet even here we may fairly say that the interpretation is likely to be correct, since the tendency is observable to equate 'the Holy Spirit' with 'the mind of Christ' (see Luke xi. 5–8).

The conclusion to be drawn from the exegesis of these passages is, as will be seen, somewhat startling. So far from Jesus having ever taught or practised petitionary prayer of the type 'O God, change things according to my will or needs', he appears to have both taught and practised the very opposite, and his exhortation 'Ask and ye shall have' must be interpreted accordingly in this sense. Moreover, Christian prayer includes much besides petition. Indeed, the latter is a mere fraction of all that is included under the heading of prayer. Adoration, confession, meditation, quiet, communion, listening, acts of will and surrender – all these are forms of prayer, but none of them is petitionary. Even when petition occurs, in its *Christian* form it is, or should be, shaped after the pattern of the words of the well-known hymn:

> Father, hear the prayer we offer:
> Not for ease that prayer shall be,
> But for strength that we may ever
> Live our lives courageously.

This involves the conclusion that a very considerable part of existing institutional Christian prayer and liturgy still lags at the sub-Christian level; and this is no mere opinion, but is based upon a scientific observation of the materials available. The prayer of many Christians has not yet reached habitually the level inculcated and practised by their Leader. At the same time it will generally be found that the most vital and arresting teachers of vocal and mental Christian prayer have expressed themselves correctly enough on the matter. The failing lies, then, rather in the sphere of popular practice than in that of the experts, though the latter may be blamed for not undertaking more earnestly the conversion of the public to their standpoint.

The development of the Hebrew nation into a church after the exile and return has left the church central also in Christianity. It is not that Jesus founded such a body, but that he merely expanded tacitly what already existed. St Paul describes the community of Christian believers as the body (*soma*) and the Fulness or fulfilment (*pleroma*) – that is, if the Epistle to the Ephesians be really his. But, whoever its author was, it correctly describes the position which the common-wealth of believers, the *koinonia*, had come to hold. It was indeed the new Israel, and it claimed to enter into the position previously occupied by the old narrowly ethnic Israel. Whatever the subsequent constitution and vicissitudes of this Church, it remains to this day true that the idea of an isolated Christian is a contradiction in terms. To make sure that one is not blinded here by denominational bias, let me end with some quotations from a new syllabus recently issued under the auspices of a County Education Committee for use in Council Schools, and written by a Free Churchman.

'The Christian religion is not vague religiosity, but a way of believing and living revealed in the concrete stuff of history, and mediated from generation to generation across the continents and the centuries in well-defined forms of thought and practice. Psychology has much to teach us, but Christianity claims to be altogether more than a little sanctified psychology. It is not a colourless and inoffensive piety to suit all tastes, but a Word of judgement, and forgiveness and blessing proceeding from a Person in history, to believe in whom is to believe in the living God ... Our religion is indefeasibly social ... all Christians know, irrespective of their denominational differences, that they cannot have for ever or for long the Christian experience of God without the divine society which is its necessary vehicle and abiding guarantee. The Christian life is not accidentally corporate; it is so by its very nature. "Catholics" and "Protestants" are alike aware that the evangelical experience of the saved soul is always ecclesiastical experience ... In short, Christianity as the universal fellowship of believers is not an "extra", a luxury for those who are gregariously inclined.'

The Church, as thus defined, cuts across the life of all States and although it may sometimes come into partnership with one or more of them, and form concordats, yet it can never be identical with any State, since it is the repository of the Christian conscience, and proclaims a standard of conduct which is possible only for those who are being regenerated, and in its fulness is beyond the attainment even of those whom the world sees fit to call saints, for these are always conscious of their own inescapable unworthiness.

Out of a world-population of about 1646 millions, it was estimated that in 1920 there were about 564 million professing Christians. Reckoning gains and losses, there can be no great difference in the proportions today in a world population of some 2400 millions, still on the increase. But quantity is far from being the same as quality: 'Many,' said Jesus, 'are called but few are chosen.'

NOTE

It has been suggested that the Buddha-Dharma also makes an imperative demand upon the whole man. But the Buddha-Dharma is hardly Deity in the transcendent sense, and the prime object of surrender to the Way of the Buddha-Dharma is really anthropocentric, the attainment of one's own beatitude; it is not theocentric, i.e. the promotion of the glory of God. This reverses the order of things. It is not a question of whether Buddhism or Christianity is to be preferred. The point is that the doctrine in the two instances is different; cf. the First Spiritual Exercise of St Ignatius Loyola with the earliest recorded sermon of Gotama, and the difference will be seen at once. But Buddhists in recent years have shown an increasing tendency to assimilate their beliefs and institutional practices here and there to those of Christians. Both in Thailand and in Vietnam they talk about 'the Buddhist Church'. They speak of Gotama as 'the true Light of the world'. Some notable Buddhist leaders have been educated in Christian colleges. Syncretism, as we can see from the Lotus Sutra, began at an early date, but it is undoubtedly still going on. What the end will be, no one can say. Perhaps there will be Christian Buddhists in the same way that there have certainly been Christian Platonists.

CHAPTER X

Islam

THE Arabs are a Semitic people, who, becoming isolated from other Semitic stocks in the large and today partially arid peninsula which bears their name, have preserved great purity of breed. The Semite is not a natural monotheist, as was supposed about the middle of the nineteenth century. He is an animist. At the beginning of the seventh century A.D. the Arabs were still polytheistic in the expression of their religious beliefs, and, so far as we can judge, the images they revered were not anthropomorphic statues, but megaliths of the type we associate with the Bronze Age in the past, and with some of the Naga tribes of Assam in the present. Yet there were traces of other influences at work. A significant feature of Arabian life about the year A.D. 600 was the presence of a number of wandering hermit ascetics with a monotheistic tendency and a craving for solitude. Passages in the writings of the Old Testament prophets might fairly well describe their behaviour. Even the fasts and retirement of Christ and St Paul and of the hermits of the Nitrian desert in the fourth century A.D. were not unlike those of these solitaries. The name by which these men were known was *hanīf*, and their development seems to have followed lines known to psychologists. The story of George Fox the Quaker, indeed, to some extent illustrates it, when we read 'At the command of God, the ninth of the seventh month in the year 1643 I left my relations, and broke off all familiarity and fellowship with young or old', and when we find that at the time he went and denounced the bloody city of Lichfield he was in a highly feverish condition of mind. These considerations must be born in mind when we come to consider the story of Mohammed, the founder of Islam. He was himself the posthumous son of a certain Abdulla, a member of the Arabian tribe called the Quraish, to which was entrusted the guardianship of the national sanctuary at Mecca, with its sacred megaliths. The Quraish were not pastoral nomads, but an urban community, engaged in commerce and handicrafts. Mohammed was born about A.D. 570, but of his early youth and manhood little is known that can be called history. We learn that he was brought up by his uncle Abū Tālib, and from the age of twelve onwards accompanied him on journeys into Syria, where he appeared to have heard and even seen much of both Jews and Christians, though it is unlikely that he knew Christianity in anything but a rather corrupt guise, probably among some sects who used apocryphal gospels. Up to the age of forty he lived in Mecca, a comparatively obscure individual, engaged in trade and business, and conducting the affairs of a certain wealthy widow, Khadīja, whom after a time he married. She bore him six children, two of whom died early, and after their deaths Mohammed became restless and wandering. He ceased to eat regularly, and became feverish and hollow-eyed. His clothes were ragged, and his appearance unkempt. Yet it is said that this kind of behaviour was not unfamiliar to Meccans, who respected it, and said, 'Our Mohammed has joined the *hanīfs*'. To become a *hanīf* was therefore not unusual. It was like becoming 'fey' among the Scotch. Other *hanīfs* were well-recognized at the period, and passages in the Old Testament prophets (such e.g. as the call of Ezekiel) might well describe their behaviour.

After repeatedly wandering in the barren deserts round Mecca, Mohammed's ill-health increased, and he began to hear voices, especially one which said: 'You are the chosen one, proclaim the Name of the Lord.' Finally one night (known afterwards as the night El Qadr) he had a kind of seizure in a cave, where a voice called to him, '*Iqra*', 'recite'. It is like the verse in Isaiah* – 'The voice said "cry".' Then came the vision of Sura I, † written in fiery letters on a cloth, spread out. Mohammed, when it vanished, stepped out into the open, and then believed that he heard the voice of the archangel Gabriel, and saw his two great eyes. He fled in terror, and seemed incapable of shaking off the visual hallucination of these eyes, until he was embraced in bed by Khadija, when the paroxysm ceased. If this story is not fiction, we may conjecture the occurrence of some neurotic seizure, of a type which is soothed and dissipated by normal sex experience.

Yet the remarkable fact remains that Mohammed's credit was not weakened by these strange events, which may perhaps have amounted to no more than the frequent 'ill-health of the mystics', the price which sensitive souls have to pay for the intensity of their vision. At any rate the blind *hanīf*, Waraqa, continued to believe in the veridical character of Mohammed's spiritual experiences; and Mohammed himself recovered from his ailment without losing any of his convictions. Shortly after this night in the cave, the second sura was revealed to him in the wilderness, and from that time onwards he came to expect that he would receive at intervals these strange intuitional 'openings' (as George Fox would have called them). His feverish attack came to an end and he resumed his ordinary dress and mode of life as a merchant of Mecca, though he continued to talk to a few of his associates (including his wife) about certain ideas which had come to him, chiefly with regard to the unity and absolute sovereignty of Deity, the fear of hell, the iniquity of idolatry and the reward of the faithful in paradise. At first he and his friends remained an insignificant

---

*Isaiah xl. 6; the same verb is used.

† Some scholars now regard the first five verses of Sura XCVI as the first revelation.

sect, but after a few years he began to preach more boldly, and to aim at forming a powerful party. There seems no doubt of his indebtedness to Hebrew prophetic ideas, for, as we shall see, he had Jerusalem and the Jews running through his mind for a considerable time, until finally he found co-operation with them less desirable, and decided upon an independent line of his own. As soon as he opened his attack on the cults of Mecca he saw himself opposed by the leaders and guardians of the local sanctuary with its megalithic idols. His followers scattered, and he himself appeared in the courtyard of the sanctuary, and made a kind of recantation. Almost immediately he regretted this weakness of his, but the mischief was done. Here he was, a man of fifty: his wife Khadīja and some of his friends had died: and when he fled from Mecca to a neighbouring town he was stoned and driven back. And then, in the year A.D. 622, came his chance. In an oasis to the north of Mecca lay a city of 14,000 inhabitants, called Yathrib. It was largely Jewish, with some Christian elements as well, and had been founded by Jews. The area was a rich date-producing one, and the city had also many goldsmiths. Here Mohammed was received, and after a hazardous journey, in which he narrowly escaped assassination, he established himself at Yathrib, which subsequently took the name of Madīnat-un-nabī or Prophet's town. He believed the city to be one where Jews and Christians would readily co-operate with him, but he encountered disappointment, and was greatly chagrined when these two groups of monotheists rejected his advances. Indeed, he gained far more support from his own Arab compatriots, with polydaemonistic antecedents. This perhaps shows that the Jews and the Christians did not feel his message to be sufficiently new and original or sufficiently in advance of their own, to make it worth while transferring allegiance to him. They regarded him as a nationalistic charlatan, and not as a genuine religious pioneer. Certain familiar technical

terms first occur at this point. The '*muhājirūn*' are Mohammed's fellow-exiles, migrants from Mecca to Yathrib. The
'*ansārs*' are young new converts. The '*munāfiqūn*' are always
'*hypocrites*' – perhaps who accept Islam without real conviction.

For several years Mohammed lived at Medina, and kept up
a series of typical Bedouin raids upon his neighbours, who at
length raised an army of 10,000 men in the hope of sacking the
prophet's stronghold. With the aid of a Persian engineer,
Mohammed fortified the town with a deep trench (a sort of
tank-trap) and refused to give battle. By indulging in Fabian
tactics he prolonged the campaign, the rains began to fall,
the besieging army grew discontented, and finally the leading
men of Mecca came over and suggested a treaty of compromise. It is at this point that we seem to see a deterioration
in Mohammed's character. Up to the time of the establishment of his small theocratic community at Yathrib, Mohammed appears sincere. But now he seems to visualize the necessity of using *force*, in order to compel the rest of Arabia, and
ultimately the world, to come into line with his ideology. He
therefore declares that he has had a revelation of the solemn
duty of *Jihād* – holy war. He revokes the necessity of observ-
ing the sacred month, in order to gain an advantage over his
more scrupulous enemies. Then come the raids mentioned
above – attacks on Mecca caravans, ending in the success-
fully conducted battle of Badr. This is followed by coercion
of the Jews, who are ordered to conform to Mohammed's
system, or massacred if they refuse. After the raising of the
siege of Medina, the Prophet declares that he has had a revelation permitting him the privilege of more than nine wives –
see Sura XXXIII. Finally he determines to subjugate Mecca
by trickery. He poses as an orthodox pilgrim, and makes a
treaty with the Meccans, ostensibly recognizing their old
divinities. When this has been signed, instead of publishing the
correct text, he saves his face by issuing a garbled version of it

T – C.R. – K

throughout Arabia, from which it appears that the entire Meccan ceremonial of the Ka'ba has been taken inside Islam. Thus did Mohammed make a treaty with the local ethnic religions. In time, however, it appeared that his respect for the Ka'ba was exaggerated. He takes the occasion of an alleged violation of the treaty by the Meccans to resume hostilities, overthrows the Meccan aristocracy, and conquers the city, making it the central place of pilgrimage, but destroying its idols.

I have dealt at some length upon the career of this extraordinary man because it presents certain analogies to that of a nationalist leader nearer to our own day. The facts seem beyond dispute, though some have declared that Mohammed was logical rather than inconsistent, and merely followed out the implications of his earlier assertions. Yet in spite of what it is hard not to interpret as a lack of principle and an unscrupulous opportunism, it must be reckoned that Mohammed succeeded in fastening upon his people, and extending throughout the Middle East, 'a broader, clearer, fresher, more vigorous political and social ideal than that of the decadent Byzantine Empire'. His teaching was better than his conduct. He had a curious way of attracting and holding friends. Almost his final speech concludes with the words: 'Ye people! hearken to my speech and comprehend the same. Know that every Moslem is the brother of every other Moslem. All of you are of the same equality.' At the end of this life he conceives the idea of a universal Empire and universal faith. 'One Prophet, one faith, for all the world!'

Even his personality is in need of fair treatment by those who approach him with prejudice. Tradition, which there is no special reason for doubting, paints him as a man of striking appearance, with a fine intelligent face, black piercing eyes, and a flowing beard. (Perhaps portraits of Emir Faysal may give the type.) He was taciturn in speech, possessed of unusual insight and gifted with a kind of rugged eloquence; at his best kindly, and a lover of children. In later life he develops polygamous tendencies, and this may have a physiological explanation; but in any event it is only fair to point out that the majority of the wives he acquired after the age of fifty-two were elderly widows, the relicts of companions who had fallen in the wars, and for whom he in this way provided homes and (so to speak) pensions. At the same time the episode of Zaid's wife, who was divorced on the authority of a *sura* in order that she might marry the prophet, is an uncomfortable one. Mohammed expressly rejected all claims to work miracles, and he despised grandeur, and lived on principle an extremely frugal life, though he was no ascetic, and loved sweet perfumes (perhaps an Arab trait, since the chief foreign trade of the Arabia of antiquity was in incense, extracted from vast groves of trees growing in the south, and exported chiefly for ritual purposes). He is reputed to have behaved very simply, and there is no reason for not supposing that he did. He performed the most menial tasks with his own hands, and was essentially puritan, saying that Divine revelation forbade him to wear either gold or silk. Though not a radical reformer, and, as has been said, 'a gradualist', he succeeded in changing the barbarous customs of his countrymen in several particulars, notably in the abolition of infanticide and cruelty to animals. It is of course possible that modern Moslem thought is rationalizing when it declares that Mohammed was working towards the abolition of polygamy and the establishment of monogamy, and that he had to move slowly, because the Arabs of his own day were quite unready for these things. It is certain that he was practical, and as an example of his method may be quoted that he first forbade the drinking of wine before coming to prayer, lest the worshippers should not understand what they were saying, and that he then subsequently prohibited it altogether. Finally, it must ever be recognized that Moslems never accord any worship to

Mohammed,* and should never be referred to as 'Mohammedans' – a word they never use. Islam is the worship of Allāh, and submission to Allāh, and Mohammed, though inspired by Allāh, is regarded as in himself a fallible and even sinful man.

For the present purpose three main points are of major importance: (1) the nature of the message proclaimed by Mohammed, (2) the sacred book in which it is embodied, (3) the development of the movement both as to institutions and theology.

(1) *The Message*. – This is not simply that Deity is One. It is the character of the one Deity that matters. 'Allāh' is not a proper name, but is the contraction of Al Ilāh, 'the strong' or 'mighty One'. The other primitive Moslem name is 'Rabb', or 'Lord'. From these it is plain that Mohammed's basic conception of Deity is that of stark absolute transcendent power. The phrases recur with almost monotonous frequency: 'It shall be as Allāh pleases', 'If Allāh will'. 'If Allāh pleases'. The will of Allāh is entirely arbitrary, and can be changed at His pleasure in a contrary direction. There is thus no fixed moral standard at all. If a Moslem is asked: 'Did not the Prophet sin in the matter of Zainab?' he will reply 'He did not sin, because Allāh commanded it'. Allāh is separated from His creatures by an impassable chasm, and the whole duty of man is Islam (submission). Moslem means 'the submissive'. To quote from the Qur'ān itself: 'Allāh leads astray whom he pleases and guides whom he pleases, and no one knows the hosts of the Lord save Himself. And every man's destiny have we fastened on his neck.' This overpowering sense of the majesty of the Unconditioned Disposer expresses itself in a

* The Hadith or Sunnat (tradition) embellishes Mohammed's life with miracles, so as to make him resemble Christ, i.e. wonders like the multiplication of food, etc. In Sufism we have also a kind of Islamic Logos-doctrine, in which the Logos is incarnate through Mohammed. (See R. A. Nicholson, *Studies in Islamic Mysticism*.)

variety of names, which purport to set forth the various aspects of the being and action of Deity. 'Most excellent names hath Allāh; by these call ye upon Him, and stand aloof from those who pervert His names.' These 'beautiful names' are said to number ninety-nine, and Moslems use rosaries of ninety-nine beads to aid in their recitation; but it is difficult to determine without prejudice how much they involve. Christians have contrasted their use with the simplicity of the believer who can stand upright without cringing, and address Deity as 'Father'. But Moslems counter this by pointing out that the two commonest attributes of Allāh are 'the Compassionate' and 'the Merciful', and that Deity as seen in nature *does* appear arbitrary. The natural rejoinder to this is that the mind of man is a part of Nature, and that the mind of man demands more than arbitrary despotism of a Deity it is called upon to respect and esteem. The Moslem doctrine of God is thus somewhat vulnerable to criticism, yet not perhaps more (or less) than the Christian predestinarian ideas which are still found among Calvinists. If we remember that Islam began in A.D. 622, we shall reflect that it is still 600 years younger than Christianity, and that in another 600 years it may have changed or developed very considerably. But against this may be set the allegation that the most correct Moslem doctrine is of a rigid fundamentalist order – that of the Wahabis of Arabia – and that such believers repudiate forcibly the attempts of so-called liberal Moslems to deduce Christian attributes for Allāh from the Qur'ān, and to blur the distinction between the two faiths. At its best Islam produces a dignified and restrained type of character, perhaps not unlike that of some Scotch Calvinist Christians. At its worst, it makes for a non-moral craftiness. But this is perhaps not an unknown phenomenon in other religions than Islam. The phrase 'Moslem fanaticism' is sometimes heard. It is a curious fact that even not very strict Moslems will work themselves into a fury of indignation at the very idea of they themselves or any of their co-believers changing to another creed. Kraemer describes this as due to what he calls the 'super-heating' of the concepts of Revelation and Omnipotence in Islam. It is, he says, theocentricity, but in a state of white-heat. 'Allāh in Islam becomes white-hot Majesty, white-hot Omnipotence, white-hot Uniqueness. His personality evaporates and vanishes in the burning heat of his aspects ... To speak of a voluntarist conception of God in Islam is properly speaking inexact; one ought to speak of a "potentist" conception, if such a word existed. It is the depersonalized aspects which are the objects of real religious devotion, and thus the surrender is quite different from the surrender so often spoken of in Christian revivalist circles.' The ideal believer is the *'abd*, or slave (Hebrew *ebed*), and is personified submission and nothing else. Religion for the Moslem centres upon *Wahy* or revelation. It is wholly given, and nothing remains but to accept it in its immutable majesty.

(2) *The Book*. – We are now entering upon a new period of higher criticism in regard to the sacred book of Islam. The word 'Qur'ān' means that which is uttered or recited. Primarily it denotes those utterances of Mohammed in which he was believed to be under the influence of direct inspiration. This distinction is not confined to Islam. Readers of the New Testament will recall St Paul's '... not I, but the Lord', showing that the apostle, like Hebrew prophets, sometimes felt himself speaking as an ordinary fallible man, and at other times controlled by the Divine 'down-rush from the super-conscious'. Mohammed's revelations were usually preceded by some sort of neurotic seizure, in which his body began to tremble and beads of perspiration appeared on his forehead. But the members of the Society of Friends were called Quakers for the same reason, and George Fox's 'openings' were accompanied by considerable bodily disturbance. Mohammed's earlier revelations were relatively brief. Later *suras*

(as they are called) seem in general to be prolix and more artificial. It is to be feared that the Prophet may have yielded to the temptation to produce paroxysms of deliverance when the occasion demanded: but in the earlier *suras* he is undoubtedly sincere. At his best he taught at Medina in short pithy sentences.

> 'The best and most beautiful of my creations is a compassionate man who gives alms. If he does so with his right hand and hides it from his left, he is more powerful than all things.'
>
> (Notice an echo of the Sermon on the Mount.)
>
> 'Anything that will bring a smile on the face of others is a good deed, and is the love of one's neighbours.'
>
> 'How can I honour the memory of my mother?' asked a disciple (or *ansār*).
>
> 'By water,' answered the prophet. 'Dig a well in her memory, and give water to the thirsty.'

The earlier theory (Rodwell's) was that the various remnants of the Prophet's teachings were in the first instance collected by his friend Abū Bakr, about a year after Mohammed's death, at the suggestion of another friend, Omar, and that the actual work was entrusted to Zaid Ibn Thabit, an *ansār* of Medina, who gathered together the fragments from every quarter: 'from date leaves and tablets of stone, and from the breasts of men.' But this conflicts with the apparently explicit intention of the Prophet himself to leave behind him not simply a mass of disjointed fragments, but a Qur'ān.

And so we come to the newer theory of Richard Bell. According to this, there were probably three periods in the composition of the Qur'ān:

> i. An early period, from which only fragments survive, consisting mainly of lists of 'signs' and exhortations to the worship of Allāh.

ii. The 'Qur'ān' period, covering the latter part of Mohammed's activity in Mecca, and the first year or two of his residence in Medina, during which he is producing a written record or 'Qur'ān' giving the gist of previous revelations.

iii. The Book-period, beginning somewhere about the end of the year II, during which Mohammed is definitely producing a Book, i.e. an independent revelation.

This, however, still leaves unanswered the question 'What is the Qur'ān as we have it today?' It would seem as though there must have been at least *two* recensions. The first, the Qur'ān as it finally left the hands of Mohammed at his death after passing through stages, i, ii and iii. The second, the Qur'ān as put together by Zaid and his coadjutors, who gave it the same name, but added to it many of the shorter pieces. Rodwell's arrangement puts the *suras* in a (hypothetically) chronological order, which virtually agrees in making Bell's collection earlier in date than Mohammed's artificially constructed Qur'ān, whereas the traditional order is the reverse of this. Indeed, the traditional order seems to imply that an artificially constructed Qur'ān was Mohammed's idea, but that a complete corpus was the idea of his followers. But here again we encounter a problem, especially if we accept Bell's analysis of the longer *suras*, for these to him appear to be full of conflations and interpolations. If Bell is right, the collection and stringing together of shorter *suras* to make longer ones was begun by Mohammed himself at Medina, and Meccan and early Medinan utterances thus became incorporated in longer compositions of later Medinan date. The Prophet reserved the right to cancel earlier *suras* by later ones, if he received instructions from Allāh to do so. The book as finally arranged contains, therefore, what appears to be inconsistencies. It is a rambling work in which the main themes recur over and over again, i.e. the transcendent and arbitrary power of

Allāh, the iniquity of coupling gods with God, or of idolatry, the inevitability of the day of Judgement, the wrath of God, hell-fire, and the bliss of heaven reserved for those with whom Allāh is well pleased. Sporadic references to the Gospels make it plain that Mohammed regarded Jesus of Nazareth as a kind of prophet similar to himself, but that he believed in his Virgin-birth, though elsewhere confusing the Virgin Mary with the Holy Spirit. He imagines Christians to be tritheists who worship God the Father, Jesus and Mary as a triad, and says that in the day of judgement Jesus will repudiate them with indignation.

(3) *The Development of the Movement.*

(a) *Institutional.* – Islam has proved attractive not least because of the ease and precision with which its devotional exercises are performed. The good life is one of disciplined submission, abstemious in food and drink, though not in sex matters, and motivated by a very definite paradise of physical delights. There are five compulsory practices, or pillars of Islam as they are called:

    i. Kalima or the recital of the creed, 'There is no Deity but Allāh, and Mohammed is his prophet'.

    ii. Salāt, or the recital of the five daily prayers, accompanied by ablutions.

    iii. Fasting, especially during the lunar month of Ramadān.

    iv. Zakāt or almsgiving.

    v. Hajj or pilgrimage to Mecca.

To these some would add as a sixth, 'Jihād', or the Holy War. There is denunciation of usury and games of chance, and of the consumption of pork and alcohol. Polygamy is granted to all. Special attendance at the mosques on Friday for a sermon is also required. The first Qibla, or directing of the body in prayer, was towards Jerusalem (not, as now, towards Mecca), which shows again that the Prophet certainly began by trying to win Jews and Christians for his disciples. The first mosque, or Moslem place of prayer, at Yathrib, was a very simple affair. A piece of ground 100 ells square was surrounded with walls made of dried bricks. Palm trees were planted in the square so formed, and one-third of the enclosure was roofed in with palm-leaf thatch. Three doors were placed in the walls, one in the direction of Jerusalem, one 'for Gabriel', and one, 'in the name of mercy', which led in the direction of the Prophet's private quarters. The courtyard was used for prayer, for assemblies and for sheltering the homeless. This place, the Masjid-un-Nabi, was the mother of some of the most beautiful buildings of the Orient.

Islam is not a sacerdotal religion. It does not believe in any mediation between man and his Maker 'who knew him before he was born, and is closer to him than his jugular vein'. Any Moslem of decent character can lead the prayers in the mosque, though in practice this is done by a leader recognized for his piety and scholarship, called an Imam, and devoted to the service of the particular mosque in question. Analogies from Protestantism will occur to the reader. Moslem worship is simple and dignified, and follows a set formula of postures and devotions, with petitions or versicles and responses faintly recalling an unintoned Litany in the English church service. The worshippers do not uncover their heads, but remove their shoes or sandals, and perform certain ceremonial ablutions, and then line up in a row facing towards Mecca, the leader taking up a position a little to the front of them in the centre. An individual who prays at the stated times during his ordinary day's work will spread his prayer-mat, and then go through the same devotions alone. There are in the Old Testament two indications of such prayer: 'At evening and in the morning and at noon-day will I pray'; and 'Seven times a day do I praise Thee because of Thy righteous judgements'. This

latter has been made a pattern for Christian monasticism, with
its seven canonical hours of prayer – matins with lauds, prime,
terce, sext, none, vespers and compline. But Moslems have a
cycle of their own, to wit five times a day – i.e. dawn, midday, mid-afternoon, sunset and bed-time. The plain object of
these hours of prayer is to ensure that the believer is never long
without God in his thoughts. Indeed, the question arises in all
forms of religion. What is the minimum recollection of God
which is necessary to save the individual from the charge of
practical atheism? People who are busy naturally find such
recollectedness difficult. An English nobleman of the seventeenth century is said to have prayed: 'O God, Thou knowest
how busie I have to be this day; If I forget Thee, do not Thou
forget me.' There is also a pleasant story from India of a holy
sage, Narada, who was asked by the god Vishnu what he
thought of a certain peasant, and who replied that he was
impious, because he called upon Ram, the incarnation of Vishnu, only morning and evening, 'while I, my Lord, remember
thee all the day'. He was then made by Vishnu to carry a jar
full of oil round the city for a day, and was asked, 'How often
have you remembered me?' 'Lord, I could not, for my whole
time was taken up in seeing that not a drop of oil was spilled.'
'Then, Narada, you were not so pious as yonder peasant, for
he, though burdened with many family cares and much labour
in the fields, remembers me twice daily.'

The object, then, of the five times of prayer is to ensure that
the believer is mindful of Allāh, and Moslems claim that this
compulsory practice is more effective than the rather incon-
spicuous devotional practices of the average Christian. In
theory this should be established by testing the integration of
character which results under the various systems, and it is
desirable not to condemn (let us say) the Afghans of Jell-
alabad for not displaying the Christian virtues. The point will
be, do they show a high average of Moslem virtue? And

again, do these places in Europe where the attendance of men is common at High Mass – e.g. certain parts of France, Germany and Ireland – show a high average of Christian virtue?

To return to the Moslem prayers. Each complete set of prayers is called a rak'a, and consists of eight separate acts of devotion. In the first posture the worshipper stands upright with the palms of his hands raised to the level of his ears, rather in the manner of a priest at Mass. Standing thus he says certain prayers and acknowledgements of the Divine Majesty, ending with the refrain: 'God is greater than all else.' In posture 2, still standing, the arms are lowered and the right hand placed over the left one, while the worshipper recites, 'Glory and praise to Thee, O God. Blessed is Thy Name, and exalted is Thy Majesty. There is no one worthy of worship and service but Thee'. And then follows the recital of the famous First Sura, with an act of surrender, and again the refrain, 'God is greater than all else'. In the third posture the body is bent forward at right angles, and the hands are placed upon the knees. Each time that this bow is made, the worshipper says, 'Glory to my Lord, The Exalted'. In posture 4 the standing position is resumed, with the words: 'God accepts him who is grateful to Him. O our God, all praise be unto Thee. God is greater than all else.' Posture 5 is that of kneeling supported with the hands on the ground, palms downwards, the body bowed forward so that the forehead touches the ground. In this position the worshipper says three times with a bow: 'Glory to my Lord, the Most High. God is greater than all else.' Posture 6 is a sitting-kneeling one, with the hands resting on the knees, with similar acts of worship, and postures 7 and 8 are repetitions of postures 5 and 6, and with the same prayers. This completes the rak'a, and prayers sometimes consist of two, three or four rak'as. To end with, a prayer is said for the Prophet, for the faithful and for the congregation, with the plea for forgiveness of sins, and at the conclusion a bow to left and to right and the words: 'Peace be with you, and the mercy of Allāh.' This salutation is intended for the two recording angels, whose presence, though invisible, is thus acknowledged.

Space has been devoted to an account of these devotions, partly because text-books on Islam always speak of 'Moslem prayers', but without saying what they are (and it is unfair to assume that the reader will infer their form from general accounts of doctrine), partly also because these prayers are perhaps the most important post-Christian attempt to regulate human devotions which has so far taken place. The innate psychological skill with which they are planned is remarkable, and the nearest parallel is to be found in the system of *yoga* postures in India. Nothing is more nicely calculated to create in the worshipper the habitual submission to the Inscrutable and Autocratic Majesty of Allāh, and the difficulty which the average human being finds in concentrating on prayer for more than a short time is as fully recognized as in the scheme of the Catholic Mass or in the offices of the English Book of Common Prayer. It must also be noticed that there is in these prayers little or no petition. This is easy of explanation, since the practice of submission to an inscrutable and arbitrary Divine Will leaves no room for petitionary prayer. So far as any request is made from Allāh, it is for forgiveness and guidance.

(b) *Theological*. – As Islam expanded from Arabia, it had, like Christianity, to adapt itself to wider horizons, and in the course of time to decide what might be regarded as proper developments from teaching originally given by the Prophet, and what might be rejected. Three lines of development thus came to be recognized:

    i. *Ijma'*, or unanimity of opinion among teachers at all times and in all places.

ii. *Sunna*, or custom, certified by a succession of teachers, and based upon the hadith or tradition regarding the works and deeds of the Prophet.

iii. *Qiyās*, or inferences and deductions from the original teaching. Some would add as a fourth, *ijtihad*, or interpretation.

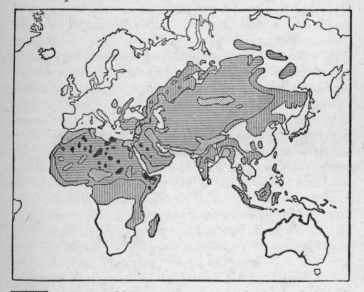

▐ Centres of the Senussi (a modern N. African revival of Islam).
▒ Thickly populated Moslem countries.
▥ Countries with a minor proportion of Moslems.
▤ Countries where Islam prevails.

5. MAP OF DISTRIBUTION OF ISLAM

Naturally some kind of unity has always existed among Moslems, and in the main it has depended upon allegiance to the supreme head, or Caliph. But in 632, when he was in his

sixty-second year, Mohammed died, and in A.D. 656 a wretch-
ed quarrel began over the succession. The first two Caliphs
were completely in earnest, but after that deterioration set in.
Finally allegiance became divided between an elected and an
hereditary successor to the Prophet, and the Moslem community to this day remains split into Sunnis, the larger body,
who do not limit the Caliphate to the heirs of Mohammed,
and the Shi'a, who maintain that the family of Ali, the prophet's nephew, have the sole right to office. The situation since
1918 has been still further modified by the forcible abolition
of the Sunni Caliphate by Kemal Pasha, the Turkish nationalist leader. This leaves the larger proportion of Moslems without any visible head corresponding to the Christian Pope, and
Islam is in consequence more than ever like other Oriental
religions, formless and devoid of organization, the chief
denominational test being now the ability to pray under the
guidance of a particular leader or Imam. A modern development of it is Bahaism, which is a development from Shi'a
Islam, combining the idea of successive incarnations of God
in Imams with a liberal Unitarianism.

Though primarily an Arabian nationalist movement, Islam
has either by coercion, trading, colonization or pure propaganda expanded in many directions. Map 5 will show its main
distribution, and will demonstrate how it is largely an equa-
torial or heat-belt religion. It does not make converts easily
in the colder or more temperate regions. As we have already
seen, it has established itself firmly in India. It has also been
strong in North Africa, Persia and East Africa, and indeed
wherever the Arab element is dominant in the population.
In Spain, Sicily, Malta and Greece it made no permanent
settlement, and although the Turks (both Seljuk and Otto-
man) adopted it, recent years have seen a strong reaction
against Islam on the part of the Ankara republic.* In more

* There are strong Moslem groups in Albania and Yugoslavia.

recent times Islam has spread among the Malays, and also in Central Africa. On the other hand, it is proving more vulnerable than Christianity to the modern spirit, and is losing ground among the younger generation not only in Turkey but also in Persia, Egypt and East Africa. In 1920 it was said to number some 221 million adherents, and, allowing for shrinkage, but also for increase in population, may now amount to 300 millions. In any case, account must be taken of the large number of animists, especially in Morocco, but in parts of Arabia as well, who, although professing to be Moslems, still retain a strong belief in a plurality of daemons small and great. Popular Islam (as seen in the Arabian Nights) has always overstressed the existence of superhuman beings such as Angels and Jinns, and these, though creaturely, are soon regarded as demigods, by the ignorant.

A modern scholar has ventured to draw some comparisons between Islam and fundamentalist evangelical Christianity, and has pointed out that both ultimately depend upon the dogma that Deity is an arbitrary Being, who expresses his Almightiness by flouting our reason and ignoring our sense of justice. In both cases 'God', as the Moslems say, 'is not to be inquired of as to what He does'. This provokes thought, for it is easy to see that, regarded in certain aspects, the power in Nature *does* appear to be arbitrary and lacking in justice. Yet, as has been observed elsewhere, the human reason and the human sense of justice – of what *ought* to be – are a part of Nature. What is Nature's place in mind? It is evident that no constructed natural religion can be self-consistent which does not attempt a reconciliation between reason, justice and the forces apparent in external nature. It is the claim of Christian theism that it can and does effect some such reconciliation. Whether it has succeeded in making good that claim is not the proper concern of the treatise, which must confine itself to scientific description.

A few brief notes on recent observations of Islam may not be without interest. From visits made during the last three years to Jordan (once) Libya (twice) and India (once) I have gleaned the following:

1. In Jordan I notice that the call of the muezzin is now often mechanized, and is broadcast by loud-speakers in many places, the chant being taken from some such centre as Cairo, and the intonations being very well and elaborately done – as someone said to me: 'with a good deal of coloratura'.

2. In Libya I noted that Islam had been written into the constitution of the new Arab state, so that it has in fact become 'established by law' (as I imagine it also is in Pakistan). The effect of this may be seen during the fast of Ramadan, since failure to observe its discipline is a punishable offence – e.g. if a policeman finds a Moslem smoking, or eating during the prohibited hours, the victim incurs a penalty, just as a person might in the reign of Queen Elizabeth I have been fined a shilling for not attending his parish church on Sunday. And this, in the twentieth century!

3. In India I found some educated Moslems seriously concerned about the necessity of re-examining the theology of Islam, in order to re-state its essential doctrines. One such has written:

i. The theology of Islam must be re-examined in all its aspects, and modern philosophy, metaphysics, ethics, psychology, and logic should be applied to formulate and re-state its essential dogmas (*sic*).

ii. Wherever the ancient scriptures or traditions speak of natural phenomena or scientific facts, their dogmatic character should be questioned. The passages should be interpreted and accepted, modified, or rejected, in terms of modern science, including anthropology, biology, physics, mathematics, chemistry, and medicine. The concept of the world, time, and the universe has changed radically since the days of Copernicus. Islam must take heed of these changes, and scientific absurdities should be removed from the main fabric of religion.

iii. The modern science of comparative religion should be a primary aid for the proper understanding of the religion of Islam,

and so on.

One hardly dares to think what might be the effect of such modernization upon the original faith of the Prophet.

Important recent works about Islam, on the Christian side (yet appreciative ones) are:

The Reverend Kenneth Cragg's *The Call of the Minaret*, and Miss Constance Padwick's book on Muslim Prayers. The latter gives a remarkable wealth of quotations from small manuals of devotion circulating among Muslims, and includes some extremely beautiful prayers, not at all unsuitable for Christian use.

NOTE

Perhaps this is the point at which to insert a note upon Manichaeism, though, so far as we know, there are no Manichees alive today. The chief impact of East upon West from the direction of India which occurred during the centuries immediately following the birth of Christianity was through a medley of sects, all of which claimed to give salvation to man by means of *gnosis* or occult knowledge. A large part of this consisted in prescribing methods of inducing states of consciousness similar to those of Hindu *yoga*, and in giving information about the emanations from the Absolute Deity or Prime Mystery. Most of it today seems to us rubbish, but we must not be too contemptuous, since it represented, no doubt, what was believed to be the secular science of that period. To do justice to Gnosticism we must try to think of it as an honest attempt to relate Christianity to a larger complex of Eastern religion. Among these attempts one of the most famous and typical is that of Mani, the son of a noble

Persian of Hamadan, who was born in Babylon in 215. Mani derived his cosmology from the ancient civilizations of the East. He took from Zoroastrianism cosmic and eschatological principles, and from Indian teaching the ascetic ordering of life. To these he added certain elements from Christianity which powerfully increased the effect of his system. The result is an independent religion, quite as independent, in fact, as Islam. Where Manichaeism is in contact with Christianity it tends to become more Christian; where it has contact with Buddhism, as in Turkestan, it tends to approximate to the Buddhist point of view. But always it is a distinct creed, showing a certain constructive genius, even if to us it seems bizarre. In the fourth century A.D. the Manichaeans were both numerous and influential, and they succeeded for a time in making a disciple of St Augustine of Hippo. Something very like Manichaeism continued to exist in Eastern Europe for many centuries afterwards, and there seems little doubt that vestiges of it were embodied in the notorious Albigensian heresy.* Modern theosophy is in no sense a direct descendant of this movement, but it undoubtedly is the residuary legatee of the same group of queer oriental religious philosophies as that which includes Manichaeism. For further information readers are referred to Professor Burkitt's Donnellan Lectures on Manichaeism, and also to his lectures on Gnosticism. Our knowledge of Mani's teaching has been recently much enriched by the discovery of documents at Turfan (edited by Polotsky), and of others in Egypt, which were being edited by Mr C. R. C. Allberry of Christ's College, Cambridge.† For those who can read French, one of the best recent works on Manichaeism has been written in Paris by Professor Puech, and published in connexion with the Musée Guimet.

* I know this is disputed, but I judge from Albigensian documentary evidence.

† I record with deep regret that Mr Allberry was reported killed in action over the Ruhr, while serving with the R.A.F. It is to be regretted that no one in Cambridge is continuing Mr Allberry's work. Dr Henning has published some articles in the *Bulletin of the London School of Oriental Studies* which contribute to our knowledge of the history of Mani, but the most outstanding work since 1945 has been done in Paris by Professor Ernest Puech, whose monograph on Manichaeism has been published by the Musée Guimet.

CHAPTER XI

Mysticism

MYSTICISM is a term which has come into common use from about the year 1900 onwards. It has since then been terribly overworked. The term itself is derived from a Greek word, *mustēs*, which means a person who has been admitted to secret knowledge of the realities of life and death. It is only natural that those who have once attained to such a state should desire to prolong it or to reproduce it at intervals. It has been suggested that all mystics, whether Christian, Moslem, Hindu or Buddhist, are agreed on a few fundamentals: (1) that all division and separateness is unreal, and that the universe is a single indivisible unity; (2) that evil is illusory, and that the illusion arises through regarding a part of the universe as self-subsistent; (3) that time is unreal, and that reality is eternal, not in the sense of being everlasting, but in the sense of being out of time. This may be so, but when once we have said that, we are bound to recognize that on almost everything else the mystics are much divided. How is it, then, that up to a point they are agreed? The explanation given for some time was that fundamentally mysticism is an advance upon all other religion, especially upon that which is rooted and grounded in the reality of events, like that of the Romans, the Jews and the Christians. Since that answer was given, we have come to know more about the way in which the various types of mysticism developed. It is not simply that this way of looking at life and religion makes a strong appeal to people of a certain temperament, or that it is gradually coming to supersede other types of religion. What is actually the case is that the

main streams of mystical religion are two, specifically Christian and specifically non-Christian. The true Christian form of
mysticism accepts the whole Hebraeo-Christian position, and
finds communion with God through the living Christ, so that
as St Paul, its earliest and perhaps its chief exponent, says, 'I
live, yet not I, but Christ liveth in me', and speaks about
'Christ being formed in' us. Non-Christian mysticism starts
from entirely different presuppositions. Although sometimes
superficially Christian or Moslem, it really depends upon a
doctrine of Deity and the world which derives from what is
called Neo-Platonism, a philosophical religion of the fourth
century A.D. which, though claiming relationship with the
original doctrines of Plato, is really in its turn derived from
India. Its chief exponents were Ammonius Saccas and Plotinus,
and for a time it attracted St Augustine, when he wearied of
Manichaeism. (It is significant that in the end he left it for
Christianity.) This system, which certainly has for its cardinal
tenets the three principles of mysticism with which we began,
was in no sense Christian, but had much in common with
Upanishadic Hinduism. It did, however, get lodgement within the borders of the Christian Church, owing to an unknown
eccentric, who took the writings of Proclus (another Neo-
Platonist who died in 485), conceived the idea of dressing his
philosophy in Christian draperies, and by fraudulently calling
it the work of Dionysius the Areopagite, passed it off as the
work of a companion of St Paul. This pious outrage led it to
be accepted, though with some head-shaking, by many who
would otherwise never have agreed to its doctrines, since a
writing by a reputed disciple of the great Apostle of the
Gentiles carried nearly as much weight as if it had been Holy
Writ. Pseudo-Dionysius, as it is now generally called, was
translated into many tongues, and travelled all over the
Christian world, being received by the credulous Christians
of the medieval Church in much the same way as the spurious

letter of Jesus to the Prince of Edessa. It became a text-book for solitaries and hermits, and, indeed, for monastic devotees in general, and its main ideas can be discerned in the writings of the Christian medieval mystics, such as Eckhart, Lady Julian of Norwich, Tauler, Henry Suso, Catherine of Genoa and many others. Whether the adoption of this treatise as a pendant to the Bible led these holy souls into logical inconsistencies, we cannot here discuss, but it is certainly a fact that Eckhart, through imbibing the doctrine and reproducing it in sermons, drew so near to pantheism that the Pope had to appoint a commission to deal with him, and he was condemned as a heretic, and made a recantation. A more critical age is able to see that the pseudo-Dionysius is only superficially Christian, and has quite a different religion as its real basis.

But this is not the end of the story. Mysticism of the non-Christian type is perfectly at home in the religious life of Indians. Hence those parallels to the Christian mystics of the Middle Ages which have been found in Hindu and Buddhist literature and to which attention has been drawn, are not in the least surprising,* and do not mean that the Christian mystics in question have an affinity with the Hindus by virtue of their Christianity, but are simply the consequence of their having steeped themselves in a particular apocryphal writing, which is based upon the writings of the Levantine pagan mystic, Proclus. It is high time that this misunderstanding was cleared up, for a good deal of inaccurate and sentimental rubbish has resulted from the failure to realize the true parentage of quasi-pantheistic Christian mysticism.

But further. Pseudo-Dionysius, or at any rate Neo-Platonism, had its influence outside Christianity, and echoes of it occur in Islamic mysticism. In the chapter on Islam no mention has been made of the Sufis, since it seemed better to reserve it

---

* E.g. Quietest Christian mystics have sometimes spoken of 'the spiritual sleep' (see p. 126, on *sushupti*).

for this point. Moslem theology does not naturally lend itself to such an immanental doctrine of the relation of the soul to God as is found in pseudo-Dionysius. But human nature revolted from the severity of Mohammed's proclamations, and this led to the development within the bounds of Islam itself of a rich variety of mystics, especially Persian, who are grouped together in Moslem circles under the term 'Sufi'. The meaning of this word is uncertain. Some think that it refers to the white woollen garment (*suf*) worn by these mystical ascetics, others to the Greek word, *sophia*, wisdom, and there are, it is true, certain affinities with Gnostics such as the unknown author of the extraordinary work entitled the Pistis Sophia. But it is hard not to conclude that the influences which led to the development of Neo-Platonism and so to the writings of Proclus and his Christian adaptor, extended themselves into early Islam, and through the centuries following led to a rich outcrop of teachers (of whom perhaps al Ghazāli is the chief), whose main object was to show how to attain absorption in the Divine. As summed up in Hughes' *Dictionary of Islam* the doctrines of the Sufis are almost exactly the same as the three quoted at the beginning of this section, though slightly expanded.

i. God alone exists; He is in all things, and all things are in Him.

ii. All things are emanations from Him, and have no real existence apart from Him.

iii. All religions are indifferent. They serve a purpose, however, as leading to realities. The most profitable in this respect is Islam, of which Sufism is the true philosophy.

iv. There is no distinction between good and evil; for God is the author of all.

v. It is God who determines the will of man; therefore man is not free in his actions.

vi. The soul existed before the body, in which it is confined as in a cage. Death is to be desired, for it is then the Sufi returns to the bosom of Deity.

vii. Apart from the grace of God no man can attain to this spiritual union; it may, however, be obtained by fervent prayer.

viii. The principal duty of the Sufi is meditation on the unity of God, the remembrance of the Divine names and progressive advancement in the *tariqat*, or journey of life so as to attain union with God.

In spite of the above, it must be strictly maintained that mysticism is not a natural growth in Islam, but is a foreign element which has worked its way into it, and is really inconsistent with the original dogmas. It is perhaps a revolt of some Moslem souls against the extremity of Islamic transcendence.

Mysticism of a certain sort also penetrated into Judaism in the early Middle Ages. It is chiefly expressed in the book of Zohar (brightness) and other similar works to which the generic name of Kabbala (tradition) has been given. Though fantastic in their magical use of numbers, and associated with theosophical ideas which may seem to many both irrational and superstitious, the Kabbalists were nevertheless responsible for much that was admirable in the prayers and hymns of the medieval synagogue, and it has been said that these, by their sheer beauty and devotional power, have won their way into practically universal use among Jews. Nevertheless it must be admitted that the main elements in the Kabbala are drawn from outside Judaism proper, and belong to the world of Gnosticism, Neo-Platonism and Alexandrianism. Martin Buber's revival of Chassidism in the twentieth century has brought into prominence a most impressive type of mysticism, which developed in Eastern Europe in the seventeenth and succeeding centuries, and has never died out.

The various types of what Schweitzer has called 'god-mysticism' are so much alike that writers such as Dr Geden have maintained that they are independent and natural products of minds which, possessed of similar characteristics, have all the world over tended to evolve similar results; and he notes that the essential features of mystical doctrine are the same in every country. The evidence which has come to hand since he wrote in 1913 seems to show that a *diffusionist* explanation of the wide distribution of such similar mystical doctrines and technique is the more probable one.

We may note in conclusion that an entirely different use of the term 'mysticism' sometimes occurs. According to this it is the equivalent of '*immediacy* in religious experience', and may be correlated with 'intuition' in the Bergsonian sense, as distinguished from the rational or intellectual apprehension of Deity. It may be granted that all 'mysticism' of the kind described in this chapter is 'immediacy', but without an undue stretching of the scope of a word we cannot allow the converse, i.e. that all 'immediacy' is therefore 'mysticism'.

NOTE

The most convenient edition of pseudo-Dionysius is that of C. E. Rolt, published by the S.P.C.K. in 1920, which gives the reader two out of the four surviving works of the author in an English translation. Not only are Rolt's own introduction and bibliography valuable, but Dr Sparrow-Simpson's appendix on the influence of the Areopagite in religious history gives clearly the main facts in the astounding story of these pious forgeries. Thus he points out that the famous Parisian theologian Hugh of St Victor (1096–1141) wrote a ten-volume commentary on the *Heavenly Hierarchy* of pseudo-Dionysius, while Aquinas wrote one on *The Divine Names*, and quoted the Areopagite repeatedly as one of his favourite authorities. It was not until the seventeenth century that French scholars began to question the identification of the author with the disciple of St Paul, and to challenge his orthodoxy. Even then he found champions in the Universities of

Paris and Louvain and among the Jesuits. Baur in 1842 and Vacherot in 1851 subjected his system to a very searching and hostile analysis, and the Roman Catholic writer Bach, in his *History of Dogma in the Middle Ages*, agrees with their conclusions. Bishop Westcott in his *Religious Thought in the West* confirms their judgements, and uses the phrases 'not wholly of a Christian type' and 'very faulty and defective', adding: 'Many perhaps will be surprised that such a scheme of Christianity as Dionysius has sketched should even be reckoned Christian at all.' It is not unreasonable to suppose that if the apocryphal and spurious character of the Dionysian books had been recognized from the first, Christian mysticism and theology would have pursued a very different course.

For further information on Chassidism the reader may refer to (i) Martin Buber: *The Hasidim*, and *Die chassidischen Bücher*. (ii) *The Hasidic Anthology*, compiled by Louis I. Newman and Samuel Spitz, Scribners, New York, 1934. See also the appropriate section in my *Sacred Books of the World* (Pelican Books No. A283).

CHAPTER XII

General Theories: Epilogue

OUR survey is finished. But some may be interested to know what has been done so far to frame a 'general theory of religion', as Comte described it.

First and foremost comes the theory of radical abandonment. All religions being based upon illusion, their study can be no more than a branch of anthropology, archaeology, psychology or sociology. This is the theory of Feuerbach, Frazer and Freud.

The second we may call that of radical exclusiveness. This need not be Christian. It may be Buddhist, Hebrew or Moslem, but its general method of classification is into 'true' and 'false'.

The third we will call that of radical relativity. This is well exemplified in the Hibbert Lectures of L. P. Jacks, where he speaks of the religions of the world as hospitable caravanserais in which the traveller may rest for a brief space, and then awake refreshed to pursue his journey of exploration. It is also the view of Spengler.

The fourth type of classification is detached and descriptive. Of this there are many examples, some showing a belief in the adequacy of one special religion, others maintaining a measure of impartiality to the very end.

Tiele, for instance, began by adopting a classification according to date and distribution, and then abandoned it for a division into nature-religions and ethical religions.

Hegel, and Principal Caird following him, divided the field into three sections: (i) nature religions, (ii) religions of spiritual individuality, (iii) absolute or universal religion.

Siebeck also adopted a tri-partite division, into (i) primitive religion, (ii) morality religion, (iii) redemptive religion.

Orelli in 1899 divided the religions of the world into seven groups, Turanian, Hamitic, Semitic, Indo-Germanic, African, American and Oceanic. This was meant to be a racial classification, but even at that was open to serious amendment.

Bishop Gore, following the Canadian scholar, Dr Hamilton, discriminated between 'discovery' and 'revelation', and limited the latter to Hebraeo-Christian religion, involving 'a unique downrush from the super-conscious'.

Other groupings, such as those of Berthelot and Lehmann, or Jeremias, are obviously only sortings-out which may be convenient for purposes of study, but are devoid of any basic principle.

A very neat and brief sub-division was that of Dr Oman, who based it upon the relations between the Natural and the Supernatural. When the latter is merged in the former, he says, we have idolatry; when the former is merged in the latter, we have pantheism; when the two are related by some kind of moral victory, we have at least some kind of theism.

The late Archbishop Söderblom, in his Gifford Lectures of 1931, after dealing with religion in its primitive stages, then discussed its greater creative developments under eight headings.

    i. As method: Yoga.

   ii. As psychology: Jainism and Hinayana Buddhism.

  iii. As devotion: Bhakti.

  iv. As a conflict against evil: Zarathustra.

   v. As the practice of a good conscience: Socrates (also the Chinese sages and the Hebrew prophets).

  vi. As revelation in history: Hebrew religion.

 vii. As culminating in once-for-all revelation: Christianity.

viii. As ever-present revelation, continued and flowing forward from vii.

It would, of course, be possible to add a ninth category to Söderblom's list, and to regard religion as a continuous discovery and a continuous revelation, pressing forward into the infinite future, all of it equally being revealed and equally all discovered, though perhaps in varying ratios.

The reader must take his choice; but if he elects the ninth classification, he must reckon that in this case the fullest knowledge of Deity may be reached only when there are no more human beings on earth to enjoy it!

It is therefore possible to choose an entirely different grouping, and to say that in the great age of religious creativity a peak, X, Y or Z, is somewhere reached, round which all other types group themselves, and to which they are all in some degree capable of being related, but which in itself is as absolute and final for religion as the work of Pheidias and Praxiteles is for sculpture, or the work of the nineteenth and twentieth centuries for science.

Or again, we may adopt what is called the theory of polymorphous truth, and say that each religion is suitable to the people among whom it has developed, but is an exotic elsewhere. This, of course, would exclude the possibility of a common world-faith of any sort.

As an alternative, a federation of existing faiths has been proposed, with the idea that their mutual tolerance and improved acquaintanceship may pave the way for a new common world-religion in the future, even though this may not as yet have arisen above the horizon. It is urged that the advent of such a new faith need not be the source of apprehension, since it would not involve the loss of any real truth already in the possession of mankind, but would merely put such truth in a larger setting.

But none of the foregoing theories takes any account of what is called existential thinking, i.e. reflection in which one is not detached and aloof from the matter reflected upon, but shaken to one's very depths by it, since one is on trial one's self, and in no position of security from which one can be an impartial critic. Willy-nilly, the thinker himself stands under judgement. It would be dangerously unfair to ignore this way of regarding religion, since, whether one agrees with it or not, it is certainly widespread today, and one has something to learn from it. According to this standpoint, all the religions of the world are forms of human, creaturely activity, and, as such, faulty, infected with that basic infirmity of the human race, self-centredness. No one form has any advantage over another. There is, and can be, therefore, no natural approach to Deity from the human side. So-called discovery can discover nothing. Only Deity himself can make his nature known. This is the old radical exclusiveness in a new dress, with 'vertical' revelation as its central point.

Those who reject this last standpoint believe that human intelligence, though an imperfect instrument, is more to be trusted than its critics aver, and that the future will see the development of a new realism in which man's quest for God may be as much appreciated as God's approach to man. This they hold, will bring us back to a sympathetic and unprejudiced study of all forms of religion, and it is the conviction of the author that out of such a study must inevitably come at last some conclusions which will command as general a consent as the main conclusions which have been reached regarding the physical universe. He must leave his readers to speculate which of the various general theories so far propounded claims his allegiance.

Our survey would be incomplete if we did not take account of a novel attempt which has been made in the last year or two to place the ideas of the various religions in series. It is frankly a Christian one, and as such may be deemed biased, but, even if we take its system of classification, we are not necessarily bound to adopt its conclusions. The author is Dr F. H. Smith, of the University of London.* Beginning with sacred literature and theories of revelation, he groups his data under six heads:

   i. Naturalistic records.

  ii. Records treated as revelation by a later age.

 iii. Records associated with an original claim to revelation.

 iv. Records associated with the belief in a personal theophany.

  v. Records associated with the belief in a divine personal or rational manifestation.

 vi. A record with an original claim to direct revelation involving the belief in a supreme revelation by Divine Incarnation.

Proceeding then to ideas of God and reality, he groups these under seven heads:

  i. Elementary religion.

 ii. Advanced religion.

    (a) Personal idea of God.

    (b) Impersonal idea of reality.

    (c) Impersonal tendencies within personal religion.

    (d) Personal idea of God within impersonal religion.

    (e) Triune Personality.

The implication, of course, is that the final term in each of these series is the highest, and that they represent an ascending hierarchy of forms. The same is postulated in dealing with cosmology and cosmogony, where a series of emanation-doctrines is succeeded by another of creation-doctrines, ending with the Christian doctrine of creation. It would be improper for the author of this book to express any opinion as to whether he considers Dr Smith to have made his case good. His own business is to describe as objectively as possible what work is being done, and he must leave those who are interested to examine his thesis for themselves, and to form their own conclusions.

* Dr Smith subsequently became Professor of Comparative Religion in the University of Manchester, and has since died.

The plan of placing features of religion in series is sometimes adopted quite independently, and has been done in respect to the idea of Incarnation, somewhat as follows:

Incarnation of the Sacred in sub-human creatures of exceptional or terrifying form or power.

Incarnation of the Sacred in men of unusual endowments.

Incarnation of the Sacred in a king, or dynasty of kings.

Incarnation of the Sacred in a priest or line of priests.

Incarnation of the Sacred in a prophet or series of prophets.

Discontinuous Incarnation in a number of unusual human beings.

Discontinous Incarnation once-for-all in Jesus Christ.

A somewhat similar method was pursued by the late Professor van der Leeuw of Gröningen, who, also regarding the world through Christian eyes, placed the various types of religion in series, as follows:

The religions of remoteness and flight.

The religion of struggle.

The religion of repose.

The religion of unrest.

The religion of strain and of form.

The religion of infinity and of asceticism.

The religion of nothingness and of compassion.

The religion of will and of obedience.

The religion of majesty and of humility.

The religion of love.

And the various types of founder of religion as:

The reformer.

The teacher.

The philosopher and theologian.

The example.

The mediator.

while religious experience is classified into:

Avoidance of God.
Servitude to God.
Covenant with God.
Friendship with God.
Knowledge of God.
Following of God.
Being filled with God.
Mysticism, the love of God, being children of God, enmity to God.
Conversion, rebirth, and the unitive life of adoration.

But by far the most attractive way of dealing with the problem of comparison is that proposed by the late Dr K. J. Saunders in his *Ideals of East and West*. Here the question is asked: 'What sort of human being does a particular human group admire?' and the answer is expected to indicate not only its ethical ideals, but also its conception of diety.

Taking up Dr Saunders' suggestion, and developing it, we get something like this:

Group	Ideal human being admired by it
Greeks of Plato's day.	The handsome and virtuous man.
Aristotle.	The high-minded man who contemplates the universe (*megalopsuchos*).
Stoics.	The wise man who is self-controlled.
Chinese.	The princely man (*chün-tz˘*).
Japanese.	The disciplined warrior (*samurai*).
Hebrews.	The righteous man (as in Psalm i and Tobit).
Romans.	Much the same as the Japanese.
British.	The gentleman.
Germans.	The self-respecting man.
Indians.	The ascetic (*sadhu*).

T–L

Group	Ideal human being admired by it
Christians.	The saint (who, penetrated by the spirit of Jesus, seeks to transform the world, and is yet at home in it).
Moslems.	The man who is completely surrendered to Allāh the omnipotent, as his slave or 'abd.

The details need working out in a way which would take up too much space here; but the mere outline will provide food for much thought. Various points will occur straight away, such as that almost all the ideals are in effect masculine except the Christian one, which is possible to both sexes. This in itself seems to put a barrier between Christianity and other systems. We recall the prayer of the Jew: 'Blessed art Thou O Lord, who has not made me a woman', and also that Socrates did not cultivate women in his symposia. Stoic sages like Epictetus seem to class women, as has been said, 'with rich soup and dainty cakes'. In the scheme it will be noticed that Buddhism has been left out. As a matter of fact, Buddhism has made room for nuns, but Gotama himself is represented as very dubious whether he should allow his followers to cultivate the society of women. In fact, no religion but Christianity, and even that not always, has stood for the emancipation of woman, though it is plain that in principle from the outset Christianity has been open to both sexes, and has in fact enhanced the position of woman, and actually made emancipation possible. If in this it is mistaken, it errs in company with the new cultus of the Dialectic Process, but is condemned by the Fascist type of religion, whether in Germany or Japan.

Other classifications which should be considered here are Reinhold Niebuhr's thought-provoking one into

(1) Religions which expect no messiah
(2) Religions where a messiah is expected;

and that which is implied throughout Dr Kraemer's great work: 'The Christian Message in a Non-Christian World.' He in effect carves religions into two classes: those which are really at bottom man-centred, and those which start from God and are centred upon God. This, of course, is intended by him to sever what he calls 'Biblical realism' from all other so-called religion, but obviously there are types of empirical Christianity which must be classified as man-centred, while some non-Christian religious seekers are quite as much God-centred as any Hebrew prophet or Christian saint. The classification involves therefore much more than Dr Kraemer perhaps would assent to, and he does not fend off its drastic effects merely by saying that a vast mass of even what appears to be exceptionally spiritual non-Christian religion is thinly veiled ethnic secularism. Side by side with it we must set Professor Hocking's confession as to the God-centred experience which he has found in devout souls all the world over, outside as well as inside the sphere which is actually touched by Biblical realism. It seems, indeed, best to quote what he says: 'The religion of the people (all over the world) has a sound kernel. The universal sense of the Presence of God, and the intuition of the direction in which the will of God lies, comes often to evidence among them. It is seldom that the crust of superstition and dehumanizing fear or corruption becomes so fixed that a glow of genuine religious life does not live underneath it.' He then quotes some examples from Shintoists in Japan and Hindus in Bengal, and continues: 'To find a similar directness of the consciousness of God in our own tradition, we should have to look to men like Augustine or Anselm, who write their diaries or conduct their philosophies as a dialogue with God. What is a deliberate form in such writers is the staple of life among many of the common folk of Asia. It is because of this soundness of substance that the lay mystics ... emerge in such numbers from their ranks.' Another experienced missionary and liberal

Christian scholar who has taken a line opposed to that of Dr Kraemer is Dr E. C. Dewick, in his recently published Hulsean Lectures.

Let no one feel discouraged at the incompleteness with which one seems to be faced when one considers the pageants of religion throughout the past millennia. The end certainly is not yet. Humanity is still too young, and the future of its continuant product may well lie elsewhere than within the leasehold of the earth itself. We have travelled far, and in a few pages have dared to bestride many centuries. Judged in such a manner, the sweep of man's quest for the Eternal and the Real seems a fine and venturesome and not wholly fruitless endeavour, and those who proclaim a Response and an Initiative upon the part of the Eternal have an even nobler tale to tell, whether we assent to it or not. Since the publication of the second edition of this book an important work has appeared from the pen of Emil Brunner, the noted Swiss theologian of Zurich, entitled *Revelation and Reason*. It is of course written from the standpoint of a neo-Protestant Christian, but it deals very fully with the general theory of religion, especially in Chapter XV. The gist of its contents may be summed up as follows:

(1) Knowledge which *comes from God* is different from the knowledge *of* God, e.g. mathematical or scientific knowledge comes from God, but it is not the knowledge *of* God, though it may be knowledge *about His works*.

(2) Knowledge of God can be had only on God's own self-disclosure, just as two human beings cannot *know* one another, as distinct from knowing *facts about* one another, except by mutual self-disclosure.

(3) The reception by man of such knowledge from God is rendered harder by man's inherent taint of self-centred waywardness, which we call sin. Hence man's quest for God, who

desires Himself to be understood, is hampered and leads man to 'hold down the truth in unrighteousness', as St Paul says. Knowledge of God through the works of His creation tends in consequence to be a warped or distorted knowledge (broken lights, or fitful gleams of truth).

(4) Fuller knowledge is possible only by God's personal initiative, which is the content of the Christian revelation, but it is more than mere *information about* God, since man needs more than information, he needs Divine action to redeem him from his waywardness. Hence God discontinuously intervenes, and under particular spatio-temporal conditions enters history in order to free mankind from the domination of the evil circumstances in which it has entangled itself. Hence, also, although Justin Martyr is justified in saying that since there is but one God, 'whatever men have said or done well belongs to us Christians', the converse is not true, i.e. that whatever Christians have is *fully* accessible to adherents of other religions than the Christian. Brunner concludes, in his own words: '... the facts of the history of religion ... show us that the common assumption that the Christian claim to revelation is opposed by a variety of similar claims of equal value is wholly untenable. The amazing thing is the exact opposite, namely that the claim of a revelation (by a Revealer) possessing universal validity in the history of religion is rare. The claim of revelation made by the Christian faith is in its radicalism as solitary as its content'.

This argument deserves careful consideration, but it seems to ignore the consideration that if man is sinful, his reception of God's full revelation is just as likely to be warped as his appreciation of the knowledge derived from God's works in creation or in the mind of man. It may, however, be admitted that the type of revelation recognized in the Bible literature is of a quality and kind to which there is no parallel elsewhere, but this should not involve the rejection of the belief that all knowledge can be in some sense revelation, nor of the notion that revelation may be and probably is progressive. Indirectly the creative evolution of humanity is part of the self-disclosure of God, a doctrine which is precisely implied in the Christian scriptures. The validity of Brunner's argument stands or falls with the axiom that the condition of man is abnormal and pathological.

With the above may be taken the assertion of Professor D. G. Baillie in his book *God was in Christ* that the specific feature of the Christian Doctrine about God is that it represents Him as One who does not wait to be discovered, but goes out to look for men.

An additional classification which I do not think has been explicitly included above is the three-fold one, into

(1) Religions which seek to affirm the world.
(2) Religions which seek to escape from the world.
(3) Religions which seek to transform the world.

It would seem that only those in class (3) can set up any effective opposition to Marxism.

Perhaps the best way in which to finish will be with a quotation from Dr van der Leeuw's preface: 'No religious experience is a mere tendency. On the contrary, it is not man himself who is the active agent in the situation, but, in one mode or another, God. A Divine activity sustains all phenomena alike, from their more primitive types to their culmination in Christianity, as well as those religious movements which are now concealed by our largely secularized civilization.' The author must not commit himself to any biassed assertion about the nature of the culminating point (for in such a work as this it would be improper to do so), but he would agree in the main with the quotation, and confess that it represents the thesis of this small book, which here has an end.

A LIST OF BOOKS FOR FURTHER STUDY
(Selected from a vast multitude of works)

GENERAL

Die Religion in Geschichte und Gegenwart, 3rd ed. (a comprehensive German encyclopedia).

JAMES HASTINGS, *Encyclopaedia of Religion and Ethics*.

Professor G. VAN DER LEEUW, *Religion in Essence and Manifestation*. George Allen & Unwin, 1938.

CHANTEPIE DE LA SAUSSAYE *Lehrbuch der Religionsgeschichte*. Ed. Bertholet and Lehmann. Tübingen, 1925.

Archbishop SODERBLOM, *The Living God*. Gifford Lectures, 1931. Oxford Univ. Press, 1933.

E. O. JAMES, *Comparative Religion* (Methuen, 1938), and its full Bibliography.

EDWYN BEVAN, *Symbolism and Belief* and *Holy Images*. George Allen & Unwin, 1933 and 1940.

EMIL BRUNNER, *Revelation and Reason* (especially Chapter 15). S.C.M. Press, 1947.

NATHANIEL MICKLEM, *Religion*. Home University Library, O.U.P., 1948 (a general text-book with an excellent bibliography).

A. C. BOUQUET, *Sacred Books of the World*. Pelican Book A 283, 1954 (a companion source-book to the present volume).

The Christian Faith and Non-Christian Religions. Nisbet, 1958 (useful also for a detailed discussion of general theories).

Also the following text-books:

The World's Religions, essays edited by J. N. D. Anderson, O.B.E., Lecturer in Islamic Law, School of Oriental and African Studies, University of London, pub. Inter-Varsity Fellowship, 1950. (Written with a conservative evangelical background, but clear, serviceable, and fair, and the essay on Islam shows special first-hand knowledge.)

The Great Religions of the World, edited by E. J. Jurji, Associate Professor of Islamics at Princeton Theological Seminary. Princeton University Press, 1946 (a somewhat similar work from across the Atlantic).

A Short Comparative History of Religions, by T. H. Robinson, D.D., Professor of Semitic Languages at University College, Cardiff. Duckworth, 2nd edition, 1951. (The work of a veteran British Baptist scholar of eminence, clear and scientific.)

PRIMITIVE RELIGION

PAUL RADIN, *Primitive Religion*. Hamish Hamilton, 1938.

VERRIER ELWIN, *The Baigas*. Oxford Univ. Press (a careful account of an Indian jungle-tribe).

W. H. R. RIVERS, *The Todas*. Macmillan, 1906.

Professor E. O. JAMES, 'The Emergence of Religion' in *Essays Catholic and Critical*. S.P.C.K., 1926. *The Origin of Religion*. Unicorn Press, 1937. *The Origins of Sacrifice*. Murray, 1933.

Professor J. G. D. CLARK, *World Prehistory*. Cambridge Univ. Press, 1961, paperback.

Professor JOHANNES MARINGER, *The Gods of Prehistoric Man*. Weidenfeld and Nicolson, 1960.

Miss ALFORD, *The Traditional Dance*. Methuen, 1935. *Pyrenean Festivals*. Chatto & Windus, 1937.

Professor E. O. JAMES, *Prehistoric Religion*. Thames and Hudson, 1958.

J. G. FRAZER, *The Golden Bough*. Macmillan. Several editions and an abridgement.

CHRISTINA HOLE, *English Folklore*. London, 1940. Methuen.

GEOFFREY PARRINDER, *West African Religion*. Epworth Press, 1949.

MESOPOTAMIA

The works of the late Sir LEONARD WOOLLEY, Professor LANGDON, and Dr REGINALD CAMPBELL THOMPSON.

L. DELAPORTE, *Mesopotamia: The Babylonians and Assyrian Civilisation*. Kegan Paul

E. W. ROGERS, *Cuneiform Parallels of the Old Testament*. Oxford Univ. Press.

The Intellectual Adventure of Ancient Man (various contributors). Chicago Univ. Press, Chicago, 1947. See also *Before Philosophy*. Pelican Books A198, Harmondsworth, 1949, edited by the late Henri Frankfort, and *The Epic of Gilgamesh*, a new Penguin translation.

EGYPT

The writings of Professor ADOLF ERMAN, Sir E. WALLIS BUDGE, Professor J. H. BREASTED, and Mr A. W. SHORTER (all, alas, now deceased); also *A Short History of Ancient Egypt*, by ARTHUR WEIGALL. Chapman & Hall, 1934.

Dr MARGARET MURRAY, *The Splendour that was Egypt*. Sidgwick & Jackson, 1949.

HENRI FRANKFORT, *Ancient Egyptian Religion*. New York, 1949.

IRAN

The works of the late Dr J. H. MOULTON, esp. *The Treasure of the Magi*, Oxford Univ. Press, 1917, and also his Hibbert Lectures, 1913.

J. DUCHESNE-GUILLEMIN, *Zarathustra*. Paris, Maisonneuve, 1948. The Hymns (Gathas) of Zarathustra in translation. George Allen & Unwin, 1952.

Professor R. C. ZAEHNER, *The Rise and Decline of Zoroastrianism*. Weidenfeld and Nicolson, 1961.

FRAMROZE BODE, and NANAVUTTY, *Songs of Zarathustra*. George Allen & Unwin, 1952.

INDIA

Pandit JAWAHARLAL NEHRU, *The Discovery of India*. Meridian Press, 1946.

Sir CHARLES ELIOT, *Hinduism and Buddhism* (3 vols). Arnold, 1921.

Professor J. B. PRATT, *India and its Faiths*. Macmillan, 1915.

The Religion of the Hindus, a series of essays by Indian scholars edited and published in New York, 1953, by Professor K. W. Morgan of Colgate University.

C. F. ANDREWS, *The True India*. George Allen & Unwin, 1939.

C. L. O'MALLEY, *Popular Hinduism*. Cambridge Univ. Press, 1935.

Dr BHARATAN KUMARAPPA, *The Indian Conception of Deity*. London Univ. Press, 1934.

Professor BERRIEDALE KEITH, *The Religion and Philosophy of the Veda* (2 vols). Harvard Univ. Press, Cambridge, Massachusetts, 1925.

Professor SARVEPALLI RADHAKRISHNAN, *Indian Philosophy* (2 vols), 1927. *The Hindu View of Life*, 1912.

Professor W. S. URQUHART, *The Vedanta and Modern Thought*. Oxford Univ. Press, 1928.

Professor J. ESTLIN CARPENTER, *Theism in Medieval India*. Hibbert Lectures, 1921.

A. C. BOUQUET, *Hinduism*. Hutchinson, 1966.

W. G. ORR, *A Sixteenth-Century Indian Mystic*. Lutterworth Press, 1947. And the following texts:

Dr NICOL MACNICOL, *Hindu Scriptures*, J. M. Dent (Everyman's Library), 1938, and *Psalms of the Marathi Saints*, Calcutta, 1919.

Dr E. J. THOMAS, *Vedic Hymns* and *The Song of the Lord*, 1931. (Both in the 'Wisdom of the East' series.)

Professor R. E. HUME, *The Thirteen Principal Upanishads*. Oxford Univ. Press, 1931.

Dr M. A. MCAULIFFE, *The Sikh Religion*. Oxford Univ. Press, 1909.

CHRISTOPHER ISHERWOOD, *Life of Ramakrishna Parahamsa*. Methuen, 1965.

BUDDHISM

Sir CHARLES ELIOT, *op. cit.*, and also the 4th (posthumous) volume on Japanese Buddhism. Arnold, London, 1935.

NALINAKSHA DUTT, *Early Monastic Buddhism* (2 vols). Calcutta, 1941.

Professor J. B. PRATT, *The Pilgrimage of Buddhism*. Macmillan, 1928.

Professor SUZUKI, *Outlines of Mahayana Buddhism* and *Essays in Zien Buddhism*, 1937.

E. STEINILBER-OBERLIN, *The Buddhist Sects of Japan*. George Allen & Unwin, 1938.

IQBAL SINGH, *Gautama Buddha*. Boriswood, London, 1937.

Dr E. J. THOMAS, *Early Buddhist Scriptures*. Kegan Paul, 1935.

Mrs RHYS DAVIDS, *Buddhism*. Home Univ. Library, 1934. *A Manual of Buddhism*. Sheldon Press, 1932.

Miss I. B. HORNER, *The Early Buddhist Theory of Man Perfected*, Cambridge Univ. Press, 1936, and *The Book of Discipline* (Publications of the Pali Text Society).

Lord CHALMERS, *Buddhist Sermons*, 2 vols in the same series of Publications. (The introduction to these is a fine piece of ripe scholarship.)

Sir CHARLES BELL, *The Religion of Tibet*. Oxford Univ. Press, 1931.

F. HAROLD SMITH, *The Buddhist Way of Life*. Hutchinson, 1951.

CHRISTMAS HUMPHREYS, *Buddhism*. Pelican Book A 228.

T. R. V. MURTI, *The Central Philosophy of Buddhism*. George Allen & Unwin, 1955.

JAINISM

Dr A. Guérinot *La religion Djaina* Paris (Louvain Pr.), 1926.

Mrs Sinclair Stevenson, *The Heart of Jainism*. Oxford Univ. Press, 1915.

Jagnanderlal Jaini, *Outlines of Jainism*. Camb. Univ. Press, 1940.

Mohan Lal Mehra, *Outlines of Jain Philosophy*. Jain Mission Society, Bangalore, 1955.

CHINA

P. J. Maclagan, *Chinese Religious Ideas*. Duff Lectures. S.C.M., 1926.

E. D. Harvey, *The Mind of China*. Yale Univ. Press, 1933.

Marcel Granet, *La Religion des Chinois*. Paris, ? 1934.

L. Wieger, *Histoire des croyances religeuses et des opinions philosophiques en Chine, depuis l'origine jusqu'à nos jours*. Paris, 1922.

Carl Crow, *Master Kung, A Life of Confucius* (illustrated). Hamish Hamilton, 1937.

R. Wilhelm, *Confucius and Confucianism*. Kegan Paul, 1931.

Arthur Waley, *The Analects of Confucius*. George Allen & Unwin 1945.

E. D. Edwards, *Confucius*, 1940.

J. P. Bruce, *Chu Hsi and His Masters*. Probsthain, 1923.

Recent works by E. R. Hughes on the Chinese classics. J. M. Dent.

Henri Maspero, *Les Religions chinoises*, 1950.

Liu Wu-Chi, *A Short History of Confucian Philosophy* (Pelican Books, 1955, A 333).

Dr Joseph Needham, *Science and Civilization in China*. Cambridge Univ. Press, 1954.

Wing Chit Tsin, *Chinese Religion since the Revolution*. Columbia Press U.S.A., 1953.

JAPAN (OTHER THAN BUDDHIST)

Professor Mahasaru Anesaki, *History of Japanese Religion*. Kegan Paul, 1930.

Dr D. C. Holtom, *The National Faith of Japan*. Kegan Paul, 1938.

George Thomsen, *The New Religions of Japan*. The Tuttle Publishing Co., Vermont, U.S.A.

ISLAM

BERTRAM SIDNEY THOMAS, *The Arabs*. Thornton Butterworth, 1937.

ESSED BEY (pseud.), *Life of Mohammed*. Cobden Sanderson, 1938.

RICHARD BELL, *A new standard edition of the Qur'ān in English, with critical notes*, 2 vols. T. and T. Clark, 1938. *The Origin of Islam in its Christian Environment*. Macmillan, 1926.

Professor A. J. WENSINCK, *The Moslem Creed*. Cambridge Univ. Press, 1932.

Professor R. A. NICHOLSON, *Islamic Mysticism*. Cambridge Univ. Press, 1921.

M. T. TITUS, *Indian Islam*. Oxford Univ. Press, 1930.

Professor H. A. R. GIBB, *Modern Trends in Islam*. Chicago Univ. Press, 1945. *Mohammedanism*. Home University Library, O.U.P., 1949.

The Reverend KENNETH CRAGG, *The Call of the Minaret*.

AMEER ALI, *The Spirit of Islam*. Christophers, 1922. (The Shī'a viewpoint.)

A. S. TRITTON, *Islam*. Hutchinson, 1951.

W. MONTGOMERY WATT. *Muhammed at Mecca*. Oxford Univ. Press, 1926.

ALFRED GUILLAUME, *Islam*. Pelican Books, 1954, A311.

GREEK AND ROMAN RELIGION

Miss JANE HARRISON, *Prolegomena to Greek Religion*. 3rd ed., 1922, and *Themis*, both Cambridge Univ. Press.

J. D. S. PENDLEBURY, *Handbook to the Palace of Minos at Knossos*, 1933, and *The Archaeology of Crete*. Methuen, 1939.

Professor GILBERT MURRAY, *Five Stages of Greek Religion*. Oxford Univ. Press, 1925.

Professor A. B. COOK, *Zeus* (3 vols). Cambridge Univ. Press, 1914–1940.

Dr JAMES ADAM, *The Religious Teachers of Greece*. Gifford Lectures, Edinburgh, 1908.

W. K. C. GUTHRIE, *Orpheus and Greek Religion*. Methuen, 1935; *The Greeks and their Gods*. Methuen, 1950.

Professor E. O. JAMES, *The Ancient Gods*. Weidenfeld & Nicolson, 1959.

Professor VICTOR MAGNIEN, *Mystères d'Eleusis*. 2nd ed., 1938.

S. ANGUS, *The Religious Quests of the Graeco-Roman World*, 1925. *The Mystery-Religions and Christianity*, 1929.

W. WARDE FOWLER, *The Religious Experience of the Roman People*. Macmillan, 1909–10. *Roman Ideas of Deity*. Macmillan, 1914.

Professor FRANZ ALTHEIM, *A History of Roman Religion*. English edition, 1938. Trans. H. Mattinson.

Sir JAMES FRAZER, *Ovid's Fasti*. Edited in 5 vols. Cambridge Univ. Press, 1929.

CYRIL BAILEY, *Phases in the Religion of Ancient Rome*.

M. PALLOTINO, *The Etruscans*. Pelican Books, 1955.

NORDIC RELIGION

Dr VILHELM GRÖNBECH, *The Religion of the Scandinavian Peoples*, and section by him in Chantepie de la Saussaye, Lehrbuch, Copenhagen.

HILDA ELLIS, *The Road to Hel*. Cambridge Univ. Press, 1944.

SLAVONIC RELIGION

Professor A. BRÜCKNER, in Chantepie de la Saussaye, Lehrbuch.

HEBREW AND CHRISTIAN RELIGION

OESTERLEY and ROBINSON, *Hebrew Religion and its Developments* 2nd ed., London, 1937.

W. E. O. OESTERLEY, *Sacrifices in Ancient Israel*. Hodder & Stoughton, 1937.

Dr ALFRED GUILLAUME, *Prophecy and Divination* Hodder & Stoughton, 1938 (Bampton Lecture).

The Nag Hammadi documents: articles in the report of the 1960 conference of the Modern Churchmen's Union. Blackwell's, Oxford.

T. H. GASTER, *The Scriptures of the Dead Sea Sect*, English translation and introduction. Secker and Warburg, 1957.

C. F. A. SCHAEFFER, *The Cuneiform Texts of Ras-Shamra-Ugarit*. Schweich Lectures, 1936–39.

J. W. JACK, *The Ras Shamra Tablets*. T. & T. Clark, Edinburgh, 1935.

T. SKINNER, *Prophecy and Religion*. Cambridge Univ. Press, 1926.

J. KLAUSNER, *Jesus of Nazareth*, for a Jewish view of the Founder of Christianity.

EDWYN BEVAN, *Christianity*. Home Univ. Library, 1933.

Professor F. C. BURKITT, *Jesus Christ: an historical outline*. Blackie & Sons, 1932.

H. D. A. MAJOR, D.D., *Jesus by an Eye-witness*. John Murray, 1925.

Sir EDWYN HOSKYNS and F. N. DAVEY, *The Riddle of the New Testament*. Faber & Faber, 1933.

ADOLF HARNACK, *The Expansion of Christianity in the First Three Centuries*. Eng. ed. Williams & Norgate, 1905.

K. S. LATOURETTE, *Missions To-morrow*. Harper Bros., New York, 1936, and *History of the Expansion of Christianity* (several volumes). Eyre & Spottiswoode, 1939 ff.

W. E. HOCKING, *Living Religions and a World Faith*. Hibbert Lectures, 1940.

The works of Dr C. H. DODD, especially those dealing with Christianity and History, the Parables of the Gospels, and the story of the Gospels in general, should be consulted.

See also *Christianity and World Order*, by the Bishop of Chichester, a Penguin Special of 1940, and a small book on the New Testament Gospels, broadcasts by four Cambridge professors, published by the B.B.C., 1965.

MEXICO-PERU

T. A. JOYCE, Works on South American Archaeology and especially Reports on the British Museum expedition to Central America 1926 and 1928 (reprinted from the *Journal of the Royal Anthropological Institute*). See also the *Guide to the Maudslay collection of Maya Sculptures in the British Museum* (1923) and its concluding bibliography.

LEWIS SPENCE, *The Religion of Ancient Mexico*. Watts & Co., 1945.

P. A. MEANS, *Ancient Civilizations of the Andes*. Scribners, New York, 1931.

G. C. VAILLANT, *The Aztecs of Mexico*. Pelican Book A 200.

S. G. MORELEY, *The Ancient Maya*. Stanford Univ. Press, California, 1947.

MANICHAEISM

Professor F. C. BURKITT, *The Religion of the Manichees*. (Donnellan Lectures, Dublin, 1923, pub. Cambridge Univ. Press.)

ERNEST PUECH, *Le Manichéisme*. Musée Guimet publication, 1949.

MYSTICISM

EVELYN UNDERHILL, *Mysticism*. 2nd ed., Methuen, London.

C. E. ROLT, *Dionysius the Areopagite*. S.P.C.K., 1920.

W. R. INGE, *Personal Idealism and Mysticism*. Paddock Lectures, 3rd ed., 1934. *The Philosophy of Plotinus*, Gifford Lectures, 3rd ed., 1939. *Christian Mysticism*, Bampton Lectures, new ed., 1933. *Mysticism in Religion*. Hutchinson, 1947.

Professor R. C. ZAEHNER, *Mysticism, Sacred and Profane*. Oxford Univ. Press, 1961, paperback.

ADDITIONAL WORKS OF A GENERAL CHARACTER

E. L. ALLEN, *Christianity among the Religions*. London, 1960.

W. E. HOCKING, *Living Religions and a World Faith*. Hibbert Lectures London, 1940.

J. M. KITAGAWA (ed.), *Modern Trends in World Religions*. Illinois, 1959.

J. NEUNER (ed.), *Christian Revelation and World Religions*. London, 1967.

H. R. SCHLETTE, *Towards a Theology of Religions*. Freiburg, 1966.

INDEX OF PROPER NAMES

INDEX OF SUBJECTS

*Some other books published by Penguins are
described on the following pages.*

A SHORT HISTORY OF RELIGIONS

E. E. Kellett

'How many churchgoers know exactly in what way their own faith differs from the faith of others? How many know how their particular church grew, its founders, martyrs, and saints? How many Christians understand the dogmas of Mohammedanism, Buddhism, Confucianism? What exactly are the beliefs of the Unitarians, the Christadelphians, the Peculiar People, the Shakers? Many of you, perhaps, can answer questions like these. I could not, until I had read E. E. Kellett's *A Short History of Religions*.

'This is a book of such fascination that I am longing for the leisure in which to re-read it. It is a modern classic, a "must" book for every thinking person, whether believer or agnostic' – Pamela Hansford Johnson in the *Sunday Chronicle*

'For width of range, clarity of statement, and acuteness of analysis Mr Kellett's survey of the religions of the world . . . takes a foremost place' – *New Statesman*

WORLD RELIGIONS : A Dialogue

Ninian Smart

If religion is largely founded on faith, and faith on revelation, which of all the revelations are we to believe? Why make the Christian leap of faith, rather than the Muslim or Buddhist one?

Very different answers to such questions would be given in different parts of the world. And in this imaginative addition to the comparative study of religions Ninian Smart has adopted the form of a dialogue between a Christian, a Jew, a Muslim, a Hindu, and two Buddhists (from Ceylon and Japan) to demonstrate how the most influential creeds differ and on what they are agreed.

The result is a fresh and at times surprising insight into the religions of the world, as the protagonists exchange their fundamental beliefs about God and the Trinity, salvation, incarnation and good and evil.

RELIGIOUS FAITH AND
TWENTIETH-CENTURY MAN

F. C. Happold

Religion, it is easy to believe, has been blown sky-high by the discoveries of modern science. But millions of people are undoubtedly waiting for the pieces to fall. When they do, what new pattern will they form?

In *Religious Faith and Twentieth-Century Man* Dr Happold examines and analyses the major influences which must determine a modern picture of reality. Whatever new worlds have been charted by quantum physicists, radio astronomers, and depth psychologists, the great mystical experiences of individual men cannot be excluded from any total view of the universe. Dr Happold's search for a satisfactory synthesis leads him to a religio-philosophy of the mystical as a way out of the spiritual dilemma of modern man. From this develops an entirely fresh attitude towards the world – an attitude he terms 'Intersection'.

The spirit of Dr Happold's book, which he modestly contributes to the current controversy about religion as 'the fruit of one man's experience', is summed up in the title of his Epilogue: 'He who sees not God everywhere, sees him truly nowhere.'

This is the second volume in a 'mystical trilogy', of which the first volume, *Mysticism: A Study and an Anthology*, is already available in Pelicans.

THE SURVIVAL OF GOD IN
THE SCIENTIFIC AGE

Alan Isaacs

Is there a God?

On the one hand we have man's obstinate faith in the existence of God, a faith so powerful that, as Voltaire said, 'If God did not exist, it would be necessary to invent him.'

Against this stands the evidence of modern science – physics, biology, cosmology – explaining in its own terms the universe and the presence within it of life. With their observations on human thinking and behaviour, psychology and philosophy frequently confirm the findings of science.

In this volume Alan Isaacs reviews the opposing cases. For many he sees religious faith as a private necessity: for society as a whole, even in the nuclear age, he acknowledges that the concept of God may serve a useful function in the enforcement of moral codes. And if his conclusion is a frank 'I don't know', his path to it follows the profoundest issue of this, or any, age through the spectrum of twentieth-century thought.

THE ENGLISH CHURCH: A New Look

Leslie S. Hunter

The English Church makes a critical examination of the Church of England's function in relation to the State and People . . . as it was in history, as it is today, and as it may be in coming years.

Dr Leslie S. Hunter, who edits this new Pelican and contributes four of the chapters, was the Bishop of Sheffield for over twenty years. His team of contributors includes some of the most distinguished Anglican thinkers of the day. Dr Carpenter and Canon Warren are both senior canons of Westminster Abbey; Canon Milford is the Master of the Temple; the Rt Rev. E. R. Wickham is the Bishop of Middleton and the Very Rev. Alfred Jowett is the Dean of Manchester.

Collectively they possess an unrivalled experience of the church's work in industrial areas and their observations, based on an understanding of modern sociology and a faith in the special relationship between Church and State in England, must make a considerable impact on present religious discussions.

THE PELICAN HISTORY OF THE CHURCH

The following volumes of this new history
have so far been published